F

Sightings:
UFOs

Susan Michaels

A FIRESIDE BOOK
Published by Simon & Schuster

FIRESIDE
Rockefeller Center
1230 Avenue of the Americas
New York, NY 10020

FIRESIDE and colophon are registered trademarks
of Simon & Schuster Inc.

SIGHTINGS is a trademark of Paramount Pictures

Designed by Kathryn Parise
Manufactured in the United States of America

1   3   5   7   9   10   8   6   4   2

LIBRARY OF CONGRESS CATALOGING-IN-PUBLICATION DATA
Michaels, Susan (Susan H.)
Sightings : UFOs / Susan Michaels.
p. cm.
1. Unidentified flying objects—Sightings and encounters.
I. Title.
TL789.3.M55 1997   97-19475
001.942—dc21   CIP

ISBN 0-684-83630-0

All photos not credited are courtesy of *Sightings*.

Acknowledgments

This book is a compendium of UFO reports, stories, and apocrypha, which originally appeared in an abbreviated form on the *Sightings* television series. The accounts in this book are based on interviews conducted by *Sightings* during the last five years, and I am deeply grateful to the hundreds of experts and eyewitnesses who have agreed to share their thoughts and feelings with *Sightings*. I hope I have presented their words in the spirit they were intended.

I am again grateful to Stephen Kroopnick, the co–executive producer of the *Sightings* television series. His humor, flawless judgment, and unflagging confidence in my ability as a writer have remained a constant source of inspiration (not to mention the free office space). I must also again thank Henry Winkler and Ann Daniel, the executive producers of *Sightings*. They started it all for me and continue to support without question my work on the television and book series. Tim White, the host of *Sightings*, has also been a tremendous support and subtly continues to make me a better writer. And I extend grateful acknowledgment to my editor, Cynthia Gitter, who has finally learned the difference between a Gray and a Reptilian.

This book would not have been possible without Cole Metcalf, *Sightings'* postproduction supervisor. He never said no, even when I asked for research materials buried in the deepest, darkest corners of the *Sightings* vaults. I couldn't have done it without you, Cole.

I would also like to acknowledge the contributions of Director of Research Jonathan Jerald, for whom no question was too obscure to answer. He is definitely the brains behind the operation. Supervising Producer Michelle Davis was again the light at the end of every tunnel. I believe Michelle has total recall of every story ever done on *Sightings.* I am also grateful for assistance from segment producers Ruth Rafidi, Phil Davis, Kim Steer, and Joyce Goldstein; researchers Curt Collier, David Green, and Blake Grant; and Executive in Charge of Production Mark Vertullo. Special thanks to Debra Matlock and Brad Grossman for the reproduction of pictures from video sources and the graphic design elements. And fast, too!

A special acknowledgment must go to Writer's Assistant Rich Hayworth. His help was essential to the completion of this book. Rich arrived in the nick of time, and I hope to repay the favor by buying his first novel (full price) very soon. Caroline Chai provided essential research, organizing five years' worth of transcripts in a few weeks as part of her summer internship. I am also grateful to Rich Brandt, who inspired me from afar (but not too far).

And finally to my family and friends, who didn't mind that I wasn't home very much: to my daughter, Sophie, my mother, Lila, and my friend Josephine Vandermey. Last but certainly not least, I must acknowledge my husband, Frank Hoppe, who is my champion, partner of twenty years, and (perhaps most important at this moment) proofreader. Thank you, darling.

For Stephen Kroopnick

Contents

Contact

Airborne Encounters

Abduction

Beyond Belief

Foreword

I think I was fourteen years old when I began to think that there must be another dimension beyond this planet, and surely there were other people who believed in, and could sense, the presence of this unseen dimension. This was not a sudden epiphany. The heavens didn't open up with a great light. Nor did I hear a voice that said, "Henry, there's more to this world than meets the eye." Actually, I had a very real experience that opened my eyes to the possibilities of the paranormal.

As a teenager, I was absolutely fascinated by the idea of ESP. When we are younger, we convince ourselves that we have special abilities. I thought ESP was mine. Like a lot of people, I would think of somebody and then bump into them on the street. I would think of a person whom I hadn't heard from in a while, and *ring* goes the phone and there they are. Coincidence? Perhaps. But I didn't think my psychic abilities could be explained away so easily—especially on the day I lost a very special fourteenth-birthday present.

During soccer practice at school one afternoon, I was completely unaware that the silver bracelet I received for my birthday had fallen off my wrist. When I was growing up, the silver link ID bracelet was really popular and I had bugged my parents for months to get me one. Well, they finally did, and now I went ahead and lost it! I was confused. My mind was racing; I needed a story, an alibi—a really good excuse. What was I going to tell them? I felt guilty—what were my parents going to say? I was panicked—what would my parents do to me? At this moment, maybe a heightened sense of fear, coupled with self-preservation, activated a psychic sense in me that, up until this point, I had never put to the test.

The field where I lost my bracelet was immense. I couldn't just go back and look for it—that would take hours, and it was getting dark. I visualized where I thought the bracelet could be. I returned to the field, stood at the perimeter, then actually saw the bracelet in my mind once again. I walked to another spot on the perimeter and then I took three, maybe four, steps onto the field, looked down, and there it was. Relieved and happy, I clasped it back on my wrist.

The confusion, the guilt, the panic all disappeared at once. I was convinced that this had to be some special power of mine. I was batting a thousand in the world of ESP, and was now hooked on the idea that there were hidden powers to be unlocked in each of us.

So now you've picked up this second in a series of *Sightings* books by author Susan Michaels—*Sightings: UFOs*—and you're asking yourself, How do ESP and psychic ability relate to UFO phenomena? To me, the connection is an easy one to make. Both subjects go right to the very heart of the mysterious and unexplained phenomena that permeate our lives and our world. Science would, of course, say that these areas are not quantifiable or identifiable phenomena at all, since so much of what we call paranormal (psychic ability, UFOs, ghosts) cannot be documented. I say, let's at least be open to the possibilities and let's explore the mysteries.

The serious exploration of possibilities was more than a point of departure; it was, and is, central to the idea for the television show *Sightings*. In 1991, I was in partnership with producer Ann Daniel. We were both equally fascinated by paranormal phenomena. Not the tabloid "I had Bigfoot's Baby" type of experience. But rather, could people really be cured by hands-on healers? Why were so many average people the world over saying they were having UFO encounters? These were the kinds of stories that we felt deserved to be investigated.

Paramount Television had faith in our ability to produce a serious program that explored paranormal phenomena. After six years and more than one hundred episodes we are still exploring . . . on television . . . on our Web sites . . . and again in print with this book, which provides a comprehensive look at the UFO experience from the earliest part of this century to the present.

The topic of UFOs was once the stock and trade of the masters of pulp fiction and fantasy. But fantasy has, in many ways, become fact. I think back on the great science fiction of this century and how much of it smacks of reality today—from H. G. Wells's turn-of-the-century description of lunar travel to Arthur C. Clarke's vision of instant global communication via a network of earth-orbiting satellites.

One of my favorite *Sightings* segments was a story we called "Sci-fi Prophets." It was about the great French visionary and author Jules Verne, whose book *Paris in the Twentieth Century* was written in 1863 and remained unpublished until 1995. The book presented Verne's vision of Paris, circa 1960. Verne saw a city illuminated by electric lights. He saw a city crowded with horseless carriages propelled by internal combustion engines. He saw a device that was capable of transmitting written information over communication wires—i.e., phone lines, capable of sending faxes. What Verne's publisher saw was something that the public would laugh at and find completely unbelievable.

The stories that have surfaced about UFOs, particularly since 1947, are viewed in a similar light. Most of us have been taught to believe that the topic is laughable and entirely unbelievable. But isn't it at least possible that people who say they have had UFO close encounters are connecting with something that most of us are incapable of understanding or appreciating at this time? It's an easy topic to brush off. After all, contact with alien intelligence is just *another* science fiction story—the stuff of Steven Spielberg movies. But perhaps one day this science fiction story will become fact in the same way that reality eventually caught up with Jules Verne's vision of Paris in the twentieth century. Validation often comes slow to fringe ideas and experiences.

I have always looked to the sky with a sense of hope and wonder. When I was younger I had recurring dreams that a UFO would, one day, land in my general vicinity. If I were really faced with this encounter I had no doubt what I would do. I'd hop on board the UFO and take off to visit other worlds. As I've grown older, had children, and raised a family, I've become much more reluctant to even think about this kind of adventure—I couldn't leave my family behind. But isn't this the type of great adventure that we hope awaits our children, their children, and their children's children? With each day and each new discovery, we move closer to this becoming their reality.

Sightings: UFOs looks at all the possibilities. Are we being observed by alien visitors? Has extraterrestrial contact occurred? And, certainly, the most haunting question of all: Are we alone? In some ways, asking that question and hoping to find an answer is very much like my experience visualizing and eventually finding my lost ID bracelet in an empty field. We can visualize the possibilities, but we haven't found the proof just yet. Maybe one day we'll discover we are not alone, and in doing so, it will be like finding that ID bracelet on a much more cosmic level.

Henry Winkler
Los Angeles, 1997

SAUCERS

1952

Saucers over Washington

The Great American UFO Flap

> The Air Force has never denied the possibility that interplanetary spacecraft exist. There are many people in the Air Force who believe in UFOs.
>
> —Al Chop, former press liaison, United States Air Force

There were more reported sightings of UFOs in 1952 than in any other year before or since. The Air Force Project Blue Book had just been established to collect and analyze reports of UFO sightings, and, as if on cue, an unprecedented wave of new sighting reports began accumulating in the Project Blue Book office. By the end of that year, there would be 1,501 confirmed UFO sightings by civilians, military personnel, and commercial pilots, a 1,000 percent increase over the previous year. The saucer invasion was dubbed a "flap," shorthand for a sustained wave of multiple UFOs.

The culmination of this historic UFO flap of '52 would occur on two consecutive midsummer nights, when high-ranking Air Force personnel, air traffic controllers, and members of the national press huddled over the radar screens at Air Route Traffic Control at Washington National Airport. For more than five hours, they watched in amazement as a spate of unidentified blips tracked across the restricted airspace above the White House, the Capitol, and the Pentagon. What were these objects, capable of generating solid radar returns over the nation's capital?

The UFOs began their sweep across America in March of 1952. The sightings did not inspire wonder and amazement; instead, the anomalous craft were immediately perceived as a serious threat to national security by both the public and the government. It was the middle of the cold war, and the likelihood of imminent attack from the Soviet Union was on everyone's mind. It was an election year, and Harry Truman was running on a rigid cold war platform. Senator Joseph McCarthy was in the middle of a bitter reelection campaign and was fomenting anti-Communist hysteria. The military was about to detonate the world's first H-bomb at Eniwetok in the Central Pacific. Air-raid sirens blared routinely at noon in cities and towns across America; air-raid shelters were replacing the backyard barbecue as suburbia's most sought-after home accessory; and schoolchildren were taught to dive under their desks for protection in the event of a nuclear blast.

It was against this backdrop of suspicion and fear that the great flap of 1952 descended on America. Articles appeared in newspapers almost daily recounting the latest "attack" by unidentified aircraft. The sightings began in the west, quickly moved across the country, and settled along the east coast, where the largest number of UFOs would be reported. Typically, witnesses reported the sudden appearance of a cluster of bluish-white lights that would either streak across the sky at a tremendous rate of speed or hover along the horizon. Some reports included descriptions of metallic flying saucers or egg-shaped wingless craft. Most of the sightings were made by civilians on the ground, and were discounted by the military as hysteria-based hallucinations, until a large number of UFOs were also reported by military pilots and radar operators who encountered them while tracking commercial and military aircraft.

Although none of these UFOs was ever reported to have actually landed or interacted with humans in any way, witnesses felt threatened by what they described as menacing lights in the night sky. According to UFO researcher Barry Greenwood, who has studied the flap of '52 extensively, it was only natural that Americans would assume these anomalous lights had a sinister origin. "[The year] 1952 was a time of great paranoia, great suspicion," Greenwood says, "and the concern over the flying saucer phenomenon was based partly on the idea that some of these objects might be secret weapons or spy devices, whether from a Communist country or from somewhere in outer space. There was an enormous concern that our privacy was being invaded by outsiders."

That concern was shared by the Air Force, which insisted that the flap of '52 be given high-priority status by Project Blue Book and the Air Technical Intelligence Center at Wright Field (now Wright-Patterson Air Force Base) in Dayton, Ohio. Richard Hall, a former Air Force enlisted man and current chairman of the nonprofit Fund for UFO Research, recalls that every branch of military intelligence believed initially that the UFOs must be of Soviet origin.

"At that time, the Soviet Union was ahead of us in the space race," Hall says. "Any new or different thing that happened, we suspected the Soviets were up to it. They were the bogeyman behind everything we didn't understand. So here were these funny things flying around, our pilots seeing odd lights and corresponding radar. The first thought was that the Soviet Union must have made a big technological breakthrough."

But the Air Force quickly ruled out the possibility that the UFOs were coming from the U.S.S.R. "The Foreign Technology Division in Dayton learned almost immediately that this was not anything the Soviet Union had produced," Hall explains. "We had sophisticated tracking systems, and there was absolutely no evidence that these craft were coming from the Soviet Union."

The sightings continued unabated, reaching their peak in July of 1952. According to Barry Greenwood, the Air Force was overwhelmed. "They were buried with reports," explains Greenwood. "Bases were trying to coordinate with one another, trying to document sightings that were ongoing by calling base to base, asking them to turn their radar in a particular direction. There was quite an effort to solidify the information on these reports. Not only were there more sightings in 1952 than in any other year, there were also the largest number of unknowns per raw report of any year. And I would add perhaps five to ten times to the Air Force figures because only a small number of reports were ever sent to military sources. Most people simply kept their sightings to themselves until years later."

On July 2, 1952, the military was able to capture on film a significant UFO event, typical of many more to come, near Tremonton, Utah. (See Photo 1.) A brilliant cluster of small bluish-white lights appeared in the midafternoon sky. They appeared to move west to east in pairs, eventually disappearing in the distance. Later analysis by the U.S. Navy Photograph Interpretation Center would conclude that the objects were light sources traveling at over 600 mph. Their identity remains unknown to this day. Within the Air Force, and even within Project Blue Book, there were officers who expressed openly their belief that this sighting and many others in the summer of 1952 were perhaps of extraterrestrial origin.

Among those who shared the belief that the flap of '52 might be evidence of alien visitation was veteran newspaper reporter Al Chop. In 1950 he was hired by the Air Force to act as their civilian press liaison. By 1952 he had unlimited access to the inner sanctum of UFO research at the Pentagon. Chop was charged with disseminating Project Blue Book reports to the press and to the public. When he spoke to *Sightings* in 1996, it was the first time since 1952 that he had spoken publicly about his role in the great American UFO flap.

"I was responsible for all information going to the press and the public," Chop recalls now. "UFOs, as far as I'm concerned, do exist. Personally, I feel that it's possible that they come from another planet or another star system. And the Air Force has never denied the possibility that alien spacecraft exist. They do not think it's probable, but they cannot explain about 25 percent of all UFO reports. Whether or not UFOs are traveling in space right now no one knows, and the Air Force certainly doesn't know."

During the spring and summer of 1952, Al Chop was flooded with requests from the press and the public. Based on information from Chop and others at Project Blue Book, *Life* magazine published an article in April 1952 entitled "Have We Visitors from Space?" The article reported that the possibility that the UFOs were coming from the Soviet Union had been ruled out and then went on to speculate about what the UFOs *might* be. It was the first time Americans began to suspect that the government knew more than it was willing to tell about the origins of UFOs.

Al Chop is quick to disagree with those who believe that the truth about UFOs was covered up then, or that it continues to be covered up today. "We didn't cover anything up," explains Chop. "It's just that we didn't volunteer information. At that time we were getting literally hundreds of UFO sightings reports. If it was a sighting by an Air Force pilot or engineer or a ground observer corps and it wasn't picked up by the press, we would not volunteer information, because we'd only be making our own jobs a lot tougher. To talk about every report would be opening up a real can of worms, but if people asked for specifics on a particular sighting we would give them all the information we had."

The two most alarming reports, reports that Al Chop could not keep from the press, occurred on the nights of July 19 and July 26, 1952. On those consecutive Saturdays, UFOs were tracked on the radar screens at Washington National Airport and nearby Andrews Air Force Base. They were also seen by witnesses on the ground and in the air. Some of the unidentified craft were reportedly flying as fast as 7,000 mph. Other craft were seen traveling at a very slow speed, perhaps only hovering, within the triangle of off-limits airspace above the United States government's most important strongholds: the White House, the Capitol, and the Pentagon.

"The first night [July 19] I was home, sound asleep," Al Chop remembers. "I read about the UFOs visiting Washington in the paper in the morning. Of course, when I got to my desk, we had many, many inquiries from the press, and I had no answers for them." The first thought within the Pentagon and at Project Blue Book was that these UFOs were an anomaly caused by a temperature inversion. During an inversion, cool, dry air close to the ground is blanketed by a layer of warm, humid air. This atmospheric condition can cause radar signals to bend and give weak, false returns. "With an inversion a radar operator can get what they call ground clutter," explains Chop. "They can pick up lights from the ground or even light shining on a rock. But the returns on July 19, 1952, were nothing like what we had during other inversions. These were good, solid returns. The Air Force radar expert who was present that night stated that they were solid returns, and he thought they were picking up metallic objects."

According to UFO researcher Richard Hall, there were few in the Pentagon who believed the temperature inversion theory. "When these objects just suddenly materialized around Washington, D.C., this was unheard of. Their approach into the city should have been detected. These things were highly maneuverable and seemed to fly vertically as much as horizontally. This was quite startling to the people involved, and they knew instantly—had a gut feeling—that something very weird was going on," says Hall.

The Pentagon's inability to provide a quick, definitive answer about the UFOs over Washington, D.C., caused widespread fear that bordered on panic. Barry Greenwood sums up the mood of the country in the week following the July 19 sighting: "When you see the headlines, you see how alarming it truly was." (See Photo 2.) "If I saw three-inch newsprint headlines declaring that saucers were flying over Washington, I would worry about it. People were seeing solid information important enough to be on the front page of the *New York Times* and in every national daily in the country. They couldn't help but think that the situation was out of control. They expected the military to deal with it and provide answers, but they couldn't. They invented explanations that just didn't apply."

In the week that followed, the Air Force was inundated with reports of UFO sightings up and down the eastern seaboard. They were also following up with several dozen witnesses, including commercial pilots, who had seen the "Washington invasion," as it was now being dubbed in the press. Then, on July 26, 1952, one week to the minute after the first Washington sightings, a second wave of UFOs appeared in the very same restricted airspace. This time, Al Chop was not home in bed. He was in the radar room at Washington National Airport.

"On the night of July 26, I got a call from the FAA telling me that the UFOs were back in action over Washington," Chop says. "They said that they had the press beating the doors down at National Airport to get a look at the radar scope. When I got to the airport around midnight, I gave the press entrance into the radar room. We all crowded around the scope and were observing the UFOs right along with the Air Force and the radar operators. There were two Air Force officers, four radar control experts, the controller who normally mans the station, and several members of the press. We all observed at that time fourteen or fifteen objects being picked up by radar.

"We had several other commercial aircraft flying in the area at the time. The radar operators were using little plastic markers to identify these known flights—one color for the known flights, another color for the unknowns. We had more unknowns than knowns, and the returns from both were the same. They were good, strong radar returns. And there was another radar in operation that night. We were in conversation with Andrews Air Force Base, and the flight controllers at Andrews were getting essentially the same returns we were getting. They had unknowns all over their scope, too."

The Air Force requested a scramble, the immediate takeoff of military aircraft, to investigate the unknowns. Two F-94s should have been only minutes away at Bolling Air Force Base. But they weren't there. Instead, they were in Delaware, and it took the two Air Force interceptors more than an hour to reach Washington, D.C. Precious time was lost for reasons that many UFO researchers believe were not coincidental. Chop explains: "It just happened that the air defense squadron that normally guards the capital was assigned to New Castle, Delaware, because they were repairing the runways at Bolling Air Force Base. It seems unusual that the UFOs visited the capital during the time that the jets weren't there."

Once the F-94s did arrive, there was nothing for them to see. "When those interceptors got onto our scope, all of our unknowns disappeared completely from the scope," Chop recalls. "It was kind of scary. We had nothing to show to the interceptor pilots. We had no place to vector them. So we had them circle the Capitol. They reported back they saw nothing, so we let them go back to base. The minute they got off our scope, the unknowns appeared again. In the radar room, we all just looked at each other. We were amazed." Washington National requested another intercept.

"At about 3:30 or 4:00 in the morning, the Air Force advised us that they were sending up another pair of F-94s," Chop continues. "We saw them come in on the scope, and this time all our unknowns stayed on the scope. We had one interceptor north of the Capitol, and we vectored the other to the south. The one who was flying north reported he saw nothing, although we tried to vector him into several of the unknown returns. He didn't see anything. At first, the one to the south didn't see anything either." Then, without warning, the pilot flying south radioed in that he had made visual contact with a cluster of UFOs.

"The flight controller had vectored the pilot into an area where we had a group of unknown blips," Al Chop remembers. "The pilot reported that he saw some lights and was going to close in and see if he could identify them. He flew into the cluster of lights and said, 'I see them. They're all around me.' He described them as brilliant blue-white lights. We could see his blip on the scope and the blips of the unknowns closing in on him. We just looked at each other and couldn't figure out what was going on up there. And then the blips started to move away, and the pilot reported that the unknowns were leaving." Then, as dawn broke over the nation's capital, the unknown blips on the radar screens at Washington National Airport and Andrews Air Force Base slowly began to disappear. By 6:00 A.M. the UFOs were gone. "None of us knew what to make of this. We were all very apprehensive," Chop says.

Kevin Randle is a UFO researcher who has assembled one of

the largest collections of documents and photographs relating to the Washington "invasion" of 1952. He believes that government officials were not only "apprehensive," as Chop describes, they were downright frightened and embarrassed. "It's very startling to suppose that aliens are flying all around with impunity, invading the sacred airspaces of Washington," Randle says. "UFOs were invading highly restricted areas, flying over National Airport and Air Force bases. It was unheard of for anything like this to happen, so you can understand why military planners didn't want to admit that the situation was totally out of their control."

Kevin Randle also believes that the events of July 19 and July 26, 1952, are particularly significant because of what happened in the wake of the actual UFO sightings. He suggests that the government's inability to determine the origin of the anomalous craft forced the Air Force to send its UFO investigations underground. Furthermore, Randle suggests, "After 1952, the Air Force's public stance evolved from legitimate interest and investigation into a public relations outfit to deny that UFOs exist." Certainly, the press was never again invited to huddle with Air Force officers over a radar scope.

Many UFO researchers agree with Kevin Randle's assessment of the fallout from the Washington UFO event. They point to the Air Force press conference following the July 26 sightings as evidence of a burgeoning conspiracy to suppress information about the existence of extraterrestrial visitors. On Tuesday, July 29, 1952, Maj. Gen. John Samford, director of Air Force intelligence, agreed to answer questions about the Washington UFOs. It was reportedly the most heavily attended news conference since World War II. Once again, the temperature inversion theory was trotted out to explain the flap of '52.

"At the press conference, General Samford tried to explain as best he could what the Air Force thought of these things. He said the most plausible answer was that the blips were caused by temperature inversion," Al Chop explains. "But the Air Force put out the inversion theory not knowing at the time whether there had been, in fact, a temperature inversion on either night. And we found out a couple of days later that there were no temperature inversions over Washington, so while the Air Force had in its haste given the inversion theory as a possible explanation, they never did say it was positively explained. This satisfied most of the press, and we had no further problem with them."

UFO researcher Richard Hall believes the inversion theory was offered for a more ominous purpose: as a red herring to divert press attention from the truth. Hall says, "When the Air Force came up with the rather lame explanation that the UFOs were caused by temperature inversions, this satisfied people for some reason. It's hard to imagine that it did, but this explanation threw everyone off the track."

As part of this alleged cover-up, Kevin Randle believes that certain military personnel who witnessed the Washington UFOs were threatened into changing their stories. Randle claims to have documents indicating "Captain Ed Ruppelt, who was the head of Project Blue Book, mentioned that Air Force personnel were coerced into changing their explanations. The witnesses were called into their superiors' offices and told what they had seen. It was no longer flying saucers. It was stars seen through low-hanging clouds. And they were then ordered to give this explanation to the public."

Al Chop insists that no one in the Pentagon or within Project Blue Book ever attempted to hide the details of the Washington UFO investigation. But Richard Hall believes that while Chop's office and Project Blue Book continued to operate as usual, the real work of the investigation had been transferred to a hidden agency. Perhaps it is not simply coincidence that the CIA first became interested in Air Force UFO files in 1952, Hall suggests. "I am convinced that there is a big archive somewhere of radar trackings of UFOs," Hall says, "with radarscope photographs, records, technical data that the CIA has or had. During July 1952, there were multiple radar trackings by Andrews and by civilian radar in Washington. These have never surfaced. There have been numerous Freedom of Information Act requests trying to get these documents, but they are deeply buried."

Until these supposed files surface, there is little hope that the truth can ever be known about the flap of '52 and the Washington invasion. At this point, there is only conjecture based on a pattern of government denial and misinformation. "My personal conviction is that the government knows full well that we're dealing with something alien," insists Richard Hall. "I'm using 'alien' in the broadest sense. We don't know where they come from, whether from another planet or another dimension, but I'm convinced the highest levels of government know a lot more about these things than they're willing to tell." Al Chop is amused by Hall's charge. "All the Air Force has are visual sighting reports and radar reports, which may or may not be accurate," says Chop. "They have no materials that you can pull apart and examine. There are no little bodies at Wright-Patterson Air Force Base." But Chop is quick to point out that there is one area in which the Air Force and UFO investigators like Hall do have a meeting of the minds. As Chop puts it, "The Air Force has never denied the possibility that interplanetary spacecraft exist. There are many people in the Air Force who believe in UFOs."

When the great flap drew to a close in November 1952, the Air Force asked the Intelligence Advisory Committee to appoint a scientific panel to evaluate the potential threat from UFOs. Members of the IAC (including the directors of intelligence for the Army, Navy, Air Force, State Department, Atomic Energy Commission, and the Joint Chiefs of Staff) asked Dr. H. P. Robertson, a physicist at the California Institute of Technology, to gather together the country's top scientists to review documents and films from the flap of '52. The Robertson Panel, as it was known, concluded that there was in fact a tremendous threat from UFOs. But the threat they described was not from an attack by extraterrestrial warriors. The panel warned that unfounded UFO reports were beginning to clog strategic channels of communication within the government and could eventually compromise national security. The panel wrote: "Continued emphasis on the reporting of these phenomena does, in these perilous times, [constitute] a real threat to the orderly functioning of the protective organs of the body politic." The panel went on to recommend "that the national security agencies take immediate steps to strip Unidentified Flying

Objects of the special status they have been given and the aura of mystery they have unfortunately acquired."

With that report, the military's open-door policy regarding UFOs slammed shut. Kevin Randle believes that the Robertson Panel was shortsighted and missed a golden opportunity. "We had this hard-core sighting with dozens of witnesses, radar confirmation, airline pilots, and military pilots all saying the same thing—that they did not see temperature inversions. It was an event that if we had studied it properly in 1952 we may have gotten the answer to the question 'What are flying saucers?'"

The significance of the flap of '52 is most often measured by its negatives: the inadequate military response; the inaccurate explanations given at the Samford press conference; the legacy of the Robertson Panel. But according to Barry Greenwood, there was at least one positive long-term effect from the great American UFO flap that is often ignored. "I think in a small way the manned space program can trace its origins to the saucer wave of 1952," suggests Greenwood. "After '52, toy makers realized that there was no longer an interest in the previous pop culture icons like cowboys and Indians; there was a new market for flying saucers, space beings, ray guns. I think all these toys eventually led many children to channel their interests into science, astronomy, and space travel. I think 1952 planted a seed in kids' minds: For once, beginning now, we can seriously believe that when we get to outer space we will be able to explore other worlds."

Flying Saucers Are Real

The Case for Real-Life Flying Pancakes, Doughnuts, and Hubcaps

It isn't a question of whether or not flying saucers exist.
The question is, what are they and who do they belong to?
—George Filer, Air Force intelligence officer, 1958–1978

I didn't have any awareness of a major program that could
in any way, shape, or form be called a flying saucer program.
—Alexander Flax, Assistant Secretary,
U.S. Air Force, 1963–1969

These two statements are representative of the great chasm of opinion about the existence of flying saucers even within the very branch of the military that is supposed to know what's flying around out there and who owns it. Both Filer and Flax are men of science who have reached their conclusions after careful study and years of personal experience. Both have faith in their convictions based on compelling evidence. Yet they have reached utterly opposite conclusions. Who is right? It's hard to know when the truth lies somewhere in the convoluted netherworld of bureaucracy, disinformation, and conjecture that plagues the serious study of flying saucers and other UFOs.

The confusion begins with the very words *flying saucer.* There is disagreement about who, in fact, coined the term, but the first written account of disc-shaped craft flying above Earth is generally credited to Raymond Palmer, a pulp fiction writer and the editor of *Amazing Stories,* a popular science fiction magazine in the 1930s and '40s. In 1946, Palmer began dropping hints in his magazine that he had information about the existence of alien spaceships and a government-backed conspiracy to cover them up. In an article entitled "Cult of the Witch Queen" from the July 1946 issue of *Amazing Stories,* Palmer wrote: "If you don't think spaceships visit the Earth regularly . . . then your editor's own files are something you should see. And if you think responsible parties in world governments are ignorant of the fact of spaceships visiting the earth, you just don't think the way we do." His claim is impossible to investigate now because Palmer advertised many of his stories as true, whether or not they were, in fact, true. After "Cult of the Witch Queen" appeared in *Amazing Stories,* circulation doubled, and flying saucer mania swept the country. From such origins the "classic" definition of a flying saucer developed, and to this day it continues to be the most widely sighted of all unidentified flying objects: a disc-shaped vehicle with a central dome area, powered by an unseen internal force that leaves no contrail.

The first use of the words "flying saucer" and the first documented sighting of a UFO to gain national attention occurred on June 24, 1947, when pilot Kenneth Arnold reportedly saw nine disc-shaped craft streaking across the sky toward Mt. Rainier in Washington. (See Photo 3.) Arnold, a U.S. Forest Service employee who was out searching for a downed plane, described the UFOs to a local reporter as traveling at more than twice the speed of sound and flying "like a saucer would if you skipped it across the water." In the days that followed, hundreds of additional sightings of similar craft were reported throughout the United States. Early press accounts took the sightings seriously and reported the facts of each case with little editorializing about the credibility of the witnesses or their claims about the saucers' extraterrestrial origins. So, the UFO craze was already in full swing when a flying saucer reportedly crashed to Earth near Roswell, New Mexico, on July 8, 1947.

Still considered the watershed event in the history of UFO sightings, the crash at Roswell fueled wild speculation about the purpose and origin of flying saucers. Eyewitnesses, including Roswell Army Air Field intelligence officer Major Jesse Marcel, speculated that the Roswell UFO was an alien spacecraft. The Air Force insisted that these claims were flights of fancy, that the crashed UFO was a weather balloon (much later the Air Force would report to the public that the UFO was a failed top-secret Project Mogul balloon). When press reports began to question the reliability and intelligence of UFO eyewitnesses, and official Air Force press releases denied the existence of flying saucers, popular opinion began to turn against the existence of alien craft. Evidently, the press insisted, pulp fiction had gotten the better of people. Well into the 1960s, ominous flying saucers piloted by little green men demanding "Take me to your leader" became largely the stuff of B movies and comic books.

After a series of television reports, *Sightings* has gathered enough information to suggest that pinning the flying saucer craze on imaginations born of *Amazing Stories* and Kenneth Arnold and Roswell may be putting the paranormal cart before the horse. Through interviews, declassified government documents, and obscure texts, *Sightings* has ample and compelling evidence that suggests several governments, including the United States, were building and testing real flying saucers well before the "official" launch of the saucer craze in 1946.

"There were five saucer projects that the Germans did during the Second World War," claims Henry Stevens, director of the German Research Project, a repository for research on the development of German aircraft during World War II. "There was the Fireball Project, the Vril Project, the Haunebu Project, and two V7 projects." In *German Secret Weapons of the Second World War,* published in 1959, former SS intelligence officer Rudolf Lusar writes: "Experts and collaborators in this work confirm that the first projects called flying discs were undertaken in 1941. The de-

signs for these flying discs were drawn up by the German experts
Schriever, Habermohl, and Miethe, and the Italian Bellonzo.
Schriever chose a wide-surface ring, which rotated round a fixed,
cupola-shaped cockpit. The development, which cost millions,
was almost completed at the end of the war. The then-existing
models were destroyed but the plant in Breslau where Miethe
worked fell into the hands of the Russians, who took all the material and the experts to Siberia, where work on these flying saucers
is being successfully continued."

It is possible, however, that some German saucer plans and the
engineers who laid them out did not end up in Siberia. "We had
large numbers of technical people searching through Germany,
moving right behind the troops, beginning in April 1945. And
they would send back everything they found," explains Alexander Flax, former assistant secretary of the Air Force. Flax began
his distinguished career designing and building aircraft prior to
World War II, became chief scientist for the Air Force in 1959,
and was then recruited in 1963 to be assistant secretary, oversee-
ing all Air Force research and development. "After the war, we
had a comprehensive program in which the documents that were
captured at the various research establishments were translated,
and I must have a five-foot bookshelf of them. Some of them were
very useful, some were duplicative of things we already knew, and
some were blind alleys." But, Flax insists, none of this research
ever led to the development of a practical American flying saucer.

"For a while, there was some focus on the saucer [shape] as
having some mystical advantage, which nobody ever found," Flax
says. "I mean, all the wind tunnel model tests did not show that
the saucer was necessarily superior to the pancake, or the delta
wing or any other low-aspect ratio shape. There was no unusual
or hidden technical advantage associated with the saucer shape;
it was just a possible shape for a low-aspect ratio flying machine."
According to Flax, from the very beginning, reports of flying
saucers have been, at best, civilian misidentifications of experimental aircraft or weather anomalies. He explains the saucer
craze this way: "They [UFO eyewitnesses] were seeing some of
our aircraft up there. When the reported movements didn't co-

incide with aircraft known to be flying at that time, they were seeing balloons operating at high altitude, or they were seeing high-altitude clouds with the sun, the moon, or some other light reflected from them. Ice crystals at high altitude will often give various illusions. I could not find evidence that any of these things came from other countries, and certainly not from outside the solar system."

Flax believes that many civilian UFO sightings describing flying saucers were misidentifications of the earliest vertical takeoff and landing aircraft. Flax remembers: "The first attempt at vertical takeoff and landing that I saw was in 1936 or 1937. It was a thing called the Herrick Vertiplane, and subsequently there were many, many different types. Some had movable wings with large propellers, others only rotated the engines. Some diverted jets. There were helicopters that converted to fixed-wing aircraft in flight. One could go on indefinitely." But none of these flying machines have the classic flying saucer shape.

The experimental aircraft with the greatest likelihood of being misidentified by civilians, Flax believes, was the Navy's XF5U-1, nicknamed the Flying Flapjack, or Flying Pancake. "The Flying Pancake was developed by a fellow named Charles Zimmerman at NAS [National Academy of Sciences]. It is exactly as described," Flax says. (See Photo 4.) "Anybody seeing it could have thought they were seeing a flying saucer." However, the Navy built only two XF5U-1 prototypes, only one flew, and the whole program was scrapped in 1947. So, it is unlikely that the Flying Pancake could account for the thousands of saucer sightings that continue to this day.

Could there have been other saucer programs or recovered alien craft that Assistant Secretary Flax did not know about? "If programs which started in the 1950s were still going and receiving substantial amounts of money in the 1960s, then I would have had to know about them," Flax says, "and I didn't have any awareness of a major program that could in any way, shape, or form be called a flying saucer program." However, Flax does acknowledge that there were certain aircraft programs outside the Air Force that he would not have been privy to. He explains, "There were some projects that were pursued independently by the CIA and where the Air Force had only a tangential involvement. I was only generally aware of them and not closely associated with them." In March of 1995, *Sightings* received newly declassified documents of one such project, code-named Silverbug. (See Photo 5.) The designs date back to 1955, and although there is no indication whether Silverbug did, in fact, fly, the project's secrets were apparently important enough to remain top secret for forty years. And where were the German scientists who were supposedly constructing flying saucers in Germany during World War II? At least one of them went to Canada and would eventually work for the United States. His story opens up tantalizing possibilities about real-life flying saucers.

In 1959, Avro Aircraft Ltd., of Toronto, Canada, unveiled what they claimed was the world's first manned flying saucer. Dubbed the Avrocar, the circular craft was paraded in front of the media, where it jerked, twisted, and barely levitated on Avro's tarmac. (See Photo 6.) It looked like a flop, hardly capable of inspiring dreams of interplanetary conquest, but two aspects of the Avrocar's design hint at greater accomplishments hidden within Avro Aircraft Ltd.: the U.S. Air Force had contributed $2 million to the project; and the Avrocar's designer was none other than Dr. Richard Miethe, the German scientist who was reportedly designing and flying sophisticated flying saucers during World War II.

German Research Project director Henry Stevens finds it preposterous to assume that the Avrocar was the best the illustrious Dr. Miethe could do. "When you think about Dr. Miethe working for A. V. Rowe [founder of Avro Aircraft Ltd.] for ten years and the Avrocar is all he could whip up, there's something really wrong." Stevens believes the Avrocar was unveiled to deflect attention from the real work going on inside Avro Aircraft. "The Avrocar is just a cover. You have Dr. Miethe going to work for A. V. Rowe in the late 1940s. You have Kenneth Arnold sighting something flying north into Canada which looks like a Miethe design. You have many sightings of flying craft that are classic Miethe designs that have nothing to do with hovercraft like the Avrocar. What Dr. Miethe was actually doing with A. V. Rowe is anybody's guess."

"The Avrocar could have been a cover for something different, but I'm not aware of it," Alexander Flax counters. However, Flax does admit that the Air Force and the CIA later made effective use of a similar cover story for a different aircraft. "The CIA had the Oxcart aircraft that began flying in the early 1960s. They were kept under cover. We had places we could fly them without anybody seeing, but they were inevitably going to be noticed in flight. At the same time, there were two Air Force programs essentially based on the same airframe concept with the same engines. One was the YF12A that was to be a fighter interceptor that never was bought in quantity for that purpose. When we realized that Oxcart might have been visible in one way or another, we surfaced the YF12A, the most innocuous of the three programs. And we did it with fanfare, invited the reporters, and that covered for the others for a while."

Researchers will probably never know if the Avrocar was a cover story. Even if any of the company's secret projects were to be declassified, the Freedom of Information Act does not apply to government projects built outside the United States. It is another dead end for UFO researchers, unless they can uncover people who worked for Avro Aircraft or any other concern allegedly building flying saucers. Dr. Miethe would, of course, be a tremendous resource, but according to Henry Stevens, "After the Avrocar was unveiled and filed away, Dr. Miethe dropped off the screen. I have no idea where he is now, or even if he's still alive." However, Jack Pickett, one possible eyewitness to Miethe-inspired flying saucer designs, is still alive.

Jack Pickett is a frustrated man. Pickett claims that while he was stationed at MacDill Air Force Base in Florida in 1967, just eight years after Avrocar's official debut, he saw several flying saucers on the base scrap heap and was later shown pictures of advanced flying saucers in the adjutant general's office. However, since that time he has never received official acknowledgment of what he saw or what he was shown by a superior officer. On the other hand, there has been no flat-out denial from the Air Force either, only vague promises that material will soon be declassified. Until then, Jack Pickett's word and his sketches are the only documented evidence that the United States ever flew saucers.

"My partner and I were near a restricted area of the base," Pickett recounts, "and all of a sudden we saw four aircraft parked out there, and our immediate reaction was 'My gosh, those are flying saucers. Those things really do exist!' They all looked exactly like the epitome of a flying saucer. They were disc-shaped; the pilot's cabin was dead center on top. The glass on these cabins seemed to be extra, extra thick, of whatever material it was. They were streamlined right straight into the sloping surface of the upper disc. The exhaust came out the lower surface of the disc. I have no idea how in the world they worked, but the largest one had four air intakes on it and trim tabs around the edge that I would assume were some sort of ailerons [movable wing flaps]. I have no idea what they were manufactured out of. They were very smooth and ultra-streamlined, just gorgeous aircraft to look at. And there was no mistaking what they were. They were flying saucers."

As publisher of one of the base magazines, Pickett asked for permission to write an article and publish photos of the flying saucers he had seen. "I went up to the adjutant general's office, escorted by Air Police," Pickett continues. "An amiable colonel went over to a file cabinet and got out a whole bunch of photographs and proceeded to lay these photographs out on a large table. Well, my interest perked up instantly when I began to see literally hundreds of photographs of all types of flying saucers. I pointedly asked him, 'Are these where the flying saucer stories came from? Is this what they were?' And he said, 'Yes.' Well, I was awestruck. I couldn't believe I was seeing what I was seeing. The photographs were easily identifiable as Air Force photographs. I was told that these particular aircraft could go fast enough and high enough to actually achieve spaceflight. I asked how come they were discontinuing them when they had that type of flight capability that could actually get into space, and he said they had come up with a better design. The new design didn't have some of the maneuverability problems that these did, so they'd decided to scrap the old ones."

Pickett claims he was given tacit approval to run some of the photographs in his base magazine, but when he went to collect the photos the following day, permission was denied. "The next morning, on my way to pick up the photos to go to press, I picked up the local Tampa paper and there was a report of a UFO sighting over Miami," Pickett explains. "I took the report to the colonel, and he said, 'I know what that was. It took off from Avon Park; it's a new design.' He briefed me about the UFO sightings and said the Air Force wasn't going to admit it was one of their aircraft. So I asked him, 'Is it a good idea that you're going to have a magazine [article] published right here on MacDill Air Force Base with the title *Flying Saucers: For Real* with about twenty photographs of this aircraft in there?' And he paused a bit, went out the door and up the hall somewhere. In a little bit he came back and said, 'We've decided not to release this material to you right now. Perhaps at a later time.'" Thirty years later, Jack Pickett is still waiting. The only visual record of the flying saucers he saw is a sketch he drew years later from memory. (See Photo 7.) Every request for access to the photographs he insists he saw in 1967 has been denied.

Among the allies that Jack Pickett has gathered in the intervening years is former Air Force intelligence officer George Filer. Since his retirement in 1978, Filer has been slowly amassing aircraft and military ephemera for the Air Victory Museum in Medford, New Jersey. Based on his extensive knowledge of U.S. military history and his twenty-year career in the Air Force, George Filer believes in the veracity of Jack Pickett's story. "Jack sent a letter to the museum asking if disc-shaped aircraft do, in fact, exist," Filer recounts. "We thought if there was, it would be a wonderful addition to the museum, so we started investigating. I found a number of people who remember seeing something strange out at MacDill. So there is reason to believe that something existed at one time. Additionally, there are thousands of pictures of disc-shaped craft that people have taken from the ground. It could all tie together. It isn't a question of whether or not flying saucers exist. The question is, What are they and who do they belong to?"

Epilogue:
The Ledding Factor

Why maintain deep cover for a decades-old project using World War II technology? Some researchers believe it's because flying saucer projects are ongoing and that the technology to build them has not come from a foreign country, but from an alien civilization. For many ufologists, the crash at Roswell was not the result of a military saucer project, but the birth of one. Is there any indication that the saucers Jack Pickett saw were based on Roswell-inspired designs?

It is generally believed that whatever crashed near Roswell, New Mexico, in July of 1947 was transported by secret military caravan to what is now Wright-Patterson Air Force Base in Dayton, Ohio. According to UFO researcher and Wright-Patterson historian Michael Swords, if there was a UFO, it would have fallen under the jurisdiction of the base's technical intelligence organization, known as T2. There was at least one man at T2 with an incredible link to flying saucers.

"One of the intriguing operatives in the early Project Sign—which had to do with UFO investigation—was a civilian engineer employed at Wright-Patterson named Alfred Ledding," Swords explains. "Ledding was originally part of T3 Engineering design, but was assigned very early in July of 1947 to work for the intelligence group. He was the one person who had a foot in both sides of the base. He had an office at T2 Intelligence on the Patterson Field side and an office at T3 Engineering on the Wright Field side. It's known that T2 talked to UFO witnesses. It's also possible that T3 could have known of actual crashed devices. If that was the case, nothing would be more natural than to expect some intelligence operative to try to design a flying disc-shaped craft of his own."

In fact, when Alfred Ledding left Wright-Patterson in 1952, one of the first things he did was to apply for a patent for one of his aircraft designs. It was a design for a flying saucer. (See Photo 8.) "Alfred Ledding, for reasons that we don't know, early in July 1947 designed a flying disc, which he ultimately got a patent for in the early 1950s," Swords says. "Why it was that Ledding chose to design a flying saucer with so many of the precise descriptive details in some of the Wright-Patterson reports is unknown. Possibly it's just a coincidence that Ledding's design came immediately after the alleged Roswell crash. But it is at least an intriguing possibility that Ledding may have actually seen something face-to-face, and that's what inspired him."

Who Built the Saucers?

Claims of Their Extraterrestrial Origin
Span the Century

> I had such an ominous feeling. Here were things not built
> by human hands, something from another planet millions
> of miles away made by intelligent creatures obviously more
> intelligent than us.
>
> —Bob Lazar, engineer

If disc-shaped flying machines designed and built by humans on
Earth are real, doesn't that end the flying saucer debate once and
for all? Doesn't the existence of real flying saucers confirm the
skeptics' point of view that all UFO reports are simply misidentified experimental aircraft sightings? No, insist many UFO researchers, because even if human-built saucers are real, the
inspiration for their design and construction may very well have
an extraterrestrial origin.

Were flying saucers built from wholesale imagination or because alien spacecraft showed us how? Two stories from opposite
ends of this century offer the intriguing possibility that flying
saucer technology developed from knowledge provided by extraterrestrial engineers.

The flying saucer (and its extraterrestrial origin) is generally believed to be an all-American phenomenon with its roots in the July 1946 issue of *Amazing Stories* magazine, the first confirmed saucer sighting by pilot Kenneth Arnold in June 1947, and the alleged saucer crash near Roswell, New Mexico, in July 1947. While it is true that the term *flying saucer* was coined in the United States around 1946, the first documented saucer-shaped craft to allegedly fly above the earth was designed and built in Germany in 1924. It was called the Vril Flying Machine, and the story of its development is a strange and obscure chapter in the history of ufology.

At the turn of the twentieth century, a number of secret societies with a diverse and distinguished membership were active throughout Germany. These organizations, like the New Templars and the Thule Society, had their roots in a strange mixture of politics, occultism, and science that would eventually fuel the burgeoning Nazi movement. Around 1919, members of the Thule Society formed a branch called the Vril Society, also known as The Luminous Lodge. The Vril society drew its inspiration from a nineteenth-century novel by Bulwer-Lytton entitled *The Coming Race*, in which a mysterious race of subterranean superhumans is described as having unnatural powers, including a potent type of electromagnetic energy called vril. Members of the Vril Society believed that vril was not science fiction, but that it was a real energy force that could be harnessed through paranormal means.

In 1920, Vril Society member Dr. W. O. Schumann, a scientist who specialized in the study of alternative energy, contacted Maria Ortisch, one of the era's most celebrated mediums. In a series of seances with Vril Society members, Ortisch claimed to make medial contact with "gods" who gave her instructions on how to use the power of vril to build an interdimensional flying machine. As fantastic as this story sounds, according to German aircraft historian Henry Stevens, the information Ortisch allegedly channeled from these gods did in fact lead to the construction of a bona fide disc-shaped flying machine.

"Initially the Vril Society thought they were making medial contact with some sort of gods," Stevens explains, "or creatures from another dimension. Later they believed the information was being channeled from extraterrestrials who gave them instructions to build an interdimensional machine. The craft basically would work because of the interaction of two spinning—not just alternating—magnetic fields. They believed this interaction would cause not only the craft but the entire region to function outside the physical laws that we are bound by. In other words, they felt they could surf on gravity. And indeed, the Vril Society built this machine in the mid-1920s, and it levitated."

In an article on German electromagnetic saucer projects for the August 1994 issue of *ZeitenSchrift,* researcher Ursula Seiler-Spielmann writes that after the first successful levitation, Dr. Schumann continued to work on improvements to the electromagnetic energy device, his so-called vril-drive, and in 1934 completed his first supposed antigravity effect–driven experimental saucer called the *Vril 1.* (See Photo 9.) According to Stevens, "The first piloted flight was in 1934. A man named Luther Veitz ascended in this craft, but not very well. It was hard to steer. He crash-landed and ran away from the machine, and the machine self-destructed. But they knew they had something at that point." Ursula Seiler-Spielmann's research has turned up ample evidence that the limited success of the *Vril 1* was the beginning of a ten-year German government-funded saucer project that would end only when the Nazis were driven out of power at the end of World War II.

During this ten-year period, the Vril Society members were supposedly the first group to attempt the back-engineering of an extraterrestrial spacecraft. "A German writer, John Von Helsing, describes the discovery of a crashed saucer in the Black Forest in 1936 and says that this technology was taken and combined with the information the Vril Society had received through channeling and was made into a further project called the Haunebu," Stevens says. *Haunebu 1* was supposedly the first large flying saucer developed in Germany. According to plans allegedly obtained from classified German SS files, the *Haunebu 1* was approximately seventy-five feet in diameter and probably lifted off for the first time in August 1939, a few weeks before the outbreak of World War II.

In addition, Dr. Schumann and the Vril Society were apparently not the only group working on a saucer design based on paranormal plans. Also in 1939, German physicist Victor Schauberger developed a design for a flying saucer using energy he claimed could be harnessed from the tonal vibrations, or "harmonics," of the cosmos. As far-fetched as this theory seems, Schauberger's research attracted the attention of Adolf Hitler, who offered to provide funds to build Schauberger's own antigravity saucer. But Schauberger, who was a deeply committed pacifist, turned Hitler down. His interest was in developing technology that was in harmony with nature, not hell-bent on destroying it. Whether or not Schauberger's plans ever got off the drawing board is not known.

However, perhaps based on the limited success of the *Vril 1* and the *Haunebu 1,* during World War II several other German scientists, physicists, and aircraft designers, including Andreas Epps, Rudolph Schriever, and Richard Miethe, did begin working on electromagnetic and conventionally powered flying saucer designs. These designers did not claim to have received direct knowledge from extraterrestrials or to have been involved in the back-engineering of crashed saucers, yet their work followed quickly on the heels of the early vril machines, and many of the plans for these German saucers are remarkably similar in design to the *Vril 1* and the *Haunebu 1.*

Just before the end of World War II, Dr. Richard Miethe claimed not only to have levitated an enormous flying saucer, but also to have flown it at great speed and altitude. Code-named *V7,* the saucer was said to have been launched in November of 1944 from German-occupied Prague, Czechoslovakia. Possible proof that the saucer actually flew comes from a memo to Hitler allegedly written by Dr. Miethe, which reads in part, "Today, under my direction and in the presence of two officers, the *V7* was tested over Baltic skies. On the first test flight it flew 23,800 meters and on the second 24,200 meters high. It can also be driven with unconventional energy." Dr. Miethe's allusion to "unconventional energy" seems to be a veiled reference to the kind of antigravity or vril power that began the German saucer movement.

Further evidence of Germany's saucer program can be found

in the book *German Secret Weapons of the Second World War,* published in 1955. In the chapter titled "Flying Saucers," author Rudolf Lusar writes: "Slowly the truth is coming out that during the war German research workers and scientists made the first moves in the direction of 'flying saucers.' They built and tested such near-miraculous contraptions. Miethe developed a discus-shaped plate of a diameter of forty-two meters in which adjustable jets were inserted. Schriever and Habermohl . . . took off with the first 'flying disc' on February 14, 1945. Within three minutes they climbed to an altitude of 12,400 meters and reached a speed of 2,000 km/h in horizontal flight (!)."

What happened to the *Vril 1,* the *V7,* and other craft, which may have contained captured alien technology? Most of the prototypes and plans were destroyed, often by their makers. Henry Stevens recalls the destruction of Rudolph Schriever's flying saucer: "In Prague, Schriever had a little airport with technicians and hangars all unto himself there for his work. On one particular day [in 1945], the Red Army was in the suburbs of Prague. Schriever and his men could hear the explosions and see the fires, and they decided that, essentially, all was lost. They were told by the German troops there that they were going to leave, so Schriever and two assistants pushed their prototype saucer onto the tarmac and blew it up. Schriever packed his plans and his family in his BMW and drove west and went into hiding. Soon after, someone broke into the trunk of his car and stole the *V7* plans." Later attempts to redraw the plans from memory failed.

Plans and perhaps prototypes that were not destroyed or stolen may have been confiscated by the Allies, who swept through Germany in April 1945, gathering every scrap of military material they could find. "The German patents were taken by the Allies as booty," Stevens says, "and were loaded onto boxcars—thirty boxcars full of patents for weapons, transistor technology, free energy devices, synthetic oil, and flying saucers."

Did any of the prototypes survive? Could the advancing American forces have included the crashed Black Forest saucer among their postwar booty? Current and former military intelligence officers insist the idea is preposterous, and yet the end of World

War II also marked the beginning of the American flying saucer craze and a spate of reports that aliens had landed. Among those reports was the most celebrated UFO case in history, the alleged saucer crash near Roswell, New Mexico. Was the Roswell saucer a reengineered *V7* gone awry? Were German scientists now dispersed around the world continuing to build vril-powered machines? Or was this craft another extraterrestrial saucer, a cousin to the craft that had supposedly crashed in Germany eleven years before?

These are the kinds of questions that plague UFO researchers and skeptics alike. They are questions that cannot be answered with direct evidence. There is no direct evidence. There is no saucer sitting in the National Air and Space Museum with a plaque reading: ALIEN CRAFT CIRCA 1940. Instead there are "alleged" plans, intriguing memos, and eyewitness testimony from scientists, engineers, and pilots who swear that they have seen flying saucers from this world and others. German scientists made such claims in the 1930s and inspired a multimillion-dollar Nazi saucer program. In the 1990s, many UFO researchers are making the same claims that flying saucer technology continues to be developed by back-engineering crashed extraterrestrial spacecraft.

Back- or reverse-engineering is a process familiar to many engineers, especially those in the defense and aerospace industries. Particularly during the cold war, captured weapons, rockets, and miscellaneous foreign technology were taken apart, duplicated, and reassembled in the hope of developing new technology for the United States. Sometimes these back-engineering projects were successful, but more often they were dismal failures. Claims that captured alien technology was back-engineered have been made since the 1950s and are usually associated with the secret military projects at Wright-Patterson Air Force Base in Dayton, Ohio, and the mysterious Area 51 in central Nevada.

"Wright-Patterson's role in the back-engineering of crashed discs is something that we have only rumor knowledge of," says Michael Swords, professor of natural sciences at Western Michigan University and an expert on the Wright-Patterson UFO connection. "Air Force engineers in the late forties and fifties apparently believed that it was feasible to build saucer-shaped craft, and there are two reasons why that could have been true. The simpler of the two reasons is that UFOS or flying discs were the result of some foreign technology, but the second and more intriguing reason is that engineers had seen an actual alien craft."

Swords's research has led him to believe that back-engineered alien flying saucers are certainly within the realm of possibility, but that it is highly unlikely that U.S. aircraft based on that technology have ever flown. He says, "I have a purely intuitive feeling that technology that would come across the vast distance of space is probably too advanced for us to back-engineer as far as the machinery is concerned. But as far as the structural materials, it's just possible that we could figure out how their materials were structured together and then piece together so-called space-age materials that would help us with, say, the space program."

But there is at least one nuclear physicist who claims that the U.S. military not only has back-engineered alien materials but also has flown captured extraterrestrial craft. His name is Bob Lazar, and in a rare interview in 1991 for the first *Sightings* television program, Lazar told a fantastic story with parallels to the Black Forest crash of 1936 and the vril-powered craft created from it. As Lazar foresees, this century may end as it began—with the creation of flying saucers based on an actual craft from another galaxy.

Following is a condensed transcription of the Bob Lazar interview as it appeared on *Sightings: The UFO Report*. He begins by recounting his first view of a flying saucer while allegedly working on a top-secret "propulsion project" at the U.S. Air Force's Area 51. (See Photo 10.)

> The second or third time I'd been out there, the bus pulled up in front of one of the hangars, and instead of going around the side entrance, I was told to walk directly through the hangar to the entrance on the opposite side of it. Immediately I could see the edge of a disc. This was your classic flying saucer, two inverted pie plates with a segmented larger-area dome on top. What struck me then was that this was not an alien craft, this was what explained all the sightings. Here is the experimental craft

that everyone's been seeing for so many years, and it obviously has some advanced propulsion technique that fortunately I'm going to get to work on. That's what I thought was going on.

But within minutes of that I realized for the first time that this had absolutely nothing to do with what the government was producing. There were no edges at all. It looked like something that had been made out of wax and heated until everything just began to melt into one another and then cooled. It looked like the entire thing was a vacuform mold on a gigantic scale. There were no welds or rivets, it was just a molded high-strength metal of some sort. The hatch was removed from it and I could see inside. What I saw was quite shocking. This was a full-sized craft— thirty, thirty-five feet in diameter—and yet everything inside it was small. I was looking at seats that were eighteen inches off the ground, obviously made for something small; certainly not made for children to play in.

Then, at the briefing, we began talking about gravity propulsion and antimatter reactors. They [Lazar's superiors at Area 51] said the craft was basically gravity powered. There was a tremendous power source, which powered three independent gravity amplifiers producing gravity waves that were then phase-shifted. This was the basic idea of how the craft operated. We then got into the specifics on how things worked—how the phase shift takes place, how the basic gravity wave is generated, and the fuel for the reactor, which is an element known as 115. It's an element that doesn't appear on the periodic chart, because it's never been synthesized and probably never will be. We talked about how energy was extracted from that element and on and on and on. It was just mind-boggling.

I knew this gravity reactor was not Earth technology, because we know nothing about gravity at all, zip. We know its effects, and there are a couple of theories about gravitons—particles that account for gravity—which are completely wrong. But even if we could develop a gravity amplifier, the power required to produce this gravity field would be astronomical. We're talking about terawatts of power, sizable banks of multiple nuclear power plants, and yet the reactor in this craft was the size of half a bowling ball and a two-foot-square piece of metal. We haven't even developed a fusion reactor, much less an antimatter reactor.

Eventually I would see nine different spacecraft, each in its own separate hangar. Each one was completely different in size and shape. There were a couple dozen of us and our job was basically to look at these recovered discs—and I say "recovered" because I don't know whether they were given to us, we found them, shot them down, who knows what—to start with a finished product and go backward and see how it was fabricated and try and duplicate some of the technology with earthly materials. I had such an ominous feeling. Here were things not built by human hands, something from another planet millions of miles away made by intelligent creatures obviously more intelligent than us. What else could you feel? And they're sitting there with people who don't know how it works, won't tell me why it's here, and haven't told anybody else more than just "something is going on." I had almost a feeling of dread that something was wrong.

What I firmly believe will happen is that when they finally find a way to incorporate the alien technology into our craft, they'll release this technology but never admit the alien connection. Anything to do with flying saucers or discs, they'll just claim it was always theirs, and any sightings are related to our test craft, which they've developed "by themselves."

I know for a fact that it [the technology at Area 51] is of extraterrestrial origin. There are no ifs, ands, or buts. Many people have said, "Well, maybe he isn't exactly sure of what he saw." No, I am exactly sure of what I saw. I know what mainstream science is like. I know where physics stands. I know all of that. There is an extraterrestrial craft. The technology is hundreds and hundreds of years in advance of us. That's the end of the story.

Bob Lazar said he had no idea how long the flying saucers at Area 51 had been there or where they had been acquired. If Lazar can be believed, the nine craft he saw and the antigravity device he worked on could have been either crashed or captured alien technology, or perhaps a crashed or captured *Vril* or

Haunebu or *V7*, the result of back-engineering of an earlier crashed extraterrestrial craft.

But can Bob Lazar be believed?

George Knapp is an investigative journalist who contributed extensive research material for the *Sightings* episode in which Bob Lazar originally appeared. He is well aware of Lazar's detractors within the ufology community who have characterized Lazar as everything from delusional to a slick con artist. Knapp sums up Lazar's credentials and credibility in this way: "It's been extremely frustrating, because much of Bob Lazar's life has just disappeared. I've always thought that the key to his story was Los Alamos National Laboratory. If he worked there as a nuclear physicist, as he says he did, it's conceivable that he could go to work in another top-secret program. The lab has always denied that they have any records on it, but they won't give me anything in writing. All it would take to get me off their back is one letter that says he never worked here, leave us alone. They will not give me a letter in response. The same thing has happened with the subcontractor who supposedly hired Lazar to work at the lab. They will not give me a response. Yet I've spoken with people who worked with him. I found his name in a Los Alamos phone book. I found his name in a Los Alamos newspaper article referring to him working there at the time he said he worked there."

With neither a confirmation nor a denial that Bob Lazar has indeed worked at any of the institutions he claims, Knapp has had to seek out people who can confirm Lazar's story. This has proved equally frustrating. "I've got more than a dozen people who have contacted me with bits and pieces of information confirming Bob Lazar's story, about what was going on out in the desert, about secret government programs. And one after another, after contacting me, they have been contacted by government personnel who have basically intimidated them or told them to back off."

Knapp's research is ongoing, but he has reached this preliminary conclusion: "What was going on there [Area 51], I believe the government was testing, experimenting with alien craft. Now whether we built our own based on models, or whether we built our own based on ones that we've recovered, I'm not sure. Lazar tells me he saw nine flying discs up there, all of them different. It wasn't like we cranked them out on an assembly line. These things came from somewhere. And I would say it's fairly certain that it came from somewhere other than Earth."

Bob Lazar claims that he left the Area 51 project both angry and frustrated. It was the veil of secrecy and the slow pace of progress that in part have led to his coming forward. Finally, it is this aura of mystery that is a haunting reminder of another saucer program in another era that we will never be able to see or touch or understand. "These are the secrets of the universe we're talking about," explains Knapp, summing up the frustration of so many who have studied the saucer phenomenon. "It's an insult to the American people that this technology should be stuck in the middle of a little desert base with maybe two dozen scientists working on it. If this technology is out there, it could change life for everyone, and here they are sticking it out there, keeping it to themselves for some power trip. What motive? I don't know, but it seems to me that it would make more sense to open the darn thing up. Let everybody work on it and let everyone enjoy the benefits of that technology."

THE
NUCLEAR
CONNECTION

1964

Deliberate Deception
UFO Intercepts Nuclear Warhead

> For thirty years I've held that image in my mind. What I
> saw was a circular object that looked like two plates put on
> top of each other with a golf ball on top. It was a classic fly-
> ing saucer, and it shot a beam of something at our war-
> head.
>
> —Lt. Robert M. Jacobs, U.S. Air Force

On a crisp fall day in 1964, United States Air Force Lt. Robert M.
Jacobs was ushered into the office of his superior, Maj. Florenz J.
Mansmann. Two men in gray suits sat silently in a corner of the of-
fice, watching intently as Major Mansmann turned off the lights
and snapped on a movie projector. Together, the men watched
six minutes of film that would forever change the way Lieutenant
Jacobs looked at the universe and his place in it. According to
Lieutenant Jacobs, the film had captured a UFO intercepting an
Atlas F missile shortly after liftoff from Vandenberg Air Force
Base in southern California. Soon after the intercept, the missile,
equipped with a dummy nuclear warhead, crashed into the Pacific Ocean. Lieutenant Jacobs was shown the film because he
had been in charge of the photographic unit that shot it. More

than two decades after the incident, he is still haunted by the images of that close encounter; the implications, if that warhead had not been a dummy; and the personal repercussions he has suffered ever since 1964.

"I liked science fiction books and films, and I thought they were fun," explains Dr. Robert Jacobs, now an associate professor of communications at Bradley University in Chicago. "But I certainly didn't believe we were being visited by intelligent creatures from somewhere else or sometime else or some dimension else. I didn't believe that until after I saw the film in Major Mansmann's office that day. The hair's going up on the back of my neck right now thinking about it, just remembering that day. I saw something that was so strange it changed my life."

From 1963 to 1966, Robert Jacobs was a first lieutenant in charge of photo-optical instrumentation at Vandenberg Air Force base. Simply speaking, it was Lieutenant Jacobs's job to photograph every missile that left Vandenberg and went down the Western Test Range. "The job was serious," Jacobs explains. "Sequential photography is something that engineers use to assess how well a rocket is working or, in many cases, how well the rocket isn't working and what made it go wrong. My job as director of a 135-person section was to provide photographic documentation from thirty or forty different camera positions for each launch."

In August of 1964, Jacobs was charged with finding a new camera position for an upcoming series of launches of the Atlas F rocket. "The engineers wanted to see all three stages of powered flight. From our positions at Vandenberg, we were essentially looking up the tailpipe as the missile flew away from us. While we could sort of make out the three stages of powered flight, the vapor trail was always in the way, so they wanted to get a side look." Jacobs scouted locations for a new camera position and found Anderson Peak, a rocky outcropping 3,000 feet above the Pacific in Big Sur, California. "Big Sur was north and farther west than Vandenberg, so we did a test and discovered that sure enough, we could see all three stages."

For the Atlas F tests, the Air Force not only wanted to photograph their new rockets from a new angle, they also wanted to test a new camera mounted on a high-powered telescope. "I was told they were sending out a very high-powered telescope, from Patrick Air Force Base," Jacobs recounts. "It was called the BU, or the Boston University telescope, invented by a guy named Walt Manning. On August 26, 1964, we went up to Monterey Naval Air Station, and a giant Hercules airplane landed and this huge telescope came off. It was the size of an eighteen-wheeler, looked like a moving van. We hauled it up to the site in Big Sur and began photographing missiles with it.

"The biggest lens we had up to that point had a focal length of 180 inches. The BU telescope had an effective focal length of 1,200 inches, so you can see that it was enormously bigger. It was so big, in fact, that when the missiles left Vandenberg just the bottom three engines on an Atlas F filled the frame. And that was from a distance of 130 nautical miles. We were quite astonished by the image size. We could count the rivets on the skin of the missile."

Robert Jacobs remembers camping out with his unit in the shadow of the gigantic telescope throughout the month of September 1964. Several missile tests were photographed. On or about September 15, 1964, the BU telescope filmed one missile launch that would be significantly different from the rest. This would be the missile launch, Jacobs claims, that was intercepted by an alien technology. "It was early morning. There was a low-lying fog bank about 1,000 feet below us. Suddenly, out of this huge white expanse below, the missile appeared. The BU telescope locked on to it. I was excited and said, 'We got it boys, let's stay with it.' We locked on and filmed all three stages of powered flight," remembers Jacobs. The telescope operated through a radar link with Vandenberg and was set up to be operated and to record blind. The members of the photo-optical team on-site could only watch the missile through their own binoculars.

"Through our binoculars we saw the first stage drop away," Jacobs continues. "We saw the second stage drop away, and we saw the third stage drop away, and then it went on into infinity." But the BU telescope was still filming. "At about T-plus 400 seconds, our film was winding down and Vandenberg locked off the telescope. We all started shaking hands and congratulating each other that we had got the missile. Now what we didn't know at the time is what else we got besides the missile. We got something that changed the way I think about myself, about our planet, about everything, because before that day I didn't believe in UFOs.

"I took the film back to Vandenberg Air Force Base for processing, and the next day I was called into Major Florenz J. Mansmann's office. When I got there, there was a film projector and a screen set up. I remember two men in plainclothes who didn't say anything to me. Major Mansmann said, 'Sit down and watch this.' He turned on the projector, and there was the film that we had photographed up at Big Sur. I was quite delighted. The three engines of the Atlas F filled the frame at the beginning. We could count the rivets on it. I was sensationally happy. I said, 'Wow, this is great!' We saw it through all three stages; then we could see the warhead flying along. We were testing an antimissile system at that point, and we had a dummy nuclear warhead in there with a small rocket about the size of a drinking glass. On the film, we saw the nose cone with the warhead deploy. It was amazing to look at because it was so clear, and the detail was so vivid."

It was just after the deployment of the warhead that the film took a historic and frightening turn. Jacobs recalls what he saw next: "As the nose cone opened, a fan of radar chaff spread out. The idea was that the Russians would fire their antimissile missiles at the chaff while the small rocket on the warhead fired, putting it into a higher orbit than the chaff so it could go on undetected. Well, during this test, as the chaff spread out, with the warhead quite plainly visible, something flew into the frame. It flew in and fired a beam of light at the warhead and hit it. Then it flew up and shot another beam of light at the warhead and hit it. Then this thing flew around to the other side and shot something out and hit the warhead again. And this is all happening as the rocket is traveling at five or six thousand miles per hour. Then the thing flew down and fired one final shot and hit the warhead again. Then it flew out of frame and the warhead tumbled out of space.

"Well, the lights came on and Major Mansmann said, 'Were

you guys screwing around up there?' And I said, 'No, sir.' And he said, 'What was that?' And I said, 'It looks to me like we got a UFO.' And he said, 'You are never to say that again. As far as you're concerned, Lieutenant Jacobs, this never happened.' I was sworn to silence, reminded of the severity of the security breach, and told to leave the room. For thirty years I've held that image in my mind. What I saw was a circular object that looked like two plates put on top of each other with a golf ball on top. It was a classic flying saucer, and it shot a beam of something at our warhead. There wasn't anything in the world capable of that kind of performance in 1964. There still isn't. We still can't do that. What the hell could do that? It became obvious to me as a relatively rational person with some intelligence that this was something from somewhere else.

"I was a firsthand observer to something that was real, solid, intelligently guided. I was told by my superiors in the Air Force to cover it up. I was part of a United States Air Force cover-up. At that time, I intended on making the Air Force a career. I was doing good work, and I felt good about my job. I thought we were doing important things back then, that developing missiles in space was something worth everything I had to give. I had hoped to get into NASA and maybe work with the space program. So I thought seriously about a security breach. They said, 'Don't talk about it,' and I said, 'Fine.' For eighteen years I never talked about it. I didn't tell my best friend. I didn't tell my wife."

When Robert Jacobs did begin to talk about his UFO encounter, the consequences were startling. In 1982 Jacobs was no longer a military officer. He had taken his photographic expertise into the private sector and would eventually become a university professor and an Emmy-nominated television producer. When Jacobs finally spoke out on a late-night-radio talk show, he knew that the Air Force could not censure him. He felt that the worst that could happen is that they would deny the incident had ever happened. Indeed, the Air Force did deny that an alien spacecraft had fired on an Atlas F rocket armed with a dummy nuclear warhead. They also denied a few other things, namely the very existence of Robert Jacobs.

"A very good researcher by the name of Lee Graham was the first to get on my story and attempt to prove or disprove it, to find out if I was lying or not," Jacobs explains. "He went to the Air Force and tried to track down the incident, beginning with, was I ever in the Air Force. The Air Force denied that I was ever there. There was no Lieutenant Robert M. Jacobs. I was never at Vandenberg. If I was at Vandenberg, I was never in charge of the photo-optical instrumentation section at the 1369th photographic squadron. They denied that there was a tracking site at Big Sur. They denied that there was a BU telescope. They denied everything. I never existed."

However, Robert Jacobs provided *Sightings* with an official Air Force document proving that not only does he exist, but that he was a U.S. Air Force lieutenant at Vandenberg Air Force Base in charge of the BU telescope project on Anderson Peak in Big Sur, California. (See Photo 11.) "Researcher Lee Graham methodically tracked down all my officer efficiency reports," says Jacobs. "He tracked down the fact that there were many Atlas launches during September 1964—and finally that not only did we photograph missiles with the BU telescope but also that we photographed an anomaly."

Further evidence of the BU telescope project was first aired on a *Sightings* television program in 1996. Through Robert Jacobs, *Sightings* obtained film of the telescope being transported to Big Sur and film of Jacobs himself standing in front of the telescope after it had been installed at the tracking site. (See Photo 12.) *Sightings* asked Dr. Jacobs if he felt the broadcast of the film would endanger him in any way. He responded that "the Air Force is probably not going to like this film, but there's nothing they can do about it. It exists. It documents the telescope, the people who were there, including me, and if there are any ramifications about it, I guess I just don't care anymore. I think it's important for people to know that there's something going on and [the Air Force] doesn't know what it is."

Perhaps the most compelling evidence to support Dr. Jacobs's extraordinary claims comes from an unlikely source. *Sightings* researcher Curt Collier wrote to Maj. Florenz J. Mansmann and asked him to confirm the details of Jacobs's account. Major Mans-mann, now retired, sent this astonishing confirmation:

> ... The story by Dr. Robert Jacobs, it is all true as presented. ... I have responded only after Dr. Jacobs released the details of the sightings, negating my secrecy bond. By the time of this missile launch, I was a trained officer in Aerial Ob-servation and a Combat Radar Navigator in World War II, a Di-rector of Operations for the Ground Observer Corps during the Korean and Cold War conflicts, a trained Aerial Reconnaissance Officer, and photo interpreter for clandestine operations [in both Korea and Vietnam].
>
> The image orthicon system we used in capturing this Uniden-tified Flying Object on film had the capacity to photograph the nuts and bolts of the missile launch and its supersonic flight. In retrospect I regret not being able to evaluate the film for more than three showings. The two government agents confiscated the film and placed it in a briefcase and departed after I had checked their authorization to leave with the film. ... I was instructed by ... my Commanding Officer to consider the incident top secret.
>
> I am writing to confirm Dr. Jacobs's account as he described it.

Florenz Mansmann's letter offers several remarkable clues to the reality of the incident as Robert Jacobs describes it and to the whereabouts of that film today. Mansmann, who has an impres-sive list of credentials that relate directly to the identification of aircraft from World War II through the Vietnam War, confirms that he saw the same unidentified flying object on film that Ja-cobs claims to have seen. He confirms that the film was shown in the presence of two "government agents" with the authority to confiscate the film. And Mansmann also supports Jacobs's claims of a government cover-up by referring to the "secrecy bond."

If the identity of the government agents—or even their branch of service—could be uncovered, the controversial UFO film might still be found in a dusty vault somewhere in the vast storage facilities of the U.S. government. Unfortunately, neither Jacobs nor Mansmann was told who those two men in civilian clothes were. "They were not in the Air Force," Jacobs says. "They were from somewhere else. They never identified themselves. They could have been CIA, OSI, OSS. They could have been from Disneyland, for all I know. I haven't any idea who they were, and that's part of the problem with our country today. We don't know who is in control of things like UFO investigations. I'm not sure anybody does."

UFO researcher Robert Hastings has spent twenty-two years trying to answer troubling questions about who controls UFO information inside the U.S. government. In the course of his research, Hastings has uncovered documents that indicate the UFO intercept of a dummy nuclear warhead was not an isolated event but part of a pattern of UFO encounters that the government has systematically concealed from the public. (See the chapter "Clear Intent.") "There is an adequate record indicating that UFOs have repeatedly maneuvered around nuclear weapons–related facilities," Hastings reveals. "The documents describe in great detail the presence of disc or saucer-shaped objects capable of hovering and performing high-speed maneuvers. I must say that the majority of the persons I've interviewed who were at sites during these incidents are of the opinion that—in fact to quote one—'Our missiles were zapped.' Someone was demonstrating that they had the ability to shut down a nuclear launch.

"I am fully aware," Hastings continues, "that at face value these stories are rather fantastic to believe, but if you look at the documents and listen to the persons who were there, like Robert Jacobs, they're describing incidents involving UFO interference with our nuclear weapons systems. I think it is not a coincidence that the UFO phenomenon emerged precisely at the time in human history when we acquired nuclear weapons."

The correlation between U.S. nuclear weapons and weapons-related facilities would seem to indicate that the UFO Dr. Jacobs claims to have seen was not from another planet but from another country, probably the U.S.S.R. However, both Mansmann and Jacobs have indicated that the technology necessary to perform the maneuvers observed on the BU telescope film was not possible in 1964. "We weren't into high-tech stuff at this point in our career," Jacobs says, referring to the state-of-the-art missile technology of 1964. "We called ICBMs inter*county* ballistic missiles; some of them even made it all the way to the beach. The point is, anomalies weren't unusual back in those days, but the kind of anomaly that happened on that particular day couldn't possibly have happened with the technology we had back then."

Robert Hastings concurs with this assessment of the state of space technology in the 1960s. "I have yet to see any credible evidence that any government has successfully flown craft that are capable of the speeds and maneuverability that the UFO demonstrated in this case," Hastings says. "In my opinion the least objectionable hypothesis is that we're dealing with a nonearthly intelligence. Documents from both the military and the intelligence communities describe objects whose capabilities are vastly superior to anything we have flying—anything anyone on Earth has flying. So I think what we're left with by default is something that is not quite of this earth."

Robert Jacobs has had more than thirty years to think about what he saw and the implications of his sighting. He accepts the idea that the interaction between the UFO and the Atlas F rocket may have been connected to its nuclear weapons potential. "I regard the whole thing that happened as someone firing a warning shot across our bow. What were we doing in 1964? We were throwing nuclear missiles at each other. We were pretending that we were going to throw a nuclear missile at the Russians, and they were going to shoot it down and then we would shoot theirs down—and such a thing would lead to the complete annihilation of the planet. It was a dangerous game, and I guess this philosophic humanist soul of mine hopes that perhaps this UFO was a warning shot. If this thing was guided by a race of beings smarter than we are, maybe we were to take a lesson from it."

Beyond speculation about the lasting benefits of the UFO Jacobs and Mansmann claim to have seen is one real benefit most Americans can appreciate directly. According to Jacobs, the Anderson Peak tracking site in Big Sur is still in use today with telescopic cameras similar to the BU telescope and its image orthicon system. Whenever a space shuttle lands in California, it is the camera on Anderson Peak that records the landing the public sees on television.

1965

The Edwards UFO

Proof That the Government Knows

> We supposedly are having quite an invasion over here.
> —Controller, Los Angeles Air Defense Sector

On the morning of October 7, 1965, a reporter for the newspaper in Victorville, California, stopped in at the local diner for a cup of coffee and the daily gossip. The counter waitress told him that she had just heard a fantastic story from a telephone lineman, who said he had just met a man who claimed he was chased along Highway 138 outside of town by an enormous glowing UFO just before dawn that very morning. The reporter wrote up the story, and it appeared in the paper the next day. It was a typical UFO account: few details, no names, and sketchy information based on a secondhand source as told to a waitress as told to the reporter. The story raised a few eyebrows, a couple of rumors about the witness's veracity and his level of intoxication, and some speculation about the extraterrestrial origin of the UFO. Edwards Air Force Base, ten miles north of Victorville, issued a public statement to calm the fears of the local citizenry by suggesting that the UFO was undoubtedly a classified Air Force project that had strayed into civilian airspace. After a day or two, the

UFO brouhaha died down, and the incident disappeared into oblivion.

It would have remained so, if not for the efforts of independent producer and UFO researcher Sam Sherman, who unearthed hours of previously classified audio tape that proves the UFO was not a fabrication, hallucination, or an experimental aircraft. Thirty years after the anonymous man's UFO encounter near Victorville, there is hard evidence that on that same October night in 1965, there were other witnesses, dozens of them identified by name in a secret government report, who all remain silent about their sightings. They include Air Force personnel, officers, controllers, and a pilot who tracked not one but as many as twelve UFOs for more than five hours as they hovered in restricted airspace above Edwards Air Force Base.

All of the radio transmissions and telephone calls between the Edwards tower, other Air Force bases in the region, NORAD (North American Air Defense Command), and LAADS (the Los Angeles Air Defense Sector, the regional command for U.S. air defense) recorded on October 7, 1965, were declassified in the late 1980s, but they remained undeciphered until 1995, when Sam Sherman produced his audio documentary *The Edwards Air Force Base Encounter*. With the help of military procedure experts, a declassified report on the incident by U.S. Air Force Captain John D. Balent, and pure diligence, Sherman was able to untangle a jumble of more than six hours of official military communications into a coherent, chronological account of the Edwards UFO invasion.

"I didn't put the tape together for the UFO community," Sherman explains. "I was researching a feature motion picture on UFOs, and I came across these Air Force tapes. I was stunned to find out that a squadron of twelve UFOs was over Edwards and that there was an alert status. It shocked me, because there had been nothing as far as I was concerned up to that point that proved UFOs were a real subject. It's a subject that has been ridiculed for many years, and I felt that this was proof that there were UFOs and the military dealt with them—and I felt the public should know."

The following are short selected excerpts from the official military transmissions between the Edwards Air Force Base tower, LAADS, and RAPCON (the Radar Approach Control Center) at an unknown Air Force location at the very beginning of the UFO sighting:

EDWARDS: It's moved to the north of us and one's coming over now.

LAADS: North or south at this time from Edwards?

EDWARDS: He's blinking red, and I have another red light and green light in combination in sight moving very rapidly overhead at this time.

LAADS: I'm going to check my RAPCON to see if they have any movement in that area.

EDWARDS   Okay.

LAADS: LAADS here. Say, do you have any reports of unknown flying objects over there?

RAPCON: No, we haven't.

LAADS: Okay, was wondering. We supposedly are having quite an invasion over here.

RAPCON: What area? In our area?

LAADS: No, it's over around Victorville and Edwards. I was wondering if any of your sites or any of your bunches over there have called anything in?

RAPCON: No. Nuh-uh.

LAADS: Okay, fine. Thank you. [*to Edwards*] Describe it for me.

EDWARDS: I watched it through the glasses, and at first appearance it just looked like a star.

LAADS: I see. In other words, it just fades in and out?

EDWARDS: It's a definite flashing, flashing red, now. It's similar to what aircraft anticollision lights would do, but it definitely isn't moving that way or constant enough to be an aircraft. It's definitely changing in color from white to red to green and red.

The man in the Edwards tower who first spotted the UFO and reported in at approximately 1:00 A.M. on October 7 was T. Sgt. Charles A. Sorrels. He remained silent about the Edwards UFO for thirty years and is the only person involved in the incident who has agreed, even now, to come forward. His first television interview appeared exclusively on *Sightings*, on which Sorrels, now retired, gave a compelling firsthand account of his UFO sighting.

"I spent twenty years in the Air Force, 1954 to 1974, and spent most of my time in control towers. There were times I was in radar, but most of the time I was in the tower," Chuck Sorrels recalls today. At the time of his sighting, Sorrels was working the midnight shift for the 1925th Communication Squadron at Edwards Air Force Base. He was alone in the tower. The tower was not equipped with radar. "This was strictly a VFR tower, which means that I went by visual flight rules, and my job was to control all the aircraft within a five-mile radius of the airdrome and to do it with just binoculars. You learn to be very good at distinguishing aircraft. You have to be able to tell which type of aircraft you're talking to and to identify all the aircraft in the air," Sorrels explains.

But at 1:30 A.M. on October 7, 1965, Sorrels saw a craft he could not identify. "At first I saw just a real bright light, a light green color, and it had a light underneath it that appeared to flash," Sorrels describes. "It wouldn't go completely out, but it would just kind of blink. It blinked red, and then I noticed there was a white light on top of the red. The object was quite large, about baseball size at arm's length. Well, it just sat there, stationary for a long time. And then I noticed there were three more of the same type, only smaller than the original one but still quite large, and they had the same characteristics as the large one. I kind of think of them now as a mothership and then smaller objects coming out of the mothership.

"The large one stayed in one position for a long period of time, and the three smaller ones would move around. Then, from somewhere else, three more came in and they were going north, south, east, and west, moving very fast. They could rise straight up in a heartbeat. They could be in one location and just seem to hover—and then in a moment they'd just appear thirty, forty miles away, just like that. I mean quick. They moved rapidly and in very strange ways. Nothing we had at that point in time militarywise had any of these capabilities. They kind of looked like stars, but these weren't stars. They were too low. At points they were not more than two or three thousand feet off the deck. They could go high, then low, just all over the place. Stars don't do that. I had no way to communicate with them, and to this day I don't know what they were."

Within an hour of his initial sighting, Sorrels had been in touch with LAADS and several other Air Force bases and radar control centers throughout the southwestern United States. He discovered that he was not the only person seeing the UFOs. Several personnel at Edwards and nearby George Air Force Base made visual sightings with 7x50 binoculars. In addition, at least four sites were painting the UFO on radar, some readings of which have recently been declassified. (See Photo 13.) According to a then top-secret Air Force report on the incident, "There were reports of up to twelve radar contacts from relatively dispersed sites. LAADS received reports at various times from San Pedro, Laguna, March, and Boron [all U.S. Air Force sites in California]. All were able to show contacts at one time or another during the four-and-a-half-hour period." Approximately three hours into the sighting, the decision was made to scramble an F-106 interceptor in an attempt to make contact with the UFOs.

In addition to the description of a puzzling UFO event over one of America's largest Air Force bases, the Edwards radio transmissions also reveal one of the military's best-kept secrets; the existence of special military personnel with the authority to scramble aircraft in the event of a UFO invasion. Here is an excerpt from an exchange between LAADS and NORAD:

LAADS: The UFO Responsible officer is in bed. Now, we talked to the sergeant [Sorrels] at Edwards, and he doesn't have any authority except to report to us. He hasn't requested a scramble or anything. So my question to you is, do you want us to shake this lieutenant out of the pad and see if he wants to request a survey? Now we're paying him lots up there, and everybody's seeing it, so do you think we ought to shake this lieutenant out of bed and see if he wants to request we go up and take a look?

NORAD: They haven't raised him yet? They haven't called him?

LAADS: Well, I told them to hold off until I talked to you. The sergeant's reluctant to call him until he needs to, it being three o'clock in the morning.

NORAD: If you have such a good trace and everything on them, I think it would be worthwhile if you give him a call.

LAADS: That's my feeling, too.

Later, LAADS reports that the UFO officer is now on the scene in the tower at Edwards Air Force Base:

LAADS: Okay, they've finally gotten a captain, the UFO officer at Edwards, out of bed and he said, yes, he would like to have a look. We're getting plenty of live data and visuals on these things about forty miles south of Edwards, several of them. We have a conference going with Edwards, San Pedro, Norton, and Boron; there are a number of people who've had visuals on them.

The references to an Edwards UFO officer came as a shock to producer Sam Sherman. "I was surprised that there were UFO officers at each base. The public thinks the whole subject of UFOs is a big joke, and it really isn't. There were UFO officers that were assigned to deal with UFOs, and it was not a subject for ridicule. They didn't have leprechaun officers or demon officers or angel officers for all the other paranormal subjects, but they had UFO officers." For Elaine Douglas, a MUFON (Mutual UFO Network) state director, the Edwards UFO tapes come less as a surprise than as exquisite confirmation of long-held theories MUFON has tried to prove to the public's satisfaction. "This is tape that proves two things. One, UFOs are real, and two, the U.S. government knows it," Douglas explains. "It's real. It's live. It's the U.S. government talking about seeing UFOs. We've got them on tape. They can't say they don't take UFOs seriously. We've got them on tape sending up jet aircraft after them. The military is seeing it, not civilians, and so they can't say they've never seen them, and they can't say they're not real."

According to Chuck Sorrels, an F-106 interceptor was scrambled from George Air Force Base more than three hours after his initial sighting. A LAADS radar operator who had the UFOs on his screen and Sorrels, who was watching the UFOS from the Edwards tower through binoculars, tried to direct the pilot toward the anomalous objects. "Captain Balent, the UFO officer on Edwards, was the one who actually had to say, 'Take a look,' and once he made that determination, they did scramble an aircraft," recounts Sorrels. "He [the alert pilot, Capt. Darryl Clark] made several passes with the aircraft over the base. I would line him up with the runway and then give him a heading off of the runway, and at about three different times, he reported contact. Then a minute or two later, he would lose contact. He would see a blip on his screen, but this thing—whatever it was—would not give any type of coded return. Any airliner or any known aircraft would have had a transponder to transmit a signal that would identify it, but this was not happening. As he would run on toward the target, I could observe him going under it. Regardless of what altitude he went through, the objects would move a lot higher. He went through as high as 40,000 feet, and I said to the director [at LAADS], 'He's low.' And the director said, 'Well, he's at 40,000 feet!' And I said, 'I don't care, he's still low.' We had very few things in those days that would go above 40,000 feet."

Transmissions between the Edwards tower and LAADS confirm Sorrels's account:

LAADS: Edwards, do you still have any of these UFOBs in sight?

EDWARDS: Yes.

LAADS: Okay, tower, pick out one you want us to inter-
          cept, and we'll take a zero on him.

The chase was on, but according to Chuck Sorrels, the F-106 never had a chance of catching up with the UFO. "The way it rose, as fast as it went up in altitude and the way the pilot passed under it at 40,000 feet, he didn't have a prayer. Not a chance of catching it." According to this excerpt, the interceptor pilot did face a formidable challenge:

EDWARDS: That thing is rising!
LAADS: Tower, how's things looking now?
EDWARDS: He's low. Search high. Search high. Search very
            high! That thing is rising. It's rising rapidly.
LAADS: We're at 40,000 feet!
EDWARDS: Search high!

Several researchers have suggested that the UFOs—because of their altitude, speed, and maneuverability—were actually misidentified experimental aircraft. They point out that Edwards Air Force Base was, and remains, one of America's premier Air Force flight test centers, and that seeing strange flashing lights over Edwards is standard operating procedure. However, Chuck Sorrels dismisses out of hand the suggestion that he, other eyewitnesses, and the radarscope had all made a simple misidentification.

"At one point, I was watching seven separate objects. The Air Force wouldn't have had seven experimental aircraft out there at one time, and being in the control tower, I would have been briefed that something was going to fly in my airspace. They wouldn't fly within my control zone without my knowledge, if for no other reason than so I could keep other aircraft away from it. I know it was not an aircraft. I know it was not a helicopter. I know it was not a weather balloon. It was not anything that we know of as a flying object even today that could do the maneuvers that this did. I know a lot of things it was not. But what it was I do not know."

At the time of the sighting, there was one military project flying over Edwards that Sorrels may not have known about that was utilizing newly discovered stealth technology. But according to Sam Sherman, the SR-71 Blackbird could not have been the UFO spotted throughout the high desert of southern California on October 7, 1965. "These things don't glow. They're meant *not* to be seen. They don't glow red and green. They don't get hot and have color all over them. Chuck Sorrels was pretty clever as an air traffic controller. He knew what a black project [top-secret military program] was. He knew when to call the Air Defense Command, and the Air Defense Command knew when they were dealing with UFOs and when they were dealing with a U.S. government project."

What about the possibility that the UFOs were produced by someone other than the United States? Recently declassified Soviet documents indicate that the Russians were seeing similar UFOs in their restricted airspace and were just as baffled as the American military. "They didn't know what we were doing, and we didn't know what they were doing," Sorrels explains, "and now I hear that they were seeing a similar thing to what we were seeing. They probably thought we had something that they didn't know about. We were thinking they had something we didn't know about. But now it turns out neither one of us had them, so where they came from no one knows." Sorrels further rules out the suggestion that he and other military officers were seeing a rare southern appearance of the aurora borealis. "I've seen the aurora borealis. I have seen dancing lights in the sky, and the northern lights is a fantastic thing to see. But this was not the northern lights. This was distinct, one light at a time moving rapidly and moving in strange ways."

The objects were so strange, in fact, that Sorrels remembers being almost embarrassed to report what he had seen and tells LAADS early on that he wants to make sure he isn't seeing things.

EDWARDS: I still see a red light from the three smaller ones. It's very possible we'll be observing these moving all night here. Let me get Boron back on and see if he's getting the impression from it I'm getting.

LAADS: Roger.

EDWARDS: I don't like to be the only one seeing these type
              things.

And in the following exchange, Sorrels reports back that he
has received his first corroborating eyewitness:

EDWARDS: This confirms my, uh, what I'm seeing. There's a
              weather man in Base Ops that's been observing
              these things all night. He's been using reference
              points to try to judge where they're moving, and
              he confirmed that they're very much higher now.
              They are definitely moving up.

The UFOs remained until dawn, gradually rising higher and
higher into space. "By the time it was getting twilight out, they just
looked like any other stars at that point, and by the time it was
daylight, they just faded," Sorrels remembers. The UFO officer
began to write his report, much of which *Sightings* was able to obtain after its declassification. In conclusion, Capt. John D. Balent
wrote: "No one in the Air Defense Sector could provide a plausible explanation. . . . Their experience and the sources of information available to them provide no help. There seems to be no
question that they did have radar control at several sites. The
ground observers claim definitely to have seen flashing lights for
which they could offer or find no explanation. Everyone concerned . . . seems convinced that something unusual occurred."

There remains one strange twist in the story of the Edwards
UFO encounter. On the night of the sighting, while T.Sgt.
Charles A. Sorrels watched a spectacular UFO display, 700 of the
world's greatest scientists and engineers were sleeping in guest
housing at Edwards. The day before, they had attended a technical conference about a breakthrough rocket project called the
X-15, a hypersonic experimental spacecraft still in the early planning stages, that would one day reach a maximum speed of 4,520
miles per hour and an altitude of 354,200 feet. "The scientists
were there on Edwards for a conference at the time, to observe

test aircraft and rocket propellants," Sorrels remembers, "and I've always kind of wondered, did the UFOs come here to put on a show for the scientists—or were they there trying to find out what the scientists were doing? I don't know, but it's just kind of strange that they decided to show up that night as opposed to some other night."

After *Sightings* had prepared its initial report on the Edwards UFO, Director of Research Jonathan Jerald contacted the Pentagon for an official comment. Jerald was told by the United States Air Force information office that the documents and tapes used in the *Sightings* report are "characteristic of Air Force documents of the period." Beyond that, they would have no official comment on the case.

1973

Silent Intruder

A Warning of Things to Come

It just stayed on us for what seemed like forever, and then just *zoom!* It was gone again. I mean, I had aviation training and this was nothing I'd ever seen in aviation.
                                                —Bart Burns, former U.S. Army MP

Roswell. Gulf Breeze. Area 51. Hunter Army Airfield. These are the locations of the great watershed events in UFO history. Roswell, Gulf Breeze, and Area 51 each played a unique part in propelling flying saucers into the national consciousness, and they continue to make news decades after their first appearances in the headlines. But relatively few people have ever heard of Hunter Army Airfield in Savannah, Georgia—and only a handful of even the most dedicated UFO researchers are aware of Hunter's significance in the chronology of great UFO events. The sightings at Hunter are seldom written about, but they are significant for two reasons. First, the unidentified flying objects witnessed by three Army MPs in September 1973 were an eerie harbinger of more sinister UFOs to come. The Hunter UFOs may have been a warning flight the military did not—or could not—heed, because two years later, strikingly similar craft would again appear over U.S. military installations, and this time their intent was clear: They were after our nuclear weapons. (See the next chapter, "Clear Intent.") Second, the Hunter Army Airfield events were significant because they would mark the last time active-duty military personnel were allowed to speak freely and on the record about their UFO sightings. After Hunter, the Pentagon slammed the door on speaking out.

The Hunter incident has never gained the national prominence of other historic UFO sightings because, until a recent *Sightings* investigation, very little was known about the September 1973 event. UFO researcher and coauthor of *The UFO Cover-up* Lawrence Fawcett was one of the first to unearth evidence that the Hunter sightings might be significant. He found a partial report of the incident in a sheaf of other documents he had obtained through a Freedom of Information Act request. (See Photo 14.) The document, an official Army SIR, or Serious Incident Report, states in part:

> At approximately 220 hrs, 8 Sep 73, an unidentified flying object was sighted by two military policemen, SP4 BURNS and SP4 SHADE, at Hunter Army Airfield while on a routine patrol of the installation perimeter. . . . Minutes later they resighted the "object" when it appeared at "treetop" level and made an apparent dive at their vehicle.

When contacted by Fawcett, the U.S. Army had no comment on the apparent UFO at Hunter. It was a swift and definitive dead end, but Fawcett did find several articles in the *Savannah Morning Press* and *Savannah News Press* that enabled him to track down three civilian eyewitnesses. Marcus Holland is a newspaper feature writer who was on the sports desk of the *News Press* when he sighted the September 8, 1973, UFO. "I never, ever paid attention to UFO sightings," Holland explains today. "I always figured that there wasn't much to them—until I saw one."

Holland recalls working late into the night on Friday, September 7, 1973. It was high school football season, and in Savannah the results of the Friday night games were big news. "We had to get about thirty-five or forty local games in the final edition. I didn't leave the paper until close to two o'clock in the morning," Holland recalls. "I was going out on the interstate, and I just happened to look up in the sky and up pretty high there was this light. What got my attention was the way it was changing from one color to another color. I saw red, then yellow with a kind of hue around it. It looked to me like it was coming east from the Atlantic Ocean. The speed on it was mind-boggling. There's just no plane that could fly that fast; it was too high and too fast to be anything man-made. It crossed the interstate and went down behind where Hunter Field would be, and that's where I lost sight of it. It seemed to dive down from a high altitude in two or three seconds.

"I didn't know whether to be scared or what was going to happen. I just said to myself, Could this be a UFO? Is that what I'm seeing? I just had no idea. When I got home, I called the Chatham County Police, and they said they had been having lots of sightings that night and the switchboard was lighting up real good. When I came into work the next day, I was scared to say anything about it. I was afraid I was going to be laughed at. But then I heard from some of the guys that a UFO had gone behind Hunter Field and raked some military police back there. I asked what time that was, and they told me about what time it happened and I said, 'You know, that could have been what I saw.'"

Although Marcus Holland remembers hearing that the police switchboard was "lighting up," Fawcett was able to find only two additional eyewitnesses who may or may not have seen the same craft but did encounter a UFO late on that same Friday night. Savannah resident Gerry Smith was driving with her son Albert on a deserted road when they witnessed the UFO. "I was nine years old at the time," Albert Smith told a *Sightings* team in 1995. "Back then, they didn't have many lights on the road, and there were no other cars on the road with us. And it seemed as if out of nowhere, a hovering craft just showed up over the top of the car. I had never seen anything like it before or since, just a big beam of light with no shapes or angles to it. Nothing but a bright light that lit up the entire car brighter than day. I heard a small humming sound like a small electric motor. Now, an airplane doesn't fly that low, and a helicopter doesn't have that type of sound. It had me so scared I dropped to the floorboard and hid underneath the dashboard."

Albert Smith's mother, Gerry, describes the light as bright red. "Red and iridescent," Gerry Smith recalls, "and it just lit up the car, and I thought, 'It's a UFO.' This thing was hovering over us, and the colors were going around and all blending together. I had never seen anything like this that close in my whole life. I was crying and I had goose bumps, and I was worried about Albert. He was lying on the floor and he was really frightened, and I just kept saying, 'Breathe, breathe.' I didn't know what to do, so I just started praying for it to raise up and leave. And just as I was praying, the UFO was gone."

In twenty years of investigation, a few newspaper articles, scant eyewitness accounts, and one brief government document were all that Lawrence Fawcett could uncover about the Hunter Airfield UFO incident. It was frustrating for Fawcett, a former police lieutenant, to admit that his tenacity had provided only a few tantalizing clues to the Hunter incident. Then, in 1995, *Sightings'* director of research made an important discovery. Jonathan Jerald came across an unrelated aviation article in a computer database that led him to Bart Burns, the "SP4 Burns" referred to in the original Army report. Burns, now a commercial pilot living in a suburb of Chicago, agreed to a meeting with *Sightings* and Lawrence Fawcett in Savannah. He returned to Hunter Airfield to relive a life-changing event he had not spoken about publicly in more than twenty years. His story fills in critical details, including the fact that there were multiple UFOs sighted at Hunter and that he was confined to base and ordered not to talk after the first flurry of press reports had already gone out.

Bart Burns recalls that in 1973 Hunter Army Airfield was a quiet, laid-back post, a welcome respite after his tour of duty in Vietnam. Burns was a decorated aviation specialist who was assigned to the military police once he arrived at Hunter. With little more than a year to go on his enlistment, Burns recalls his duty at Hunter as pleasant and uneventful, until the early-morning hours of September 8, 1973. Burns described the incident to a *Sightings* investigative team, while driving on the same road where he had his first UFO encounter.

"I was a patrol supervisor in the MPs," Burns begins. "Randy Shade and I were working the swing shift, eleven to six, patrolling the perimeter of the base, making sure everything was secure and operating normally. At approximately 2:30 A.M. we were patrolling the perimeter road—Randy driving—when I caught out of the corner of my eye a bright speeding object at fairly low altitude just for a flicker of a second, just long enough to grab my attention. And then it was gone. It caught Randy's attention too, because we were both looking at each other like, 'Did you see that? What was that?'

"I don't know if it was seconds or a minute, but then it came across the treetops, and this time it was much slower and I could see that there were lights around it—strobe-type lights with an amber color, a bluish color, and maybe a mauve kind of color. And as it came across the treetops, it appeared to dive at us. Randy swerved to the right and went off the pavement into the grass. I thought it was going to hit us the way it just dove right at us. I absolutely felt my safety was in jeopardy, so I dove under the dashboard. Our senses were pretty well heightened at that point. As I came back up, I saw Randy was going for his .45, and I had to tell him to holster it. He didn't know what to do. His voice got very short and loud. He was yelling, 'What was that? What are we going to do?' We didn't know what we were seeing, and it was just fear all mixed up with every other emotion.

"As I came up from the dashboard, we saw that it was now just hovering over the approach end of the runway. We tried calling the desk sergeant, but he was coming in broken. We kept trying to get through to him, but something was interfering with the radio. Randy and I were both amazed and bewildered just watching it hovering there, making absolutely no noise. It was warm that night, we had the windows down, and still there wasn't a sound. We didn't even hear the wind whistling when the thing came down. We decided to try and get a better position, so we drove around behind some bushes within a hundred yards of this thing.

It was probably one hundred feet around and one hundred feet across, larger than a semitruck, with an oval shape to it. There wasn't a lot of depth to it, but there was a rise on the top and the bottom. It was just sitting there at the end of the runway, hovering about ten feet off the ground. The amber, blue, and mauve lights were flashing."

Bart Burns's description of an enormous craft hovering at the end of the runway is almost identical to the description of a UFO sighted in 1975 by members of the security team at Loring Air Force Base. (See the next chapter, "Clear Intent.") Because none of the Loring personnel will speak on the record, Bart Burns's testimony is the only independent verification that the Loring event probably did occur just as the anonymous sources have described it.

As Burns and Shade watched the UFO hover dangerously close, "We tried calling the desk again," Burns continues. "And just when we got through, the thing just took off from zero to whatever speed it was in an instant. We were ordered to come back to the station, and as we were progressing toward the station, we saw the UFO come back over the trees and hover about one hundred to two hundred feet above the trees, tailing us by about a quarter of a mile. It just stayed on us for what seemed like forever, and then just *zoom!* It was gone again. I mean, I had aviation training and this was nothing I'd ever seen in aviation. The rate of acceleration was far too rapid. It had absolutely no noise. It didn't have wings or propellers or jets. It wasn't emitting any jet streams as a fighter jet would when you hit the afterburners.

"We returned to the station and related everything to Al Murray, the desk sergeant, and he told us that the state police had just called in and said that one of their troopers was on the highway near the perimeter road, and he had seen it also. We called the tower to see if they had it on radar, and they had negative reports on radar but one of the fellas up there said he thought he saw something. Randy and I had to sit down and fill out written reports about the incident, and Al had to notify the base commander. We got off duty at six o'clock in the morning and went back to our barracks. We were still pretty shook up about this, and we were just trying to lie down and unwind and try and get some sleep. But there was no sleep to be had.

"Back then, Hunter Army Airfield was pretty much an open base. Anybody could get on; you'd just go through a gate and sign in. There weren't a lot of personnel there, and there definitely wasn't anything top secret going on, so they just let everybody in. The gate started calling us and saying there were reporters waiting to talk to us, and then the reporters and all kinds of people were in the barracks, coming up to our rooms and trying to talk to us about what we had seen." Burns remembers that there were reporters from the Savannah newspapers, a local television station, and the *National Enquirer,* all of whom had picked up the radio dispatch between the state police and the Hunter MP station. Burns and Shade spoke freely to the reporters. No one at Hunter prevented the two from appearing live on that evening's broadcast of a Savannah news program.

Bart Burns was off duty that night but accompanied Al Murray out to the runway along the perimeter road. Burns recalls that Murray was anxious to see if the UFO would return. It did make a brief appearance, but Burns recalls that it was not nearly as spectacular as the previous night's events. Returning to the station with Murray, Burns learned that he and Shade had been ordered to return to the barracks and stay there. "We were confined to our quarters, ordered not to speak to anyone. Later in the day, we were interviewed by a ranking officer I didn't know. We were ordered to come into an office one at a time. There was a court reporter-type person there who took everything down. The officer just asked us point-blank questions, very cold and matter of fact. He never gave any indication one way or the other what he thought about what I was saying. I believe I spent about forty minutes or better with the officer. Shortly after that, someone relayed to Randy and Al and I that the Pentagon was ordering us to be quiet, period."

Lawrence Fawcett felt that Bart Burns was an unimpeachable witness who was telling the truth about a bizarre extraterrestrial encounter. "When I interview somebody like Bart, I rely on my police training and ask the basic questions: who, what, where, when, and how. In this case, you have a man who observed a spectacular action who is a trained observer, a military policeman. So his observations are very important, particularly since he has been around aircraft, and this was something he's never seen before. It makes a good case for this being a UFO." Fawcett was particularly interested in two aspects of Burns's narrative—the fact that Burns filed a written report and the serious attention paid to the sighting by high-ranking officers.

When *Sightings* attempted to obtain copies of Burns's report or the base operations logs for September 8, 1995, researchers were told that all of the Hunter Army Airfield paperwork from that era had been destroyed. Fawcett said he smelled a rat. "There was an officer on duty logging what's going on. There's a base operations log. This doesn't exist anymore? They tell you that the director's log has been destroyed? That's a record you want to keep just in case something occurs where you have to go into court and produce documents. If they say they lost or destroyed [the report of] an incident like that, they're lying.

"One of the most interesting things that came out of my interview with Bart," Fawcett continues, "is that in 1969, when the government closed Project Blue Book—its UFO probe—they told the public they weren't investigating UFOs anymore. Well, here in 1973 we see the contrary. Here we see them bringing the witnesses into a room along with a stenographer and taking down testimony, which lasted more than forty minutes."

After the original broadcast of Bart Burns's interview, *Sightings* was able to track down another eyewitness to the UFO events at Hunter Army Airfield. Al Murray, the desk sergeant on duty on September 8, 1973, came forward and agreed to share his recollections of that historic night. During Murray's interview, he also described two additional UFO sightings he made in the days following the September 8 event and revealed a new and startling connection to the nuclear weapons overflights of 1975. First, Murray began by recalling the bucolic—in his words "boring"—atmosphere at the base.

"The Vietnam War was ending, and the base was kind of closing down. It was excess and towards the end there were only a few of us, mostly in a caretaker role," remembers Murray. "I was the desk sergeant and shift supervisor for the military police. I spent most of my time at the station supervising the guys out on the road and funneling the paperwork. The night of the first incident, there was nothing going on; matter of fact I think I was talking to a girl on the phone, bored, in the middle of the night. Then Bart called in and at first I was thinking, *What the hell are they doing out there?* But then I could tell from the way they were talking that they had genuine concern, and I remember telling them, 'Well, if there is something there, then get the hell out of there!' And I remember at that point hearing over the radio their patrol car running at full acceleration and their saying, 'We can't go any faster!'

"They came running into the station, very shaken. Now, Bart, he wasn't the type to scare easily. He'd seen quite a bit of action in Vietnam and was a brave person. He was very concerned, and Shade was especially shaken, really scared. I said, 'Well, somebody's got to go back out there,' and Shade absolutely refused. He said, 'I don't care what you do to me, I'm not going out there.' So I went out with Burns, but we didn't see anything more that night. At the station, I called the county dispatch and said kind of nonchalant, 'How's it going? Anything different going on?' And I could tell in the dispatcher's voice there was something going on. I said, 'Anybody *see* anything?' And he said, 'Well, one of our guys called in,' and he told me what he had seen; and because we kept a log, I knew the county patrolman had seen the same thing Bart and Randy saw at the same time. So right away I knew this was something, not that I doubted our guys before, but this was more evidence."

Al Murray also confirmed that he did accompany Bart Burns to the end of the runway the night before, where Burns and Shade had watched the UFO hover ten feet off the ground. "We took the patrol car and drove down the runway," Murray recalls. "We turned off the lights and just sat there, hoping for something to happen. I saw the red light first. I thought it was a rotating beacon from an airplane, but it didn't flash at all. It was just a round, red light moving in a very erratic fashion with quick jerks. Then it moved away and disappeared down behind the trees. After it was gone, I looked at Bart and he looked at me, and I said, 'I guess you saw that.' And he said, 'Yes, I saw that.'

"Not long after that, I saw a white light that went down the length of the runway, like an object that was going so fast that you couldn't quite follow it. That happened twice. Something just went right down the length of the runway. It was strange, because I knew that at that point the runway was closed. They weren't using it."

Bart Burns and Al Murray both recall the instant celebrity that followed their frightening encounters. "After we reported the incident," Bart remembers, "we were the talk of the town. Everybody pointing their finger at us and laughing. It took several weeks for things to die down, and even then people were still taking potshots. I wished I never saw it. Before the sighting, I didn't believe in UFOs, and you know, I thought people who'd seen things were freaks. Now I was the freak." Al Murray encountered the same prejudice, but his vocal role in the sighting also brought him in contact with someone who provided brand-new details that strengthen the connection between the Hunter Army Airfield UFOs and the flap of 1975.

"I was in the mess hall having breakfast, and this guy came up to me," Murray explains. "He wanted to talk to me, but he said, 'Not here.' So we went outside, and I thought, being an MP, that he's maybe done something and wanted to report something. But instead he said, 'I thought maybe you would understand this after what's gone on.' He told me he had taken a part-time job as a security guard off-base—which a lot of the guys did—and he was working out where they were building a power plant; I believe it was nuclear. He said the first night he was out there, he checked in with the security guard who'd been there awhile, and he said, 'Watch out, there's some really strange stuff that goes on around here. There's weird things that fly around here.' Well, this guy starts on his rounds, doing his job, driving to different points and seeing that things were secure. And he told me he saw just what Bart did, an oblong object with the lights hovering in over the trees, and it was hanging around these transformers. He said he was petrified, just sat in his truck and couldn't move. I said, 'What did you do?' And he said, 'I just sat there until I got relieved in the morning, and then I went back and quit.'"

The story is apocryphal and unsubstantiated. But it does tie in to later events that these men could not have known about in 1973. While the testimony of Bart Burns and Al Murray has furthered the investigation of the Hunter Army Airfield sightings, there are several troubling questions that cannot be answered with official military cooperation. Do the Hunter logs still exist? Did the Army continue its investigation after debriefing Burns, Shade, and Murray? Was the UFO investigating Hunter before moving on to a nuclear power plant?

There is at least one more link to the story that could provide some answers. As of this writing, *Sightings* has still not been able to locate SP4 Randy Shade. Perhaps the legacy of the UFO for Bart Burns provides part of the reason why Shade may not wish to be found. "It changed me," Burns says. "Prior to the sighting, I thought it was all science fiction, there was nothing to the UFO thing. But my personal feelings at the time of the sighting were first fear of the unknown and then that my sense of reason was totally befuddled, because I didn't know what it was and had no way to figure it out. I have a different respect for UFOs now. Is there something beyond? For me now, I'll have to say Yes. There's something out there, but what it is I don't know."

1975

Clear Intent

Big Bombs, Bigger UFOs

> Somehow the object managed to change the tracking
> numbers on the missile. According to one witness, the mis-
> sile had to be removed and retooled to make it opera-
> tional again. And to see this information not just in UFO
> books but where I found it in government messages was a
> real eye-opener.
>
> —Barry Greenwood, coauthor, *The UFO Cover-up*

Throughout the United States, a vast underground network of
sleeping giants stands poised at the ready: a security blanket of nuclear missiles we hope we will never have to use. These weapons
are maintained and monitored twenty-four hours a day by the military's best and brightest, and America sleeps peacefully knowing
that nothing can compromise the safety of our nuclear arsenal.
Immune from misfiring—or even terrorism—the possibility of a
domestic nuclear disaster is unfathomable. But there is evidence
that someone, or, more accurately, some*thing*, has tampered with
our nuclear capability, incapacitating supposedly infallible systems. The details of these incidents are deeply buried in government files, but some information has leaked through to the

outside, leading many UFO researchers to believe that the government is hiding the degree of their involvement in the most potentially deadly UFO encounter of this century.

"There is ample evidence that the United States intelligence community has been involved in clandestine UFO research since the late 1940s," says Timothy Good, UFO researcher and author of *Above Top Secret.* "We now have documents released by the FBI, the Defense Intelligence Agency [U.K.]; the FBI; the National Security Agency; Army, Navy and Air Force Intelligence; and the Atomic Energy Commission indicating that there is no question that UFOs are treated seriously behind the scenes. Most of these agencies admit that they are withholding information in the interests of national security, and some of these documents are being withheld at an above-top-secret level."

Timothy Good's research has led him to a few documents describing unearthly incursions at nuclear missile silos, nuclear weapons storage facilities, and nuclear research centers. In his research, ufologist Robert Hastings has also found compelling documents that strengthen the UFO-nuclear connection. "My research has centered on incidents involving UFOs maneuvering near nuclear weapons–related facilities, ranging from laboratories where nuclear weapons are developed—including Los Alamos, New Mexico—to weapons deployment sites to weapons storage areas. There is a paper trail indicating that UFOs, for whatever reason, have repeatedly demonstrated an interest in our nuclear weapons sites. The documents describe in great detail the presence of disc-shaped craft that are capable of both hovering and performing high-speed maneuvers. We're obviously dealing with a technology vastly superior to anything in the United States, Russia, or anywhere else on the planet."

Sightings has part of that paper trail in its possession: authenticated Department of Defense memoranda, which describe UFO incursions at three different nuclear weapons sites during the fall of 1975. Barry Greenwood, a veteran ufologist and editor of *Just Cause,* the official publication of CAUS (Citizens Against UFO Secrecy), analyzed the documents for his book *The UFO Cover-up* (coauthored with Lawrence Fawcett). "[The year] 1975 was six years after the government had publicly declared that Project Blue Book was over. The government was supposedly out of the UFO investigation business," Greenwood told *Sightings*. "But what people don't know is that military bases were still having UFO encounters and that there were still investigations going on with respect to those bases."

During October and November of 1975, three U.S. Air Force bases, each with a nuclear arsenal, reported strange encounters with UFOs. Eyewitnesses at Loring AFB, Wurtsmith AFB, and Malmstrom AFB all described the UFOs as hovering dangerously close to high-security nuclear weapons sites, apparently under intelligent control. The first reported UFO incursion occurred on October 27, 1975, at Loring Air Force Base in Limestone, Maine, prompting the Department of Defense to issue a secret memorandum stating that the UFOs had "a clear intent in the weapons storage area [of Loring Air Force Base]." The base is now closed. To the Air Force, Loring is a dinosaur whose extinction was made possible by the end of the cold war. To ufologists it is a silent reminder that UFOs have been among us, and their intent is clear.

At approximately 8:00 P.M., an unidentified flying object appeared over Loring's nuclear weapons storage facility. The object appeared to be similar to a helicopter in size, shape, and flight pattern, but when the Loring tower attempted to make contact with the "helicopter," there was no response. The UFO circled the Loring munitions dump for forty minutes. All attempts to communicate with the craft were in vain. The next night, October 28, 1975, the UFO returned, coming in much closer and lower. Ground observers described the object as oval, with glowing white and orange lights. This time, it hovered over the munitions dump at an altitude estimated to be less than 150 feet. According to Barry Greenwood, who has interviewed one eyewitness to the Loring event, the UFO was soon joined by a second object, which hovered only five feet off the ground at the end of a Loring AFB runway.

"Loring Air Force Base at the northern tip of Maine was a nuclear bomb storage site," Greenwood explains. "One of the objects hovered to within 150 feet of the bomb igloos, and the base commander was very concerned about this. Some of his men wanted to shine a searchlight on the objects and the commander said, 'No, don't do that, because we don't want whoever it is to be blinded by the light,' thus crashing into the bomb igloos and creating a nuclear accident. They were hampered as to how they could react to this. I think that if the public had known that at the time, there would have been great alarm, but the military was very effective in keeping it quiet. Only a few press stories came out later, but by then the alarm was over. However, it alerted UFO researchers to pursue the story heavily, and we've found the extent of the incursions was quite substantial."

According to one recently declassified Air Force report of the period, "Penetration of sensitive areas during the hours of darkness has prompted the implementation of Security Option 3 at our northern-tier bases." Greenwood explains the significance of this directive: "The Pentagon invoked a Security Option 3 so that there would be a high state of awareness at all the northern-tier Air Force bases, notifying all bases that they should be on their guard. In the next three-week period there were at least a dozen U.S. and Canadian military bases that were overflown by unknown objects; disc-shaped craft, which demonstrated intelligence and a clear intent—and some of them were sighted in very sensitive nuclear weapons areas."

The second known UFO-nuclear incursion occurred just two days after the Loring events. On October 30, 1975, at Wurtsmith Air Force Base, just outside Oscoda, Michigan, base radar reportedly picked up an unidentified aircraft advancing toward the base at an extremely high rate of speed. Wurtsmith, also now closed, was a SAC base (a vital link for the U.S. Strategic Air Command) and already on twenty-four-hour alert after the Security Option 3 directive. On radar, the UFO appeared to be closing fast. A KC-135 tanker flying in the area was alerted and also picked up the UFO on radar. When the crew members made visual contact, they allegedly pursued an enormous glowing orange sphere but were unable to catch up with it. Estimates of the speed of the UFO range from 200 to 1,000 knots. Later, base security police reported a UFO hovering at a very low altitude over the nuclear weapons storage area.

One of the eyewitnesses to the Wurtsmith AFB incursion was civilian aircraft mechanic Rick Eberhardt. In 1975, Eberhardt lived directly across from Wurtsmith's main gate. He is the only eyewitness to the UFO-nuclear incidents of 1975 who would agree to appear on camera for *Sightings'* original television report. His account of the night of October 30, 1975, is a chilling reminder of just how vulnerable the U.S. nuclear defense system may be.

"That night I was awakened by a bright, glowing orange-colored light that was coming in through our sliding glass doors. It was bright orange, glowing and fluorescent. I'd never seen an orange that bright in my life. It lit up the inside of my house like we had the lights on. At the time, I thought our house was on fire, so I got out of bed to investigate. I went to the glass doors and looked out. There was a large glowing oval-shaped object hovering outside. To me it looked like it was two to three football fields long and a good couple wide. There was no noise at all, not even a whisper. It hovered over the base for three to four minutes, just sat there. Then it sped off at a high rate of speed, heading away from the base. I've seen F-16s fly high rates of speed, but this thing was here and gone from a dead-still hover in no time flat. In a blink of an eye, it was climbing and gone. I was scared, fear running through me. I couldn't believe what I had seen."

Rick Eberhardt is not an uneducated observer. He has worked on military and civilian aircraft for twenty years and has seen Wurtsmith takeoffs and landings on a daily basis. "I work out there now for a large freight company," says Eberhardt. "I work on 747s, DC-8s, DC-9s, DC-10s, L10-11, all very huge aircraft. I know in my mind that what I saw that night was not an aircraft. It was no 747. No B-52 Bomber. It was no KC-135 straddle tanker coming in. There were many nights back in the '70s when we'd be sitting outside at night watching the B-52s and the straddle tankers come in all lit up like Christmas trees. But their size didn't even compare to the size of the object I saw that night in '75. Two of them together wouldn't even come close. I thought, 'I'm seeing a UFO,' but then I thought, No, I must be seeing things."

However, a few days later, Eberhardt found out he wasn't seeing things. "I was helping out down at my mom and dad's restaurant, and I overheard a gentleman in there having a cup of coffee explaining to his buddies what he had seen a couple of nights ago. I could hear in bits and pieces what he had seen, so I took him aside and was kind of teasing him about it, not telling what I had seen, trying to find out if he was for real. He told me he had seen a great big orange object. He said he had seen it go through the air toward the direction of the base. After that I told him what I had seen, and the times matched up almost perfectly. So I know somebody else has seen what I have seen."

Eberhardt's testimony is important, because military eyewitnesses will not talk on camera. However, there are declassified military documents that speak volumes about the UFO overflights at Loring AFB, Wurtsmith AFB, and finally at Malmstrom AFB in Montana. The Malmstrom incidents are particularly chilling, because UFOs not only hovered over nuclear missile silos, they also seem to have temporarily neutralized America's missile launch capability.

In 1975, Malmstrom Air Force Base had an undisclosed number of underground Launch Control Facilities housing Minuteman missiles equipped with nuclear warheads. "Malmstrom was a site for nuclear missile silos, ICBM missiles that were to be launched at whatever country might attack us at any given time. The entire base was essentially ringed with these sites," Barry Greenwood explains. "And Malmstrom, during the first week of November 1975 had several intrusions near missile silos. Many of these incidents were primarily radar incidents. There were some visual sightings, but the most dramatic sightings occurred in connection with radar tracking. In some cases, the objects would go from a very low altitude—hovering over sensitive parts of the base—to extremely high altitudes in a matter of seconds.

"The Air Force had no explanation for the intrusions. The UFOs were in very, very sensitive parts of the base and caused great concern. In one case, a security crew saw what they described as an orange football-shaped object, certainly not a conventional aircraft, hovering very low over one of the missile silos.

It sped off very quickly after the crew arrived. They didn't even have time to react to it—and certainly no time to take pictures or scramble aircraft."

Then on November 7, 1975, the unthinkable happened. At the Malmstrom nuclear missile silo code-named K-7, an unseen force tampered with the nation's infallible missile launch system. Some time that evening, the electronic security sensors around K-7 were triggered. Malmstrom's Sabotage Alert Team was called in and reportedly observed an enormous orange, glowing object over the silo. One eyewitness would later describe the UFO as a bright orange disc the size of a football field. The UFO was also tracked on radar by NORAD. Two F-106 jet interceptors were scrambled and reached the UFO within minutes. But as soon as the interceptors came into view, the UFO rose quickly to 200,000 feet, hovered briefly, then disappeared. Inside the Launch Control Facility, military personnel made a startling discovery. During the overflight, the computer on the nuclear warhead had somehow changed its own launch code.

Greenwood explains: "Somehow the object managed to change the tracking numbers on the missile. According to one witness, the missile had to be removed and retooled to make it operational again. And to see this information not just in UFO books but where I found it in government messages was a real eye-opener. I was very surprised. I never thought that there would be such an admission of helplessness with regard to that incident and other incidents during that period. Each base reacted with puzzlement as to what was happening, and to my knowledge the cause of the incidents was never identified, but certainly something was flying around that didn't belong there."

For many UFO researchers, the incursions of 1975 outstrip Roswell and the flap of '52 in overall significance. Richard Hall, former director of NICAP, the National Investigations Committee on Aerial Phenomena, says, "The reason this is so significant is that the UFOs seemed to be focused on atomic weapons. And the objects, which the military called 'mystery helicopters,' were seen and tracked on radar flying in areas where they had no business being. These bases, because of what they stood for—our massive retaliation capability—were highly secure bases, and that is also why this is so significant. Whatever was flying around could just penetrate our defenses at will."

Ufologist Robert Hastings believes that whatever they were, the strange craft were not part of a Soviet or any other country's military strike force. "I think, first of all, that the description of the craft suggests that we are dealing with something off the earth. And if we accept that this is the case, the question is, Why are they targeting nuclear weapons-related facilities?" Although some researchers paint a terrifying picture of aliens plotting a future course toward intergalactic warfare, Hastings is more optimistic in his assessment of the 1975 incursions. "One hypothesis is that whoever is flying these craft has, for reasons that we may not be able to fathom, an interest in the future of mankind and is providing a demonstration that they have the ability and the will to interfere with weapons of destruction that can jeopardize the future of Earth."

Barry Greenwood says, "Even if you remove any hint of extraterrestrial involvement, you're still dealing with a series of major intrusions into military bases along the 3,000-mile U.S.-Canadian border. Who has the money to do this? Who has the equipment to do this? Who would want to take a chance at infiltrating bases during a time when there was really nothing newsworthy to create terrorist activity? Nothing would suggest to me why these incidents occurred, and the military feels the same way. They have no conclusions as to what was happening."

Greenwood, Good, Hastings, and many others believe that the extent of the UFO-nuclear connection is probably far greater than just the three documented events in 1975. They are frustrated by the government's refusal to declassify thousands of additional pages of documentation believed to exist on the subject. "The military's responsible for protecting the country. If they don't know what's flying over our heads, I think hard questions have to be asked. And they have been asked, and I don't think we have adequate answers yet," Greenwood says.

"I believe there is information out there of staggering implications and importance," Hastings asserts. "I think people need to be made aware of the fact that these things have taken place in American airspace and on American soil. I don't think the government should be given a blank check to decide year after year what is good for us and what are the proper things for Americans to know or not to know about UFOs. I think the phenomenon exists. It's worldwide. It is probably extraterrestrial in nature and seems to suggest by its behavior that it's bound and determined to interact in the human arena at this point in our history. I think sooner or later a public information policy needs to take hold to begin to make people aware that this is not science fiction. This is not the funny papers. This is not Hollywood. This is reality."

CONTACT

1965

Unidentified in Exeter

Congress Acknowledges UFO

Has No Explanation

> There were a few moments when I was in Vietnam that I
> thought I was going to go. But, honest to God, that didn't
> bother me half as much as what happened that one night
> in Exeter. I'm not lying to you. That scared the living hell
> right out of me.
>
> —Norman Muscarello, eyewitness

More than thirty years after Norman Muscarello's UFO encounter, he's still having nightmares. It wasn't just his memory of
the enormity of the craft or the way it maneuvered through the
sky or its eerie crimson glow. What frightens Muscarello is the unknown. He will never know what he saw or where that unearthly
craft came from, because both the U.S. Air Force and the Congress have admitted that the flying object Muscarello saw over Exeter, New Hampshire, in the early morning hours of September
3, 1965, is, and will always remain, absolutely unidentified.

Before September 3, 1965, before the UFO and the media and
the military, Exeter, New Hampshire, was a typically sedate New
England community. "It was beautiful back then," Norman Muscarello remembers. "It was rated one of the top three nicest,

cleanest, safest towns in the United States. You could leave your keys in the car. You could leave your house unlocked, go to work, and not worry about it. Come home, you'd find a note on your refrigerator that your neighbor had borrowed a loaf of bread. I can remember when you could take a sleeping bag out on Route 90 on Sunday morning around two o'clock and go to sleep and not worry about being run over." Then there was the Sunday morning at two o'clock, September 3, 1965, when everything changed for Muscarello. That was when the "thing," as he calls it, showed up in town.

Muscarello was eighteen years old. He'd been in Amesbury visiting his girlfriend and was walking the twelve miles back home to Exeter. He didn't even bother to thumb a ride as there wasn't anyone around. Coming over the last hill before the road dipped into town, Muscarello thought he saw a strange glow over by a country store, but he didn't think much about it. In hindsight, he believes that this was the beginning of the UFO's approach into Exeter. A few minutes later, an enormous ball of red and blue light seemed to appear from out of nowhere.

"I was walking though a field on the Dining family farm when this thing shot over the trees and come up over the Russells' house and scared me half to death. I didn't know what it was, but it was big as a house, with a red hue and flashing lights, sometimes in sequence, sometimes erratic," says Muscarello. He remembers hearing a few dogs bark and the horses whinnying in their stalls, and then there was an overwhelming, eerie silence. "That's what got me," Muscarello recalls. "Not a sound. Even the crickets stopped doing their thing—and crickets don't just stop like that for nothing. Something scared them, and something scared me." Muscarello says he dove into a ditch filled with leaves to hide from the overwhelming UFO.

"It meandered around and wobbled and yawed. I couldn't tell what it was, couldn't make out if it was metallic or anything. There was no silhouette. The lights were too bright. I couldn't make out a shape," Muscarello says. "And then it took off to the east. I watched it disappear, the light dimming out like when an old TV goes out and the light just gets smaller and smaller. That's what it did. I was stunned and just stayed there awhile, and then I went to the Russells' house and I pounded on the door. The upstairs lights came on but nobody would answer. So I ran down and stood in the middle of the road and put my arms up. I thought, 'Well, the next car that comes by is either going to hit me or take me to the police station.'"

When a car did come over the hill, the driver knew Muscarello. "I said, 'I've got to get to the police station. Please take me there. I can't explain it.' That's all I could say to him. And he just said, 'Okay, Norman, no problem.' He drove me to the police station and when I walked in, Scratch Toland was the dispatcher on duty. His real name was Reginald, but we all called him Scratch. I think because of the sweaters he wore. I described to Scratch exactly what I saw. I told him the whole story, and he's looking at me with this dumbfounded expression. Little did I realize that reports had already come in prior to me getting there."

Exeter had two police officers on patrol duty that night. One of the officers, Eugene Bertrand, had just taken a report from a woman whom he had found sitting, shaken, in her car. She claimed that a ball of red light had chased her car, then disappeared. "So when Gene came into the station, I told him the same thing I'd told Scratch," Muscarello continues, "and he says, 'Let's get in the cruiser.' It's maybe two-thirty, three in the morning by now, and he takes me right up to the field where I had seen the UFO. We get out of the cruiser and proceed along the side of the field, and just then David Hunt, the other officer on duty, pulls up in his cruiser behind us. He's got the door open and his mike in his hand, and he's hollering down to us, making all these funny cracks like 'How many beers you had tonight?' And he's teasing Gene about what he's doing. And that's when this thing reappeared. It shows up over the tree line and stops and stays there for five minutes. And then, *shooom*, it's gone. That's enough to freak anybody."

Norman Muscarello and the two officers were later interviewed by Raymond Fowler, a noted UFO researcher who at the time of the incident was a technical investigator for NICAP, the nation's leading UFO watchdog organization at the time. "What made this case interesting for me was the fact that an object as large as a barn was seen within 500 feet of witnesses. This was a close encounter of the first kind. Many of the sightings we had been dealing with were discs seen at a long distance. This was a close encounter, and it was seen by reliable witnesses. The Air Force was interested; therefore NICAP was interested." (See Photo 15.)

Raymond Fowler recalls Officer Bertrand's version of the Exeter UFO encounter: "He told me that they walked out into the field, and Norman yelled, 'Look out. Here it comes!' And up over the treetops comes this object right at them with red flashing lights. Bertrand's first reaction was to get down on his knee and draw his service revolver—and then he thought better of that as it got closer. He said it was as large as a barn, lighting up the whole field. The horses started kicking in their stalls, and dogs were howling. The object was making fantastic maneuvers. It was doing right-angle turns and then it left the area."

Muscarello, Bertrand, and Hunt stood in the field and stared at the empty sky. "It was like it was there and then it wasn't," Muscarello remembers. "The police officers saw the same damn thing I did, and I'm glad they did. I'm glad I went there with Gene and David Hunt, because I'd be in a nut house today if I hadn't had those witnesses." A UFO investigator and expert on the Exeter sightings, Peter Geremia, attested to the veracity and credibility of the witnesses. "I interviewed Norman, and there's no doubt in my mind that what he is saying is true," Geremia says. "Eugene Bertrand was no-nonsense. He wanted to make it clear that what he saw was unexplained, but he was not calling it an unidentified flying object in the sense of an alien spacecraft. He was just describing what he saw. You can't ask for a better witness than that, a credible guy with an excellent reputation."

After the sighting, Muscarello and Bertrand returned to the Exeter police station. Shortly thereafter, a New Hampshire telephone operator phoned to inform Scratch Toland about a call she'd received from a man who claimed he had been chased by an object with red flashing lights. The operator said that the man had asked for the police, but then terminated the call before she could connect him. Later, Raymond Fowler interviewed six different people who had all seen the Exeter UFO. "After the object left the field, there was a sighting about twenty miles away," says Fowler. "A schoolteacher, a very reliable person, was coming home from Essex to Ipswich along Route 133, and as he came to the top of the hill, he felt static electricity and the hair on his head and his arms just went up. Then, as he came over the hill, there to his left, hovering just off the road, was a round object with glowing ports. He said he was so scared that he went off the road."

The UFO was gone, but the backlash from its visit to Exeter was just beginning. Norman Muscarello remembers the scene at his house when daylight broke: "That's when the crap hit the fan. People started pounding on the door. If it wasn't the neighbors, then it was the media. And then we had a knock on the door, and it was the Air Force. A major and a lieutenant who had an attaché case handcuffed to his wrist came into my mother's kitchen. The major said, 'Where's Norman?' and just marched right into the living room. He told me, 'You. Shut your mouth. Don't you say another word. I'm going to make your life miserable.' He was trying to tell me that I didn't see what I saw. And I don't understand this. I'm a punk kid, fresh out of high school, and I don't know what's going on. What's this guy doing here? Why is he telling me to shut up? What are they afraid of?"

In a later interview with Norman Muscarello's mother, Raymond Fowler would learn details that might explain the major's anger and fear. "Norman's mother said one of the Air Force officers had a manual locked to his wrist," Fowler recalls. "She offered him coffee, and he unlocked the manual and put it on the kitchen counter and walked into the living room. While the water was boiling for coffee, Mrs. Muscarello started to look through the manual and saw some photographs, which seemed to be different types of imprints, landing areas involved with UFOs. When the lieutenant came in and saw her looking through it, he read her the riot act."

For Norman Muscarello, the lieutenant's harsh words were the last straw. He remembers, "This guy literally chewed my mother out in lavender. And that's when I got—pardon my French—I got pissed. I said, 'You guys get the hell out of here. That's it. I've had it.' I thought I was cracking up. I pride myself on being halfway intelligent and understanding what goes on around me, but I had seen something that was not earthly, and I wasn't watching a television set."

Although the identity of the major and the lieutenant are still not known, Raymond Fowler was able to confirm that two Air Force officers from nearby Pease Air Force Base (fifteen miles from Exeter) did visit the town on September 4, 1965. "Pease sent out a major and a lieutenant on the fourth, and they asked the police if they would just keep their UFO information confidential. But the police told the Air Force officers that the *Manchester Union Leader* reporter had already been there and got the story. The Air Force actually sent the lieutenant around Exeter to buy up all the newspapers with the sighting story, which I thought was ludicrous. Then the officers went on site and investigated, asking farmers if their cows were giving the same amount of milk, the chickens still producing the same amount of eggs. And there were rumors that they investigated a burned area in the field and then asked Carl Dining to bulldoze his field."

The Air Force's first public statement regarding the Exeter UFO did little to quell the community's growing concern. "The Pease AFB commander, in his attempt to explain away the sightings, called a press conference at night right there in the field where the object was seen," Fowler recounts. "They had quite a crowd out there, and he told everyone, 'Well, the latest explanation we feel is that it was the lights at Pease. So I'm going to have the lights turned on at Pease, and everybody look in that direction. You'll see it was just the lights from Pease Air Force Base.' And everybody looked, and he radioed back to Pease and they turned on the lights. And no one saw anything."

Speculation about the extraterrestrial origin of the gigantic red UFO was rampant throughout New England, but Raymond Fowler was more tempered in his judgment. "Muscarello saw a structured object as large as a barn, silent, with red flashing lights in sequence that was under intelligent control. The object showed intelligent control by its maneuvers and by chasing specific things. You can surmise that it might have been an extrater-restrial craft or something from another dimension. But when all is said and done, what you have is an unidentified flying object that was not man-made."

After the press conference fiasco at the original site, the Air Force claimed that it was launching a thorough investigation of the Exeter UFO. According to a letter to the Exeter Police Department written by USAF Maj. Hector Quintanilla, Jr., then chief of Project Blue Book, "The investigation and evaluation of this sighting indicates a possible association with an 8th Air Force operation, 'Big Blast.' In addition to aircraft from this operation, there were five B-47-type aircraft flying in the area during this period. . . . Since there were many aircraft in the area we might assume that the objects observed . . . might be associated with this military air operation." Another letter from the Pentagon written by USAF Lt. Col. John P. Spaulding suggested that a refueling operation might have been the cause of the sighting: "Refueling area 'Fur Trapper' and refueling area 'Down Date' are controlled through Loring Air Force Base and located over the area of the sighting."

In response to these "official" explanations, Eugene Bertrand and David Hunt wrote to Major Quintanilla: "As you might imagine, we have been the subject of considerable ridicule since the Pentagon released its 'final evaluation' of our sighting. . . . Since one of us (Bertrand) was in the Air Force for four years, engaged in refueling operations with all kinds of military aircraft, it was impossible to mistake what we saw for any type of military operation, regardless of altitude. It was also definitely not a helicopter or balloon. Immediately after the object disappeared, we did see what probably was a B-47 at high altitude, but it bore no relation at all to the object we saw. . . . We would both appreciate it very much if you would help us eliminate the possible conclusion that some people have made that we might have *(a)* made up the story, or *(b)* were incompetent observers. I'm sure you can understand the position we're in."

Whether or not the Air Force understood the position that Bertrand and Hunt were in, their explanation changed little.

While maintaining that the Exeter witnesses were probably seeing military aircraft, the Pentagon did issue an additional statement suggesting that the UFO may have been a misidentified
planet or star. "Anybody who's lived in the New Hampshire sea-
coast area has seen refueling aircraft," Exeter UFO researcher Peter Geremia says, "and they normally refuel at 30,000 feet. This is
not going to cause a young man to duck because he's afraid he's
going to get hit with a flying tanker. And the explanation of twin-
kling stars didn't even come close to answering what was seen.
The Air Force lost a great deal of credibility in proposing these
ridiculous answers."

Raymond Fowler agrees. "Telling the public that they were seeing stars and planets and airplanes; it was a classic case of reliable
witnesses seeing an object they couldn't identify at close range—
and the Air Force telling the public that there was nothing to it." In
fact, it was the Pentagon's incomplete and fatuous explanation of
this sighting and several others that soon followed that would lead
then Congressman Gerald R. Ford to convene a special congressional hearing on the Air Force approach to UFO investigations.

"After the incident at Exeter," Fowler explains, "the public was
annoyed with what the Air Force had done. Congressman Ford
and other men and women in Congress felt that the Air Force
was not handling the UFO problem properly, because they were
getting complaints from the public. All UFO offices on all bases
had a list of things to tell the public: stars, planets, weather balloons, you name it. I mean, they would just pick something out
just to get the public off their back. They didn't want open congressional hearings at all, because it would bring out the fact that
they were dealing with something that was violating our airspace
and that they had no control over." However, on April 5, 1966,
under public pressure, hearings began before the House Armed
Services Committee.

"My report on the Exeter sightings was put into the congressional record," Fowler says, "and they discussed the report. The Air
Force backed down and admitted that the object was unidentified
and had been unidentified from the very beginning. Unidentified

to the military means that we don't know what it is or where it came from, and we have no control over the situation."

While the Air Force's admission was a victory for Raymond Fowler and NICAP, it has done little to satisfy the nagging fear and embarrassment that continues to haunt Norman Muscarello. Official congressional acknowledgment that he was not crazy or drunk or ignorant has been no consolation. "Gene and I were both members of the Legion here in town. We still get heckled over there. It's been over thirty years, and I still get it. I'm hurt and angry, because I couldn't have done anything about that sighting. I saw what I saw, and all of a sudden I'm a nut. I wish it had never happened. I wish I could have just waltzed through life. Honest to God, it's been too much trouble and too much heckling and problems and waking up at night. And I don't even know what happened to me."

UFOs in the Holy Land
Fiery Craft of Biblical Proportions Return

Many serious people who have been studying UFOs around the world have reached the consensus that the Bible is a convincing UFO story.

—Barry Chamish, journalist

The legendary saucer crash near Roswell, New Mexico, in 1947 may be the world's most famous and most popular UFO landmark event, but, say many UFO historians, it was certainly not the first—not by a few millennia. For decades, researchers have been examining the possibility that many ancient inscriptions and passages in the Old Testament are actually documentary evidence of ancient UFO sightings and pre-Christian extraterrestrial contact.

"No one who takes the Bible literally and as a historical document can say that people in the ancient Near East were not aware of what are known today as UFOs," according to Zecharia Sitchen, historical ufologist and author of *Stairway to Heaven,* a study of UFO sightings in ancient times. "The difference between then and now," Sitchen believes, "is that back then they did not call them UFOs. To ancient people, the ships were not unidentified. They believed they knew precisely what these craft were and who was flying them. They believed they were piloted by gods; today we call them aliens."

Barry Chamish is an Israeli journalist and author who has also studied the connections between the Old Testament and modern ufology. His approach to the subject began as an attempt to expose as ludicrous the theories of Sitchen and others. Instead, Chamish became fascinated with the eerie parallels between ancient writings and drawings and modern-day sightings. "After reading the Jewish scriptures from beginning to end, I have come to the conclusion that the pillar of fire, the cloud that led the Hebrews out of Egypt, the whirlpool that swallowed Zacharias, Ezekiel's wheel within a wheel, all the way through to the prophets, were all in fact UFO-related. I came to this conclusion quite hesitantly. Only after a great deal of research have I accepted the possibility that the Jewish people may have been given guidance by forces outside of this planet." (See Photo 16.)

It's a controversial challenge to mainstream interpretations of the Bible that is unquestionably on the fringes of UFO research. However, a recent spate of UFO sightings and alleged contacts in Israel has the entire UFO community sitting up and taking notice. On the eve of the third millennium (C.E.), UFOs are being reported at an alarming rate. In fact, more UFO sightings and alien contacts have been recorded in the Holy Land in the last ten years than have been recorded in the last ten centuries. "People who have been studying UFOs seriously have reached the conclusion that the angels of the Bible are returning, and these are the aliens of Israel today," says Chamish.

When Barry Chamish first began examining the connection between ancient inscriptions and modern ufology, he made a strange discovery. "When I was researching my book," Chamish says, "the only public mention of UFOs in Israel in modern times was from 1952. There were two sightings near Haifa. That was all I could find until the Shikmona encounter of 1987." Shikmona is a beach area along the Mediterranean Sea just outside the city of Haifa, Israel. The UFO event that occurred there on September 28, 1987, is considered the Israeli Roswell, the opening act of a UFO extravaganza that continues to this day.

"It is the evening of Rosh Hashanah, the Jewish New Year, 1987," Chamish explains. "Ami Achrai, an auto mechanic, is returning from Tel Aviv to his home in Qiryat Bialik near Haifa. In the sky over Shikmona beach Ami sees a red object fly into the air, hover and dip." It was a life-changing experience for Ami Achrai, who feels it is more than coincidence that his sighting occurred during the Jewish High Holy days. "On that evening, we were between Rosh Hashanah and Yom Kippur, which is called the day of repentance and coming back to God," Ami Achrai says. "I was on my way home about 10:25 P.M. when I saw an object hovering about ten meters off the ground with sparks as big as eight meters in diameter moving in a counterclockwise direction around the object. Underneath was a glowing red spot. There were immense spotlights coming at me as if I had been spotted by this thing. There was a loud noise of whirlpooled air as if a helicopter was going to crash. I got out of my car to look, and then the next thing I remember, I was driving my car away from the beach, watching the object moving up and down far away. I am missing parts of the experience. Suddenly I could see only the red spot, and, within a matter of minutes, it was flying high above the earth. I drove home and told my wife. She laughed at me."

Achrai remembers being extremely disturbed by the night's events and his family's skepticism. At first, he tried to put his UFO sighting behind him and dismissed it as an asteroid or a comet. But something in the back of his mind nagged at him—something, Achrai says, that drew him back to the scene of his encounter. In the daylight, Achrai believes he found an astonishing remnant of the UFO. "When I went back to Shikmona, the ground where the UFO had been was clearly burned and there were red stones and other melted-looking things as well. The burned area was like an outline of a symmetric form. The whole thing looked liked a stamp on a sheet of paper," Achrai remembers. "Suddenly I felt pains in my arms, and my eyes were full of tears. I felt very bad that night, and for three days I had to stay home, because I was shaking with electric waves all over my body."

The burned-in shape in the Shikmona beach drew national attention. Observers who came to the site saw within the shape a strange silhouette that was put forward as proof that the UFO had been not only extraterrestrial but also occupied. "There was evidence of intense heat," Barry Chamish explains, "and the burning sand and vegetation were in the shape of a UFO. Inscribed in the right-hand corner, we observed a clear-cut silhouette of an astronaut in front of something that looked like a dashboard." (See Photo 17.) In addition to the indelible mark in the sand, which is still visible as of this writing, testing at the site revealed that the ground itself had taken on unusual properties. Electrical engineer Avi Grief claimed to have found that the soil and sand in and around the UFO site was 671 percent more magnetic than the surrounding beach.

A *Sightings* team collected samples from the scorched earth at Shikmona beach and sent them to biophysicist Dr. William C. Levengood for a detailed analysis. Dr. Levengood, who is best known for his studies of biological mutations within crop circles, found that the ground around the supposed Shikmona beach landing site had several inexplicable characteristics. "Over the years, I have seen many anomalies and alterations in plants and soil, but this is a new one," Dr. Levengood says of the Shikmona samples. "I have found tremendous changes in the ratio of elements. For example, ordinary zinc was increased 104 times, whereas other elements stayed absolutely the same." But that finding pales in comparison to what Dr. Levengood found while he was preparing to take a photomicrograph of one of the soil samples.

"To take this photograph, I had to use a light of fairly high intensity, " Dr. Levengood explains. "As I was adjusting the camera to get the right angle for the photograph, to my astonishment, the soil appeared to be melting. What I found was that there was a hydrocarbon coating on the soil with a very low melting point. I have since consulted with a geophysicist, and there is no explanation. This does not occur in nature. There is no natural way that this amount of hydrocarbon would be on the soil."

Could the Shikmona UFO and landing site have been an elaborate hoax? Ufologists insist the evidence was far too sophisticated to have been conjured by even the most creative special-effects artist. Ami Achrai says he knows it was not a hoax, because he continues to suffer physical effects and believes he has gained supernatural abilities since his UFO contact. "From that day on, I was reborn," Achrai says. "I was a new person with new perceptions of the universe around me. I have helped many people since then. They come to my shop, and somehow I can put my hands on them and cure them. I feel like all routes are open to me now, and they gave me a special power that I have in my hands and in my eyes."

In late February 1988, just five months after the Shikmona beach sighting and just one mile away in Haifa proper, Menachem Kalfon, his wife, Rosetta, and sister-in-law Suzan were the next to spot an anomalous craft in the sky. This time, they were able to capture the UFO with a home movie camera. (See Photo 18.) "The light was golden, like nothing I've ever seen in my life. There was a real light beam radiating out from it. It was shocking, truly shocking," remembers Menachem Kalfon. Rosetta Kalfon adds, "We were in our apartment sitting around and chatting like we always do, and suddenly my sister looks up toward the window and sees a glittering light in the air. I looked and there it was. We got up quickly and rushed to the window. I said, 'Do you know what that is? That is a UFO!' It stayed there for seventeen minutes above the sea and then disappeared very quickly until it became as small as a star."

Barry Chamish believes the Haifa home movie is the first recorded Israeli UFO in modern times. "The most outstanding feature of the film is that the camera operator was clever enough to get the background. There's no mistaking this UFO as being in the sky over the Haifa area. It's not a fraud or a natural feature on a hill or in the sky. If you look closely at the film, you can even make out windows in between the lights on the object. It moves, it has lights, and it was witnessed by many, many people, including UFO experts. This was a tremendously documented UFO."

Three years later in 1991, the UFO activity in the Holy Land seemed to move east to a largely agricultural area in and around the town of Kadima in central Israel. Eli Cohen was the first eyewitness to UFOs there. "Eli Cohen is one of the most sincere people in the whole Kadima drama," says Barry Chamish. "He is an instinctively intelligent man: young, energetic, and ambitious. One night, he's awakened by a light inside his house. He thinks it's an intruder. Eli creeps to his drawer, pulls out a gun, and starts down the hallway. The light is intensifying. He reaches the kitchen and looks out the window."

"I was standing near the kitchen window," Cohen recalls, "and I looked out the window and up toward the light. It was very clear that it was a disc. In the center there was an eye—what looked like a big eye with a tremendous light coming out of it. I didn't need anyone to convince me that it was something from outer space." The next night, around 3:00 A.M., the UFO returned. It hovered outside Cohen's window for more than three and half hours. Cohen remembers that it made no sound, but it seemed to have an influence on the electricity in his house. He would later learn that there had been mysterious blackouts in and around Kadima on the nights of his sightings.

"On the third night, I thought that I must organize some witnesses. I wanted more people to see it, not just to prove I wasn't seeing things but also because I thought more witnesses would perpetuate it," Cohen says. "I wanted to prove it happened, so I prepared my video camera. I invited a large group of friends over and made sure there was someone outside all the time to watch for the UFO to come. Suddenly, one of the girls jumped up and said she could see a light. We ran outside, and soon we started to see it. We all saw it. (See Photo 19.) It had a strange movement, a zigzag movement, and it looked as if it was hanging on a string. It was like a slow-motion dance. The UFO again looked like an eye spreading light like a fire in the sky. It was there, dancing, and then it was just sucked up into the air."

Soon after Cohen's sightings, in late November 1991, realtor Yosi Ben Ma'as saw a similar UFO while driving home from work late one evening. "There was a huge sheet of light right before my eyes," recounts Ma'as. "It was spectacular, but also what was strange is that it was a calming light. And yet I was afraid. I saw it traveling slowly toward my home in Bet She'an, and I started thinking, 'I hope it doesn't go to my town. I hope it doesn't go where my friends and family are.' And then all of a sudden, this thing changes course—as if it were reading my mind—and starts moving away from my home as if there was a kind of telepathy between us."

Unlike other eyewitnesses, Ma'as called the police right away. He convinced Yitzhak Mordechai, the commander of the Bet She'an police department, to go outside and scan the skies for himself. Mordechai saw an enormous, brilliant craft. "It looked like a boomerang, only a little thicker and about thirty meters across. It was a shape I had never seen before. It had a unique power and a unique color," Mordechai remembers of the UFO. "There was a special glow, which was very different from anything I had ever seen before. It was silent; no noise at all, not even a whisper. I didn't know how to react, but I didn't feel it was threatening us. I treated it as a friendly object." But when Mordechai queried the Israeli Air Force about the UFO, officers there did not treat the craft as a friendly object. As the object moved toward the Jordanian border, the Air Force mobilized 300 troops, who were sent in to track the unidentified craft.

"This UFO was dragging a convoy of armed men for three hours on a trail up to the Jordanian border, which is a very sensitive place," Barry Chamish explains. "But this thing seemed to know where the border was, because as soon as it got to Jordan, the UFO turns around and starts to head back into Israel. The troops followed the UFO until six in the morning. When there was daylight, the UFO disappeared in a flash. Attempts to track the object on radar were not successful. Even though there were hundreds of eyewitnesses, trained military people, giving the UFO's exact location, the object never appeared on radar."

Sightings in and around Kadima continued for more than two years, fueling speculation that there was a message in the increasing number of sightings. "Many serious people who have been studying UFOs around the world have reached the consensus that the Bible is a convincing UFO story," Chamish says. "And there were certain researchers who felt that the sightings at Kadima were prophesied in ancient texts and inscriptions. So when the contact increased in 1993, everyone felt that we had reached an important turning point in the history of Israeli UFOs."

Chamish is referring to a series of close encounters that occurred in Kadima between March and June 1993. During that time, five different women—who did not know each other and had not heard about each other's experiences—all claimed to have made contact with giant extraterrestrial creatures. These women were not claiming to have been abducted or to be remembering scenes out of their subconscious. Each woman insisted that she was fully conscious when she came face-to-face with creatures from outer space. Shoshana Yahud was the first to claim contact on March 3, 1993.

"I was asleep and woke up very early Saturday morning," Yahud told *Sightings*. "I heard a loud bang. I was afraid to go downstairs and check it out. I lay in the bed thinking I might wait until daylight, and then I saw something coming through the wall. It was a man, or a being, I should say. His face was oval shaped. His eyes were shiny like a stoplight, glittering. His nose was very small like a dog." According to Barry Chamish, "Shoshana was very reticent to be interviewed about her experience, but she's a sincere woman and she is absolutely sure that this being—whatever it was—came through her wall. It's a problematic aspect of her story, because the doors were shut tight, the windows were shut tight, and the door downstairs was not touched. The only assumption we can make is that the being did come through the wall somehow, and in fact there was another woman who had the exact same experience where a being came through the wall."

Doron Rotem is a researcher, writer, and ufologist who has studied extensively the otherworldly experiences of the women of Kadima. Rotem has been particularly interested in the bizarre aftereffects that the UFOs and beings leave in their wake. "The day after her contact, Shoshana had bad headaches," Rotem describes. "She went outside to get some air and to put some laundry on the line, and she was very surprised to see a perfect circle four and one half meters wide impressed into the ground, a perfect circular landing site. When I went to meet with Shosh, she talked to me about the incident but didn't want to talk at all about the alien. I asked her to try and draw a picture of what she had seen, and what she drew matched the description given by the other women and other eyewitnesses around the world."

Hanna Sommech was alerted to the presence of a strange being when her dog began barking in the middle of the night. "It was three in the morning," Sommech recalls. "I woke up to the sound of my dog barking, really going a little crazy. My husband was sleeping, so I went downstairs, and something told me to go in the kitchen. I saw my poor little dog fly across the room, and then he was just smashed against the wall in the kitchen with a terrible force. It was very frightening, very upsetting. I went to the window by the door and looked out. Inside the house it was dark, but outside it was bright, filled with brilliant light. I opened the curtains a little more and saw a big giant image staring at me. I don't know why, but I felt as if I was being drawn to him. I tried to get to him, but then when I was very close, instinctively, I raised my hand to push him away—but it was like pushing against a wall. This being never said anything to me. But there was a voice in my head; it was like telepathy. And the voice said, 'Go away. I could smash you like your little dog. Go back to your husband.' Before I could move, he disappeared."

Later, Sommech would find a strange circle impression in the grass outside her home. She also drew a picture for Doron Rotem, a picture like the others, of a seven-foot-tall being with round eyes and a tiny mouth wearing a metallic suit. "Hanna drew a huge being," Rotem remembers, "with a big round head and huge eyes. She said he was surprisingly slow, as if the earth's gravity influenced him to move like that." "Hanna was one of five women," Barry Chamish adds, "who didn't know each other who all described the same bald-headed giants. They could have described little ones, green ones, red ones, humanoids; they had infinite possibilities of description, but they all describe the same exact being."And it is a being, Chamish points out, that does not fit the classic, media-driven image of an alien.

Ziporet Carmel also saw the beings when something landed in

the backyard of her Kadima home. Although Carmel's sighting was one of the last to occur in early June 1993, she was the first to go public with her story. She describes her contact this way: "It was a Saturday, and I woke up very early. I looked at the alarm and it was 6:30 in the morning. There was such a strong light in the room, and something just pulled me up and out of the room. I walked outside into the yard, and I had the feeling as if something was staring at me. I turned around, and suddenly from nowhere I saw a silver crate. It looked like the kind of crate we use to collect oranges but much bigger. I stared at it, and at that moment from above, but at the same time from nowhere, I saw another crate landing on top of the first. I just stood there, staring at it in amazement, wondering if I was dreaming.

"Then, also from nowhere, a man appeared. He was almost three meters tall, and he wore a kind of astronaut suit, a silvery-colored suit. He had a hat on, and in front there were flaps so I could not see his face. Simultaneously, I saw three beams of light from the sky shine down and go right through this man. All around him there were flickering lights. It was an absolutely incredible and awesome sight. It dawned on me that this must be something from outer space. I tried to speak to him—I called out in Hebrew to this man to let me see his face. I received the answer in my head, so to speak, telepathically and in English, saying, 'This is the way it should be. You're not supposed to see more. You're not supposed to see less.' I was in utter shock, and it took three days until I managed to—literally—open my mouth and tell it to someone."

When Carmel did talk, it attracted media attention all over Israel. Reporters and UFO investigators flocked to her tiny yard to see the site of her encounter and the strange grass circle that had been left behind. It was the same type of "landing site" found outside of the homes of all five of the Kadima contactees. "In all, more than fifty-nine crop circles—or what I call fields for landing—were made between March and June 1993. Why, I don't know," says Doron Rotem. "Very strange materials were found inside all of the circles. There was some kind of transparent liquid, which flowed in a spiral wave inside the circle. Sites that we reached just after the UFO had been reported were hot to the touch. It was unbelievable."

The circle that formed in Ziporet Carmel's backyard grass had several properties that support the formation's mysterious origin. "The place where the silver crates landed," Carmel explains, "became very dry, and all the grass just fell down flat in a circle and dried out completely. The weeds were in a clockwise pattern, almost perfectly round and five to six meters in diameter. There was a very strong smell that gave me incredible headaches. What was amazing was that for almost a year, the weeds stayed in exactly that position even though it rained, there was a lot of wind, and hundreds of people had examined and walked on the site."

Some of the grass from the Carmel circle was sent to Dr. William Levengood for analysis. "I found that the internal cellular structure of the Israel crop was quite similar to what I have found in other crop formations around the world," Dr. Levengood says. "The overall indication is that the grass has been subjected to a very high transient heat that was built up rapidly and dissipated quickly. Within the nodes of the plants, the changes were dramatic. The nodes were literally blown apart. There was some kind of internal pressure within each plant that was sufficient to blow out the fibers inside the stem."

Doron Rotem collected samples of unknown materials found clinging to the dried grass in the Carmel circle. (See Photo 20.) "There were strange red stains all over the grass and little pieces of unknown material that we now know is silicon," Rotem explains. "The pieces we found were very light, very thin, and were glowing brightly. We sent samples to the national geological laboratory for testing and were told that the material found in Ziporet Carmel's field of landing was 99.8 percent pure silicon. Silicon of that purity does not occur naturally anywhere on Earth. It can only be made in a laboratory." According to research conducted by Rotem, there is only one other place on Earth where silicon of this purity has been found: at another alleged UFO landing site in Socorro, New Mexico.

Contact in Israel took a bizarre turn in January 1995 when a series of animal mutilations reminded the locals that the UFOs weren't through yet. The center of contact this time was a small Kadima-area farm owned by Amos Gueta. "Saturday morning we went to feed the chickens, the sheep, and the dogs, as usual. It was a quiet morning, and there had been no unusual sounds or even barking in the yard," recounts Gueta's mother, Rachel. "At 6:30 in the morning when we woke up, it was already too late. All the animals were already dead except the dog." Barry Chamish picks up the story from the still-distraught eyewitness: "Mrs. Gueta goes out with a bowl of bones to feed her dog. She hears him whimpering. She looks at him, and his eyes are closed. She opens his eyes, and there are no eyeballs. Fifteen minutes later, the dog is dead. She goes on to the chicken house where the chickens are literally frozen dead, about forty of them. No panic among the chickens, they're not scattered, just in their roosts, dead. Three sheep are dead. They have been shaved around the cheekbone and have had a hole drilled into the cheek all the way to the bone itself."

Doron Rotem visited the mutilation site. "No blood was found. We cut the veins of the sheep, and there was no blood in the veins. There was no blood on the ground." A few strange tracks were found near the farm. A Bedouin tracker was called in to assess the prints. He could not identify the prints as belonging to any animal, either indigenous or imported. A local veterinarian was asked to evaluate the cause of death. Doron Rotem and Barry Chamish claim the veterinarian could not identify any type of predator that could kill in that manner. "When I phoned the veterinarian to ask him to prepare for an interview with *Sightings*," Chamish says, "he reiterated his astonishment at this bizarre attack. And yet when he was interviewed by *Sightings*, he said that this was a wild dog attack! The people of the village are now asking what dog removes eyeballs without any blood? Why didn't the dog howl or bark during an attack that must have been awful torture? Why didn't the chickens panic if they knew they were about to be attacked by wild dogs? Do wild dogs stop and drill a hole in a sheep's cheek before they kill it?"

Since the attack on the Gueta farm, the sightings in and

around Kadima have spread. Strange craft are no longer being viewed by a few eyewitnesses or in isolated pockets. They're flying around in broad daylight where everyone can see them and photograph them. (See Photo 21.) Barry Chamish believes this is not a coincidence. It is fate. "Israeli ufology is divided between rationalists and mystics. The mystics believe that something extremely important is related to the landings. Beginning with Shikmona, the UFOs were announcing in black and white, 'We are here!' At Bet She'an, they were saying, 'All right now, we've got 600 of you seeing us.' Kadima was Stage Three: 'We want to meet you.'"

Stage Four, according to Chamish, has been foretold by the Old Testament. "From Kedem they shall go up to Jerusalem," he reads. "In other words, the next step toward the revelation of the UFOs is Jerusalem."

1994

Invader on the Range

UFO over America's Most Sacred Airspace

> The slap in the face is that this craft shows up in one of the most secure areas in the world, and it's like they're playing with kids.
>
> —"Bob," Nellis Air Force Base tracker

Thousands of people flock to Nevada every year to see the brilliant, dazzling lights; and not all of them are tourists cruising the Las Vegas Strip. Some sightseers come in search of UFOs, and they're finding them by camping out in the mountains between Las Vegas and Tonopah, Nevada, at campsites that overlook the government's supersecret experimental aircraft playground. The Nellis Air Force Base Bombing and Gunnery Range Complex takes up more than 3 million acres of southern Nevada and includes the officially "nonexistent" test ranges known as Dreamland, Groom Lake, and Area 51. Nellis, the sky watchers will tell you, is where the weird stuff flies.

Whether these UFOs are man-made, captured extraterrestrial craft, or vehicles back-engineered from crashed saucers is debatable; but whatever their origin, the government knows every second of every day what's flying over Nellis. They're launching them and watching them, with radar, surveillance aircraft, and remote cameras that videotape every movement on the range. The Nellis Complex is the largest, most comprehensively monitored tactical training area in the world, with more than 7,700 square miles of restricted airspace. Nothing can fly here, the Air Force insists, that they don't know about. "You won't see many objects wandering in by accident," explains Bill Sweetman, an aviation expert and aerospace journalist. "They're very careful to insure that sort of thing doesn't happen. The potential for serious accidents if something strays into the range is very, very serious."

However, in the summer of 1995, *Sightings* received a videotape that provides compelling evidence of an airborne invader on the Nellis Range that the Air Force didn't launch, couldn't intercept, and still has not explained. The videotape contains footage taken from two different classified camera locations on the range sometime during daylight hours in late September 1994. It clearly shows an anomalous craft soaring slowly over the northwestern corner of the range for more than five minutes. (See Photo 22.) On the videotape's audio track, range operators can be heard trying to figure out what or whom they are observing. The anonymous source of the footage claimed that he had obtained the tape from range operators at Nellis Air Force Base in Las Vegas, Nevada. Someone had duplicated the classified videotape, smuggling it off base and eventually into the hands of *Sightings*.

The following is a partial transcript of the videotape's audio track. Call signs and other encoded speech have been removed to make the transcript more readable; otherwise, these are the exact words of highly trained Air Force personnel reacting to a UFO in their sacred airspace:

OPERATOR 1:   Figure out what it is? This time . . . it's a helicopter?

FEMALE OP: Ahh . . .

OPERATOR 1:   That's why it's so slow.

FEMALE OP: I thought it looked kind of strange. It's not much more than a round dot, but it looks different than most I've seen.

CONTROL:	I show an aircraft headed north pretty fast.
OPERATOR 1:	I got a helo [slang for helicopter].
FEMALE OP:	At eleven?
OPERATOR 1:	Yeah, can't figure out where he's at on this thing.
CONTROL:	Be advised . . . We're filled to capacity.
OPERATOR 2:	What is that?
OPERATOR 1:	I don't know. No idea. A helo?
FEMALE OP:	Looks like one. It's way up high now. It's going, like, straight up.
OPERATOR 2:	It's a balloon, isn't it?
OPERATOR 1:	I don't know what the hell that is.
FEMALE OP:	I think it's a helicopter.
OPERATOR 2:	That ain't no helo! Forget it. Where's he at on here?
FEMALE OP:	It's straight up.
OPERATOR 1:	I'm on it!
FEMALE OP:	Oh, O.K.
OPERATOR 1:	But what the hell is it? I'm going to lose it in the sun.
OPERATOR 2:	I don't even know what it is.
FEMALE OP:	It's weird-looking.
OPERATOR 2:	What is it, Jim? That's outta here. Where's it come from?
OPERATOR 1:	Way down there . . .
[*Break in audio*]	
OPERATOR 1:	You can try to engage but . . .
OPERATOR 2:	You'll rock 'em and we'll roll 'em.
OPERATOR 1:	I'm gonna say it's an unknown airplane. T-1 over . . . There's an aircraft coming inbound, ahh, we don't know what type.
OPERATOR 2:	Whatever it is, you'll get it.
CONTROL:	[*Gives bearings of UFO.*]
OPERATOR 2:	That's strange.
OPERATOR 1:	Weird, man!

Baffled by the unknown object, perhaps assuming that it is part of a tactical training mission in progress on the range, the operators decide to simulate a surface-to-air missile strike. There is no actual missile; they are only practicing launch procedures, but it is interesting to note that their instinct is to shoot down the UFO:

T-1:   Trying to pick up that traffic.

OPERATOR 2:   Let's try it.

OPERATOR 1:   We acquired this unknown object. Aircraft of some type. We're going to put a launch up on it anyways, see what happens. It seems to be hovering there. [*Gives bearings of UFO.*] It appears to be going outbound real slow. There's hardly any range velocity. I don't know if this would impact or not . . . [*Simulated launch occurs.*] We have impact. We'll call this a kill on this unknown aircraft. T-1 Control doesn't know what type of aircraft this is either. . . .

OPERATOR 2:   That's weird.

OPERATOR 1:   Strange.

OPERATOR 2:   It's outbound?

OPERATOR 1:   Yeah, outbound. It's moving fast.

The Nellis Complex is America's premiere facility for pilot training, aircraft experimentation, and ordnance testing, and video cameras are believed to monitor every square inch of every range. The UFO videotape received by *Sightings* allegedly contains footage from two different camera positions referred to as S-13 and S-30. The first task for our *Sightings* investigative team was to authenticate the footage. A U.S. Air Force spokesperson would neither confirm nor deny the existence of camera positions S-13 and S-30, or, in fact, whether or not cameras exist anywhere on the Nellis Complex. Officially, the government has no comment. However, *Sightings* was able to find two Nellis Air Force Base range operators who agreed to discuss range cameras and the 1994 UFO. They requested complete anonymity and came forward for a 1995 interview at considerable professional and personal risk. Both men insisted that the footage was real and that the UFO sighting was big news (and top secret) at Nellis for months after the event.

"Bob" would not reveal his current assignment within the Nellis Air Force Base Complex, but did show documentation that he had been employed in the past as a "tracker" on one of the ranges. His is not one of the voices on the tape, but he claims he was present in the control room "at some time" on the day of the UFO sighting. Naturally, Bob was reticent to provide any details of his job or his whereabouts that might give superior officers a clue to his identity. Bob appeared on camera only in silhouette, his voice altered significantly.

"I was a tracker," Bob explains. "I did video tracking and simulated attacks on aircraft. There are hundreds of cameras on the range, and the identification and tracking of aircraft is done there on a daily basis. I've seen thousands of different types of aircraft—thousands—but the UFO on the S-13 and S-30 videotapes is the first instance where no one—not even range control— knew what it was. I've seen a lot of aircraft, but I've not seen anything or even any category of aircraft like this one. It was like nothing I've ever been acquainted with. Strange."

A second range operator, "Frank," echoed Bob's confusion about the origin of the craft. "I'd never seen anything like this before. This was my first encounter with anything of this nature, and I've been working on the ranges for close to ten years," Frank recalls. "It seemed to move in whatever direction it wanted to go whenever it wanted to, contrary to any aircraft I've seen in the past. I didn't feel threatened by it, because I work with strange objects all the time. But this had no assertion of being anything I've ever seen. It changed shape, changed movement, changed color—and all too rapidly to be anything we've worked with before."

"The slap in the face," Bob says, "is that this craft shows up in one of the most secure areas in the world, and it's like they're playing with kids. It's like they could come, do whatever they want, and then, 'Bye now.' And it left those that should know what it was scratching their heads. How simple it was for that craft to come in and then leave. That's scary."

Sightings called in a variety of independent experts to examine the Nellis videotape. Chuck DeCaro is a former member of U.S. Special Forces, specializing in state-of-the-art military technology and hardware. He has analyzed hundreds of hours of supposed UFO footage, identifying most as top-secret experimental aircraft. But, DeCaro told *Sightings,* he has never seen anything like the Nellis UFO. "In my first look at the tape, I said, 'Wow!' And I continue to say, 'Wow!' There are only three things that could be on that tape. One is a very elaborate and expensive hoax. I don't think that's what we're seeing," DeCaro explains. "The second is some kind of a black project, a secret project that has some very unusual aerodynamic characteristics. And third, if you can eliminate all those aerodynamic possibilities, this could be a true unknown. If you come to that conclusion, you've got a pretty interesting piece of history right here."

To rule out the possibility of a hoax, *Sightings* located range personnel (the aforementioned Bob and Frank) and also located a government subcontractor who works with the same image analysis computer used by the U.S. Department of Defense. The subcontractor, referred to as "Steve" to protect his anonymity, used this computer technology to analyze the S-13 and S-30 videotape. (See Photo 23.) "The video appears to be genuine," Steve concludes. "Specifically, I can verify that it was taken by contractor personnel operating tracking sites for the United States Air Force."

Could, then, the Nellis UFO be a rare glimpse at a military black project? The stealth bomber is one former black project tested in Nevada and misidentified by civilians as a UFO. But the military personnel *Sightings* has interviewed insist that they know the difference between experimental aircraft and a true unknown. Not necessarily, says Chuck DeCaro, who cites one apocryphal incident from the late 1970s: "In his book about the stealth fighter, Ben Rich talks about an incident where they flew a prototype over a Marine Hawk antiaircraft missile battalion to see if they could see it. They flew right over the top and they didn't see it, and Lockheed was very satisfied that their stealth technol-

ogy worked. So it is possible that the military would fly a new vehicle over a range without telling anyone."

Steve doesn't think this was the case with the Nellis UFO.
Based on his experience with the Nellis Complex, range control
is always aware of everything in its airspace, no matter how experimental. "The dialog on the videotape informs us that range control didn't have any knowledge of this object. The range is very
tightly controlled for safety reasons. When you've got a large
number of high-performance military aircraft flying at many altitudes up and down the range, you just can't have anything out
there in that airspace that isn't controlled or known, or somebody's going to get run over by an F-15. Even if it's a highly classified program, range control has to have knowledge that there's
something in the airspace. And the tape shows that when this
UFO appeared, range control had no knowledge of this object
being authorized on the range."

Steve also explained that when black projects are tested on the
ranges, the tracking cameras are deactivated. "Typically, the camera operators in the tracking sites are not exposed to highly classified aircraft. When those aircraft need to cross the range,
generally the tracking sites go into a cap mode where the lenses
are capped and the video equipment is effectively turned off."

If the tape is not a hoax or a black project, could it be a true unknown? Chuck DeCaro sat in with Steve as he began to analyze the
Nellis videotape frame by frame. "In the video we find many places
where the object appears to move in an erratic, irregular manner,"
DeCaro explains. "It doesn't have a flight profile characteristic of
most known objects. When you first look at it, it appears that the
camera is jiggling and moving, but this is a very stable fixed-mount
camera. The camera's very smooth and very controlled; it's the object that's dancing and jiggling up and down."

Another anomalous characteristic of the UFO is its apparent
ability to change shape instantaneously. "The physical profile of
the object changes almost frame to frame," says Steve after his
analysis. "Sometimes it appears almost to be a fuzzy, gassy cloud,
and then in some portions of the video it appears to be several

spherical objects surrounding a dark mass. (See Photo 24.) I observed that some parts of the object are twisting and other parts are not. There is a hump on the top, and when it turns one way, sometimes the bottom doesn't turn at all and sometimes the bottom is changing size. The object appears fluid and rubbery. It doesn't make sense. The object is less than a mile from the camera, and at that range—with the type of equipment they're using—you can easily discern a helicopter or a fixed-wing aircraft or even a balloon. At that distance you could almost read the logos on an aircraft, but this object is shifting and changing in a way I've never seen before."

But Chuck DeCaro is still not ruling out the possibility that the Nellis UFO is man-made. "My bet would be that this object is a black project, some type of UAV (Unmanned Aerial Vehicle) with new propulsion technologies and perhaps a new kind of chameleon technology. Chameleoning is the ability to change the appearance of a vehicle with a type of light-emitting diode or a liquid crystal display embedded in the skin of the aircraft. If you could control all those little emitters, you could make the object look like something else, give the impression that it's changing shape as we see with the Nellis object. That's a technology that's happening right now on a UAV that's being tested in Nevada, code-named IVY. It has a skin that changes like a chameleon. So we could be looking at IVY or a prototype for IVY here."

Is the UFO actually changing shape, or is it a trick of the eye caused by the chameleon effect? For an answer, *Sightings* brought the Nellis videotape to Chip Pedersen, a video processing and computer animation expert. He stabilized and enhanced several minutes of the footage. Pedersen has a catalog of known aircraft profiles, and the Nellis UFO does not match any of these. "At first, as a skeptic, I thought it was definitely a lighter-than-air craft, probably some sort of balloons tied together," Pedersen admits. "If all I had was the visual image on tape, that's what I would have to say. I would assume the erratic flight pattern was caused by the object drifting in the wind."

But then Pedersen noted that the range videotape contained a constant readout of the object's elevation, range, and azimuth (its position relative to the horizon). From this information he was able to recreate the UFO's flight path. (See Photo 25.) "Knowing the azimuth, elevation, and range of this object," Pedersen explains, "and some very simple high school geometry, I was able to determine the position of the object at every second along its flight path. I thought that if I did that, I could either confirm or deny that this thing was following the wind. If it did some maneuvers that were atypical of the wind, you could then assume that it was under some form of propulsion or guidance. When I did that, I realized it didn't change shape, but it did change position and direction quite rapidly.

"For the majority of the videotape, the UFO was at a constant range from the camera within one meter exactly," Pedersen continues, "and yet at the same time the azimuth and elevation was changing, which means that the object had to be under some form of guidance, intentionally keeping a consistent distance from the camera. Wind couldn't do that. It's as if the UFO is observing the ground position just as the ground position, the camera, is observing the UFO. I would really have to say I don't know what it is. The data just doesn't come together. I don't have enough information. I don't think anybody has, and it's clear that the people who were looking at it live as it happened didn't know either. So what is it? I wouldn't even want to guess."

Among the experts who were asked to study the Nellis UFO was a defense department subcontractor who also specializes in image enhancement of experimental aircraft. "Charles" believes that the Nellis UFO bears an uncanny resemblance to many of the UFOs observed over Mexico City in 1991. He is concerned that his startling conclusions could compromise his top-level security clearance, so he has also asked that his identity be concealed.

"The Nellis video had over 8,000 frames of information, and after six weeks, we probably only made a study of 700 frames out of the 8,000. It's a very time-consuming process to go in and apply mathematical techniques through the image and try to enhance the resolution. You have to be very careful when you're doing these things that you don't add information to the images that's not in the original media," Charles says. "When we did the analysis of the Nellis video, we looked at it in comparison with all known types of military and civilian aircraft, including balloons, rotorcraft, and UAVs. We never found any craft that compared at all to the object sighted at Nellis. Then we got to several frames that had a very dark black area in the center. I remembered seeing that same black area on an aircraft I'd analyzed back in 1991, during an analysis of UFO footage from Mexico City."

UFOs have been sighted on a near-weekly basis in and around Mexico City since a solar eclipse supposedly "triggered" them on July 11, 1991. The UFOs there have been observed by military and civilians alike, including airline pilots, newspaper reporters, police, and clergy. Hundreds of videotapes have been recorded and analyzed. "Both the Nellis videotape and several of the Mexico City tapes have the same configuration: a pitch-black area in the center surrounded by four little bumps and a spine area, or ridge, along the top," Charles explains. (See Photo 26.) "I think you could make a rough assumption that these objects showing up in two different places—Mexico and Nevada—in two different years—1991 and 1994—may be the same or from the same family of unidentified flying objects."

It is the black area in the center of the UFOs that is the most compelling structure within the UFOs. Charles explains: "That area is very puzzling to us, because it appears to be so highly absorbent of light. Most objects illuminated in this bright a sky, even surfaces that are way down on the bottom in deep shadow, still reflect light back to the camera. This object stops reflecting right on the forward edge, and it falls off very rapidly to pure black in the center, what we call superblack. Engine intakes for turbine engines would look similar to this, but even they would be more reflective, and there would be what we call a splinter, the center shaft or hub, which you can see without much trouble. We've gone way into the black area on the UFO footage, and we can't seem to bring out any detail. We can't find a splinter, or a center, or any kind of protrusion that'd we'd expect to see."

Charles is also baffled by the objects' seemingly amorphous

shape. The fact that the videotaped image of the Nellis UFO in particular is extremely fuzzy points to its possible extraterrestrial origin, Charles says. "We took some video of a golf ball coming up through the sky," he explains, "and it produces an object very similar to a lot of supposed UFO footage. It's a small white dot in the sky. But we were able to take that video and with very minimal work bring out the dimples on the golf ball in flight. Now, the Nellis UFO is less than a mile away from a camera that's extremely accurate. The lens on that camera could read the manufacturer's number on an aircraft at that range. So why is this thing so fuzzy? That's the question. We can't get the definition or the geometry we would expect for objects as close as this one was to a very good camera." Charles has also found that UFO videotape from Mexico City shot with a hand-held home video camera shows almost no difference in clarity. "It's very unusual," Charles continues, "that there's no difference in resolution, no matter what camera is used. Whatever the source, all the UFOs in this family have that ball-of-cotton syndrome, that fuzziness, to them."

No one interviewed by *Sightings* about the Nellis UFO was willing to say that this is definitely a spacecraft from outer space. As men of science, they are trained to keep an open mind and not jump to conclusions. Whether or not this UFO is evidence of an alien civilization invading American airspace, they allow, is up to you. Aerospace journalist Bill Sweetman sums up the feelings of *Sightings'* panel of experts best when he says, "Is there life somewhere out there in the universe that could be called intelligent in some way? Given that the universe is infinite, you'd be a fool not to say yes. Is that intelligent life building things that are recognizable as air vehicles and testing them in collaboration with the U.S. Air Force? I think that much less likely. I believe this is some kind of unusual vehicle being developed under a secret program. It's something highly, highly experimental that would never get off the drawing board if the Pentagon got first whack at it."

In the end, it is "Frank," the anonymous Nellis range operator, who sounds an extraterrestrial note about the origin of the enigmatic craft. "Several people here think it could possibly be a UFO from who-knows-where. Things have been found and tested and probed by the government for years. They could've dug something up and got it working. I've never seen anything like it before, but it is my personal opinion that the government has in the past deliberately released bits and pieces of information just to get the public's curiosity. This could be the start of a new one."

1994

Visitation in Zimbabwe

Why Would 62 Schoolchildren Lie?

> It was upsetting. The lights were big and I thought the ship
> was going to land on the school and destroy it.
>
> —Zimbabwean schoolgirl, age eleven

The Mutual UFO Network is the world's largest UFO research organization. MUFON has more than 5,000 members in over
twenty countries, including a legion of field investigators and regional directors operating in all fifty of the United States. But on
the entire continent of Africa, the grand total of MUFON coordi-
nators is one; and Cynthia Hind of Harare, Zimbabwe, has got
her hands full.

According to South African ufologist Dimitri Galanakis, sightings throughout Africa have risen dramatically in the past ten
years. During an interview in 1994, Galanakis said, "The sightings
in South Africa alone have increased tenfold in the last few years,
especially in the last twelve months. On average we receive between 500 and 1,000 calls each month with regard to UFO sightings. I'd say at least half of the sightings are genuine, the balance
being attributed to secret aircraft, meteorites, or other natural
phenomena. But at least half of the sightings reports we get are

definitely worth investigating." Investigating UFO sightings in Africa has proven to be a daunting task. Vast expanses of desert and bush, tribal superstitions, and language barriers have all conspired to keep nearly every authenticated African UFO event out of the mainstream media.

"When I have heard about UFO cases that seem genuine and are worthy of a good looking into, I have offered to pay for people to go into Kenya, to the coast, or to some outside town in Ghana," Cynthia Hind explains. "I tell them, just give me an account of your expenses, and I will give you the money to go and investigate. But sadly, nobody has wanted to do it. These areas are generally very remote, and it's scary. There are a lot of wars going on. And however dedicated I am about UFOs, I don't want to die for them. I do have hope that now that things are opening up and people are becoming more educated, we will begin to show everyone that this area is important in the worldwide study of UFOs."

Sightings in Africa are of particular interest to UFO researchers, because the eyewitnesses have not all been tainted by descriptions of extraterrestrial spacecraft and alien beings in the mass media. "Many people in Africa do not have television," Hind says. "They might have radio, but I can tell you that the reporters here don't have UFO stories on the air. So where would witnesses pick it up? I remember I once had a good case in a tribal village in Zimbabwe, where twenty-three people were involved in a UFO sighting. They didn't use words like 'saucer' and 'alien,' because they don't even know what those words mean. Instead, they described the beings as the ghosts of their ancestors. However, their descriptions of the tight-fitting suits and strange slanted eyes are the same as descriptions of aliens reported by people in the States or in Europe. Remember, in the tribal areas, the people are isolated. When I told them that men are going into outer space and that Americans have walked on the moon, they said, 'That can't be. Only God walks on the moon.' In many remote places there is no conception of what's going on in the rest of the world."

Several years ago, Hind investigated a case in a remote desert outpost in central South Africa that illustrates the area's lack of sophistication about UFOs and their place in popular culture. "In rural areas, they don't actually know what UFOs are; nevertheless, things are happening. I interviewed one man who lives in the Great Karoo, an area that's almost completely unoccupied, just miles and miles of arid land with nothing on it. This chap woke up one morning and walked out to a wall that surrounds the village where he lives. He saw what he thought was a caravan, what you call a trailer in the States. As he walked closer he thought it was strange the caravan hadn't got any wheels, just tines sticking into the ground. When he got nearer still he saw four men standing in this trailer; one was at a console where a lot of lights were flashing, and the other three seemed to be examining meters. Something alerted them to the man's presence outside. They all looked up, and with that, the man heard a click, and a light flashed on him. 'I couldn't get my breath,' he told me. 'I felt as though I was drowning. I was trying to get out of this beam of light, but it was difficult.'

"His nose started to bleed. He began to vomit. As he tried to crawl out of the light, this craft lifted off the ground, the legs folded underneath, and it took off. He said it nearly knocked over his windmill. Well, the man died eighteen months later, because he was riddled with cancer. I'm only speculating because nobody knows, but I think he got too close to that craft, and he died from the effects of radium or some kind of radiation sickness. But no one would ever examine the case. The doctors all thought he was crazy and that I was crazy."

In a more recent case in Ruwa, Zimbabwe, Cynthia Hind did not have to contend with an easily ignored single eyewitness, as in the Great Karoo case. This time, on September 16, 1994, Hind found sixty-two irreproachable witnesses who had all seen the same brilliant UFO and claimed to have made contact with the alien beings who emerged from the craft. The witnesses were all schoolchildren ranging in age from eight to twelve years old. Their account of a saucer-shaped craft and its humanoid occupants has ignited the UFO community worldwide, attracting notable researchers to the site, among them Harvard professor of psychiatry John Mack. "The children of Arial School experienced a powerful encounter with strange beings, and we're left with the rather disturbing fact that this seems to be what it is," Mack says. "And it seems to have no other psychiatric explanation."

The Arial School is located in Ruwa, Zimbabwe, about twelve miles outside the capital city of Harare. "It's a primary school for young children, quite isolated in the country, but it's a good school," Cynthia Hind explains. "It's open to all races, and there are about 250 children at the school." At approximately 10:30 in the morning on October 16, 1994, most of the Arial School children were playing outside during morning recess. All of the teachers were inside attending their monthly staff meeting. The only adult supervising outside was a woman operating the snack bar.

One of the older children (*Sightings* has chosen not to disclose the names of the Arial School children) remembers seeing some of the fourth-graders straying into the bush, outside the school's playground boundaries. As a student prefect, responsible for enforcing school rules, the older boy went to tell the younger children to come out of the dense undergrowth and return to the safety of the playground. "This thing, an object, landed with three or four things beside it," the boy recalls. "We saw this man in the musasa trees, and he looked like he was dressed in a really shiny diving suit. His eyes were down around his cheeks and he was looking really, really funny." One of the younger girls remembers, "He was definitely not a human. I don't know what he was really, but he had a big head and big black eyes, and he was dressed in a black body suit."

After the initial sighting, more children began to gather at the bottom of the playground. "I saw a few things in space," a fifth-grade girl explains. "I saw the bigger ship and then like four or five smaller ones crowding around it." An older girl corroborates her sighting. "I saw one big one and quite a few little ones scattered all around. They were very still, just hovering, and then I saw them also disappear. They went about a meter off the ground, and then they just vanished." In all, sixty-two children claimed that they had seen the UFOs and two alien creatures. No adults were present. According to Cynthia Hind, "The only adult there was the woman who ran the tuck shop [snack bar] where the children buy sweets and drinks. One little boy did run up to her and said, 'Come quickly, come quickly, there are little men in the playground.' And she said, 'Pull the other leg. You're not going to get me out of the tuck shop so you can pinch sweets.'" Another boy explains, "We went to the teachers, and we went into the office, and we started telling the teachers, and then they said maybe there's nothing. We felt very sad, because we did see something."

Colin Mackie is the headmaster of Arial School. He remembers being skeptical about the children's story. "We were all in the middle of a staff meeting. None of the staff actually saw anything. Some of the children indicated to certain members of staff that they were seeing something very strange. Unfortunately, we just fogged it off, to put it bluntly, until after the meeting. But I began to take the situation more seriously when the parents began arriving after school and the children started to take their parents to the place where they said they saw the UFO." One mother, a native Zimbabwean, says, "I believe the children, because normally children don't lie about things like that. I believe that what they saw is maybe from the spirit world, not from our world." Another mother, a recent emigré from France, said, "At first I thought it was a meteorite display, but then when my son went into a description, I thought that it must be something more. Children don't lie unless there's an adult involved encouraging them in a certain direction. In fact, I was quite upset he didn't phone me so I could run down with the camera." As to her interpretation of the sighting, the mother adds, "I don't exclude the possibility of life on other planets, but I can't say I believe until I actually see one."

When Cynthia Hind was first brought in to investigate the children's seemingly outlandish claims, she asked the students to draw pictures of what they had seen. The children created a disturbing portrait of extraterrestrial contact in pencil and crayon. (See Photos 27–29.) "I believe they saw what they say they saw," Hind asserts. "They put into their drawings many things that I don't think they could have known about. For instance, UFOs are inclined to follow electricity lines, and one little boy drew a picture with the UFO coming in along the electricity lines. There were several small details like that in the drawings, which I found to be incredible. I was amazed at the common features that occurred among quite a diverse group of children."

The drawings were extremely convincing to Hind, and her belief in the children only increased when she interviewed each child individually about the encounters. "The children strike me as being particularly intelligent," Hind says. "I interviewed them in the presence of Colin Mackie, and I can tell you that the children wouldn't lie to their headmaster. He's quite a disciplinarian, and the children respect him and are a little scared of him. He said to me, 'I don't believe in UFOs, but these children wouldn't lie because they're afraid of me.' And I agreed. Whenever I would ask a question, they would look at Mr. Mackie while they were answering. These children were not lying."

Not everyone who has since studied the Ruwa sighting agrees with Hind. "It's not a question of whether they're lying or not. It's a question of their distinction between reality and not reality being not as sharp as that of an older kid or an adult," says John Saliba, a professor of comparative religion at the University of Detroit. Saliba has researched many claims of extraterrestrial contact, discounting them all. "I think the kids knew about flying saucers. The way they drew the flying saucer and the so-called people who came out of it, now those are pictures you'd find in TV programs and movies." Hind counters: "Most of these children don't have a television. They don't go to the movies. They live in the country where their parents are farmers."

Saliba remains skeptical. "I have to admit that you have all these stories of flying saucers for the last forty years and I can't understand their goals. Why are they here? I don't know what they're doing, why they're wasting their time going around in circles talking to a few people who are insignificant." One of the young fifth-graders sums up the feelings of the children when she says, "He can believe that, but it's not going to change my idea of what I've seen or what I know."

In 1995, world-renowned alien-abduction expert John Mack became interested in the Arial School children and journeyed to Zimbabwe to interview the students, teachers, and parents. Dr.

Mack, a professor of psychiatry at Harvard's Cambridge Hospital, is also the director of PEER, the Program for Extraordinary Experience Research. PEER is currently producing an in-depth documentary on the Ruwa sightings. Dr. Mack first interviewed the children alone for later comparison. The following are three excerpts from his interviews:

I

BOY: The ship was silver, and the ring around it was red.

DR. MACK: Was red. Did light come from the whole thing or . . . ?

BOY: There were lights just above the ring on the dome.

DR. MACK: What was it doing?

BOY: It was hovering above the trees. That's when I saw the little men, and then I just couldn't see the object or the men anymore. I don't see how anything from this world could fly away so fast.

DR. MACK: What did the men you saw look like?

BOY: The hair was a bit like Michael Jackson, and they had on a black suit. They had short legs and quite long tops. Their heads were big, and their eyes were four or five times bigger than ours but they were about my height.

DR. MACK: What would you say to the idea that this was an experimental craft that landed where it shouldn't have, and these men were in spacesuits and helmets?

BOY: Well, unless kids my age got dressed up in diving suits and built a spacecraft . . . these men were my size.

II

DR. MACK: How many of the strange beings did you see?

GIRL: I saw one below the craft and another one running around, but bouncy-like. They had a longish face, and they had eyes like rugby balls. I didn't see any mouth.

DR. MACK: Was there any communication between you?

GIRL: They were kind of just like looking at us. They were like kind of astonished at what we were.

DR. MACK: How did you feel?

GIRL: I felt scared.

DR. MACK: You felt scared. What was scary about it?

GIRL: I felt scared, because I've never seen such a person like that before.

DR. MACK: How do you feel now?

GIRL: I feel now that it was valuable for me to see, because aliens are something hardly anybody gets to see. And just to see something really strange and new makes me feel good.

Not all of the children came away from their sighting with a positive feeling. Many of the children told Dr. Mack about telepathic communication that they believed they had received from the extraterrestrial visitors. It was a disturbing message that Dr. Mack had heard from hundreds of abductees in the United States, half a world away. "In the abduction process," Dr. Mack explains, "one of the most powerful elements is presentation of information about the fate of the earth and the ecological catastrophes that are brewing and accelerating. They are shown images of pollution, deforestation, Earth as a vast desert; apocalyptic scenes that have an extraordinary impact." Their doomsday scenario is being repeated to the last detail by the children of Ruwa.

III

DR. MACK: What do you imagine is his reason for visiting Earth?

GIRL: I think it's about something that's going to happen.

DR. MACK: Something that's going to happen?

GIRL: What I thought was maybe the world's going to end. They were telling us the world's gonna end.

DR. MACK: Are we supposed to do something about that?

GIRL: I think they want people to know that we're actually making harm on this world, and we mustn't get too technologized. They don't think we look after the planet properly.

DR. MACK: How did that get communicated to you?

GIRL: I don't even know. It just popped up in my head. He never said anything. He talked just with his eyes. It was just the face and the eyes. They looked horrible.

DR. MACK: And the eyes, the horrible look had that information that you just told me?

GIRL: Yes. I just felt all horrible inside. I felt all the trees in the world will just go down, and there will be no air and people will be dying. It was upsetting. The lights were big, and I thought the ship was going to land on the school and destroy it.

DR. MACK: Are you still worried?

GIRL: I worry that the man is still looking at me and may kill me.

DR. MACK: You're really upset about this.

GIRL: Yes.

DR. MACK: I'm sure no harm will come to you. Do you believe me?

GIRL: I don't know.

Dr. Mack and PEER are continuing to work with the children and their families to help alleviate the fear and anxiety that has come in the wake of the 1994 sightings. Both Dr. Mack and Cynthia Hind believe that the most important thing right now is for the parents and teachers in Ruwa to continue to support their children and to believe in the truthfulness of their extraordinary experiences. "Instead of looking at the mystery, we accuse the tellers of false memories. This is not the right approach," Dr. Mack says. Hind echoes his clinical judgment in her passionate question, "Why would sixty-two children lie?"

AIRBORNE
ENCOUNTERS

1978

Into Oblivion

The Disappearance of Frederick Valentich

> In my opinion and the opinion of a number of other re-
> searchers, Mr. Valentich is alive and well. I believe that he
> was grabbed out of the sky and taken away.
> —Robert Dean, field investigator, Stargate International

A fiery oblong UFO with no wings, no observable propulsion system, emitting a bizarre, greenish light; this was the last thing pilot
Frederick Valentich saw before he disappeared off the face of the
earth. That was on October 21, 1978, and from that day to this,
Valentich's father and a handful of dedicated UFO researchers
have searched for information about who or what was controlling
that unidentified craft. Still, nearly twenty years after his son's disappearance, Guido Valentich makes an annual pilgrimage to the
place where Frederick was confronted and conquered by a
threatening UFO. Guido Valentich returns to Cape Otway in
southern Australia every October 21, because he hopes that one
day the extraterrestrials who took his son away may decide to
bring him back.

Standing on a bluff at Cape Otway, Guido Valentich looks out
over the Bass Strait and can almost make out King Island, his

son's intended destination. "It is very emotional for me," Valentich says, "because every year when I come here it seems to be only yesterday that Frederick was alive. And when nothing happens, there are no new clues, I feel so sad and have to hope that maybe next year we will learn something new or get some sign about Frederick." Australian UFO researcher Colin Hayvice has accompanied Valentich on his annual pilgrimage. "Guido believes his son has been abducted," Hayvice explains. "And Guido believes Frederick will be delivered back. He makes this trek to Cape Otway, because 4,500 feet above this place is where Frederick was last heard from. Guido believes that this is the point where his son will be delivered back."

Guido Valentich has survived nearly twenty years of grief after the disappearance and presumed death of his firstborn son. It's only natural that he would cling to any shred of hope that Frederick is still alive. But there is nothing natural about Frederick Valentich's disappearance, and there are many researchers who believe that Guido is not simply a distraught father in denial. There is strong evidence that Frederick did encounter a UFO over Cape Otway; a UFO under the command and control of an extraterrestrial force that was being tracked by the United States government.

In 1978, Frederick Valentich was a twenty-year-old pilot with the Australian Air Training Corps. (See Photo 30.) On October 21, Valentich left Moorabbin Airport in Victoria bound for King Island, a sparsely populated outpost one hour's flying time from Moorabbin. Earlier in the day, Valentich had told his father he was going to King Island to catch crayfish and pick up any air corpsmen needing a ride back to the mainland. He would leave at twilight and make the return flight after dark in order to pick up night mileage toward his commercial pilot's license. "His future was to be a commercial pilot. He already had a Class 4 license and about 200 hours flying time. I remember the morning of the twenty-first at the breakfast table talking about the flight, and as he went out I remember his last words were 'Hey, Pa, it's going to be a beautiful day to fly,'" Guido Valentich recalls. "We talked about me going on the plane with him, but there were family things to take care of. I feel sorry now that I didn't go, because in my mind I feel that if I had been with him perhaps the situation could have turned out slightly differently."

Frederick Valentich was known to his fellow pilots as hardworking and honest, a straight shooter who knew how to fly. He filed a flight plan with the Moorabbin Airport hours before his proposed flight and attended a meteorological briefing, where he was given information on weather conditions and air currents. Valentich took off at 6:20 P.M. as the sun was just beginning to set on a cool and cloudless afternoon. His flight plan would take him along the southeast coast of Victoria and then out across the Bass Strait, an infamous expanse of ocean known as the Australian Bermuda Triangle. Valentich had heard the rumors about strange disappearances, inexplicable mechanical failures, and magnetic anomalies but told friends he never paid much attention to that kind of superstitious talk.

"Since 1904," Colin Hayvice has found, "there have been almost 350 people from boats and planes that have just disappeared off the face of the earth in the Bass Strait Triangle. And that's not including shipwrecks and plane crashes, just cases where they've found boats and planes with no personnel aboard. No bodies. No skeletons. Nothing. The strait's also where we have a lot of UFO sightings and reports of abductions." But as far as Hayvice can determine, Frederick Valentich was the first pilot to ever radio in that he was in the presence of a threatening UFO.

Forty-five minutes into the flight, Valentich contacted the control tower at Cape Otway near Melbourne, the last landfall before the Bass Strait and King Island beyond. Valentich was concerned about a high-speed unidentified aircraft, which appeared to be on a collision course with his single-engine Cessna 182. According to tower controller Steve Rovey, the radar screen was clear. The following is excerpted from the official Commonwealth of Australia Department of Transport accident report. It is a transcript of Frederick Valentich's first sighting of the UFO as recorded by the Cape Otway control tower.

VALENTICH: Melbourne, this is Delta Sierra Juliet [Valentich's call sign]. Do you have any known traffic below 5,000 [feet]?

TOWER: Delta Sierra Juliet, no known traffic.

VALENTICH: I am seeing a large aircraft below 5,000.

TOWER: What type of aircraft is it?

VALENTICH: I cannot affirm. It is four bright—it seems to me like landing lights.

TOWER: Delta Sierra Juliet?

VALENTICH: Melbourne . . . the aircraft has just passed over me at least a thousand feet above!

TOWER: And it is a large aircraft? Confirm.

VALENTICH: Er . . . unknown due to the speed it's traveling. Is there any Air Force aircraft in the vicinity?

TOWER: No known aircraft in the vicinity.

VALENTICH: It's approaching now from due east toward me . . . it seems to me that he's playing some sort of game. He's flying over me two, three times at speeds I could not identify!

TOWER: Confirm you cannot identify the aircraft.

VALENTICH: Affirmative.

TOWER: Can you describe the, er, aircraft?

VALENTICH: It's not an aircraft. As it's flying past, it's a long shape, cannot identify more than that it has such speed. . . . It's before me right now, Melbourne. . . . It seems like it's stationary right now. What I'm doing is orbiting, and the thing is just orbiting on top of me. Also it's got a green light and sort of metallic-like. It's all shiny on the outside . . . it's just vanished again.

TOWER: Confirm the aircraft just vanished.

VALENTICH: It's now approaching from the southwest . . . the engine is rough idling . . . I've got it set at 2324 and the thing is coughing . . . that strange aircraft is hovering on top of me again. It's hovering, and it's not an aircraft. . . .

After this last transmission, the report states, "There is no record of any further transmissions from the aircraft." The report then concludes: "The weather in the Cape Otway area was clear with . . . excellent visibility and light winds. The end of daylight was at 1918 hours [7:18 P.M.]. The reason for the disappearance of the aircraft has not been determined."

The actual taped transmissions between Frederick Valentich and the Cape Otway tower were classified top secret and reportedly erased. Guido Valentich was allowed to listen to his son's last words only once, in the presence of military personnel. He claims that the tapes he heard differ dramatically from the official written transcript released by the Department of Transport. A transcript that Valentich believes is far more accurate appeared in a Melbourne newspaper soon after Frederick's disappearance, supposedly leaked to a reporter by anonymous airport personnel. In this "unofficial" transcript, some of the wording is the same as the official report, but there are far more details about the size and shape of the craft. For example:

> VALENTICH: This is not an aircraft. Repeat. Not an aircraft
> known to us. An unidentified vehicle with a green
> light at terminus of upper cylinder. Outer projec-
> tion appears to be aluminum or some other light
> metal. Windows are unmistakable, and I see four
> lights from the interior. Not windows, some other
> observation area. Melbourne . . . it's playing a
> game with me!

"Valentich gave a complete description of the type of craft. He described the shape, the portholes, what it was doing," Colin Hayvice explains. As a veteran UFO researcher and author, Hayvice has made a complete study of the Valentich disappearance and firmly believes that Valentich came in contact with an extraterrestrial force. "It was buzzing him, circling him, going off at great speeds, then disappearing, then coming back. He was in constant contact with the tower over this period of time, until 7:14 P.M., when all of a sudden he said this thing was approaching him and bathed him in a green light. Then there was a metal scraping sound heard over the radio, and Frederick Valentich was gone. The plane and everything just disappeared off the face of the earth."

According to the unofficial transcript and Guido Valentich's memory, these were Frederick's last words:

VALENTICH: Do you believe me, log?
TOWER: Sure do. We know it's Valentich.
VALENTICH: Am proceeding at a speed of 110 at the same course moving up to 4,000. Wait . . . wait . . . engine faltering. I've got rough idling. She may conk. He's coming up from the rear at tremendous burst. His green light is all over here. It's not an aircraft . . . going up to 5,000, 6,000 . . . long wingless metallic tube spouting flame . . . I feel scorching . . . I feel . . .
TOWER: 229, 229, we hear something tearing . . . 229, 229, please reply.

"After the incident, Steve Rovey, the controller, said that Freddy Valentich's attitude and manner was calm and matter of fact," Colin Hayvice explains. "Rovey reported that Valentich showed no panic through his voice, except in the last few seconds. They all knew Valentich at Cape Otway. They knew him to be a stable young man with a good family background and a devoted girl-friend. They had no reason to disbelieve what he reported over the radio." Guido Valentich adds that his son was a cautious, sober pilot who had a lot to lose by misidentifying a conventional air-craft. "He would not present anything that would jeopardize him getting his commercial pilot's license. He would not want to show up for his license and be known as the man who saw the UFO."

After the control tower lost radio contact and Valentich did not arrive per schedule on King Island, a search plane was sent to the point of last contact, twelve miles off the coast of Melbourne in the Bass Strait. There was no sign of Valentich or his plane. According to Hayvice, "Even though they considered that he probably went into the water, the search and research department searched by air, sea, and land within a fifty-mile radius from Cape Otway. They searched for five days continually, twenty-four hours a day, and then continued daylight searches for three weeks before they called off the search. Then they notified all the shipping and shore patrols that went through the area for a period of three months to look out for any wreckage, anything from the plane."

No trace of Valentich or his plane has ever been found. At the very least, some shred of aircraft debris should have washed ashore. Valentich had four life vests with him at the time of his disappearance, some of which should have been recovered. There also should have been an oil slick, but the only slick found during the search period was analyzed and found to be diesel fuel from a fishing boat, not aviation fuel. Investigators at the Department of Transport hypothesized that Valentich had been flying upside down, became disoriented, and probably crashed inland. However, ground searches found no trace of Valentich, and Colin Hayvice has learned that it would be impossible for Valentich to have flown his plane upside down for any extended length of time. "Some of the experts said he got disoriented," Hayvice explains, "and that he was flying upside down. So therefore, when he thought he was going up, he was going down. But the Cessna 182 he was in has got the aviation petrol in the wings being fed to the engine by gravity. So after forty-nine seconds of flying upside down, the motor would have cut out. But Valentich was talking to Steve Rovey in the tower for more than six and a half minutes. That tells you he wasn't flying upside down. He wasn't disoriented."

Officially, there were no eyewitnesses to Frederick Valentich's disappearance. However, a small group of UFO researchers believe that there were eyewitnesses working in the Australian desert at a supersecret surveillance facility known as Pine Gap. (See Photo 31.) On the record, Pine Gap is a tracking station located twelve miles from Alice Springs in central Australia, a joint U.S.-Australia space defense facility. But according to UFO investigator Robert Dean, Pine Gap keeps its true mission well hidden, and officials there know more than they're willing to tell about Frederick Valentich's disappearance.

"We have around the planet an electronic space shield, and Pine Gap is one of the key positions in this worldwide electronic grid," Dean explains. "That means that anything that comes in from out in space is immediately picked up. They can track anything from a basketball-sized meteor to a satellite—or whatever. If it's a 'whatever,' something we don't know about, immediately Pine Gap monitors it, photographs it, and tracks it. That's what Pine Gap does. There's no question in my mind that the Pine Gap facility tracked the object that Valentich described. They were tracking Fred, they were tracking the object. God knows when the truth will come out. I think Fred was grabbed, and Pine Gap must have monitored the whole damn thing, because they monitor everything."

Robert O. Dean speaks from impressive firsthand experience. He is a retired U.S. Army Command Sergeant Major who spent twenty-seven years in the military and fourteen additional years working for FEMA, the Federal Emergency Management Agency. Between 1963 and 1967, a period that Dean claims changed his life profoundly, he was assigned to SHAPE, the Supreme Headquarters Allied Powers in Europe, the military arm of NATO headquartered in Paris, France. It was during his tenure at SHAPE that Dean claims he obtained a top-secret clearance known as a "cosmic top-secret" clearance and was shown files about NATO's knowledge of UFOs. "I learned of a study that was initiated in 1961 because of large numbers of circular metallic objects flying all over central Europe, flying at a very high altitude, at a very high rate of speed, in formation, and very obviously under intelligent control. And for a time, the Soviets thought they belonged to us, and we honestly believed that they belonged to the Soviets—and here we were looking at each other across this iron curtain with our fingers on the triggers.

"It was a very difficult time; neither the Soviets nor the U.S. knew what it was all about. The study wasn't concluded until 1964. I arrived in 1963 and read the report continually until I left in 1967. That's how I got involved in the UFO matter. That's how I learned for the first time that this was not myth or legend or fantasy. I learned that the UFO matter was not only real, but, my

God, the conclusions of the SHAPE military study indicated that the ramifications of this—the implications—were earthshaking. That was the beginning of my devoted, almost obsessed, research into the UFO matter."

Robert Dean believes Pine Gap is a significant linchpin in the U.S. government's secret UFO tracking network. "*Sightings* has got hold of a tiger by the tail when you start looking into Pine Gap," Dean says. "I must be honest with you that the Pine Gap facility and what it's involved with is probably one of the most secret installations in the world. The NSA is involved. The CIA is involved, and the National Reconnaissance Office is part of it. They call it a 'Joint Space Defense Facility,' but it's a hell of a lot more than that."

Not everyone agrees with Dean's assessment of the Pine Gap mission. Desmond Ball, the author of the book *Pine Gap* and a professor of strategic and defense studies at the Australia National University in Canberra, insists that Pine Gap is not involved in UFO tracking. "Pine Gap is the ground control station for a network of satellites, and they're involved in listening to a variety of signals, communications, and other electronic emissions," Ball says. "The primary mission involves relaying signals from missiles and other advanced weapons systems in their test phase to engineers on the ground who want to know how the missile is performing. Since the 1970s, there have been a broader range of secondary missions mainly involving interception of microwave communications." Secret UFO intelligence notwithstanding, Desmond Ball does admit that he does not know everything that goes on at Pine Gap. Ball says, "Most governments don't even publicly admit that they are involved in any type of satellite intelligence operations. That's probably about as close as any government is going to go by saying that they're involved in 'signals,' in their intelligence collection functions."

Robert Dean claims to have friends on the inside who tell quite a different story about the Pine Gap facility and the type of intelligence it is gathering. "The real secret behind Pine Gap, the real unpublished, underground operation involves the alien reality and UFOs. I can tell you as a result of thirty years of research, my experience in the military, and the fact that I still have a bunch of cronies in sensitive places, there appears to be a real paranoia among our defense establishment," Dean has found. "It's never been announced to the people that there's a threat from outer space, but officials are frightened. That's what the Strategic Defense Initiative, the so-called Star Wars program, is all about. That's why it continues, even though the Soviet Union has collapsed. And Pine Gap is an important part of this vast program."

"I think that's just nonsense," says Desmond Ball about Dean's charge that Pine Gap is part of an "alien reality." Ball's research has him convinced that "even though there's secrecy about the place, they'd never be able to hide what satellites their antennae are pointing at. There are thousands of people who work there now—and thousands more who have worked there and moved on. A secret of that magnitude would be impossible to keep."

"Eyewitnesses have seen white disc-shaped objects being flown in and trucked in to Pine Gap," Robert Dean counters. "U.S. Air Force trucks, U.S. Air Force planes, C5A Galaxies, enormous transports have been seen carrying these white objects with USAF markings, disc-shaped craft with domes on top. People in Australia, UFO watchers and investigators, sit out there in the mountains at night and photograph UFOs all over the place. There's an enormous amount of UFO activity out there, just as there is at Site [Area] 51. Possibly some of them are ours. Some of them may not be ours. That's part of the big secret."

Whether the UFOs are "ours" or "theirs" or exist at all continues to be hotly debated. While the experts are at loggerheads over the activities at Pine Gap, Guido Valentich continues his own quest for the truth behind his son's disappearance. Was there a UFO over Cape Otway for Pine Gap to see? Shortly after Frederick's last radio call, Guido Valentich received a letter from a woman in Germany who claimed that she was having psychic visions of the craft that took Frederick. She included a crude drawing of the craft. Valentich found the letter interesting, but unsubstantiated, and put it aside. Then, a few days later, he received another letter containing a photograph of an anomalous craft hovering above Cape

Otway. The UFO in the photo bore an uncanny resemblance to the one drawn by the German psychic. Amateur photographer Roy Manifold had taken the picture on October 21, 1978, just minutes before Frederick Valentich told Cape Otway controllers he was being approached by an unidentified aircraft. If the eyes and ears at Pine Gap are as powerful as Robert Dean suggests, its personnel would have known about the UFO snapped by Manifold.

"It was quite a clear night," Roy Manifold recalls. "We were at our holiday cabin on the coast. It was cool outside, and I remember we had a fire going in the front room. Everything just seemed very normal that night." Manifold was experimenting with a new motor drive and timer on his camera. He had set up his tripod outside to take a series of time-lapse photographs of the sunset. "I had taken six consecutive shots, and as I came outside to collect my camera, I heard a small airplane pass overhead."

A few days later, Roy Manifold had his film developed, and—along with the beautiful sunset—was a possible clue to Frederick Valentich's disappearance. "I picked up the film," Manifold remembers, "and the first shots were very good, and then I got to one that had a very strange object in it. [See Photo 32.] At first, I wasn't suspicious about it or making any connection with the Valentich case. I just wanted to know whether I'd done something wrong with the exposure or there was something wrong with the camera. I took it to Kodak's Victoria headquarters and asked them to explain the object if they could. They assured me that it was nothing to do with the processing or the film. It wasn't an emulsion error or anything they could explain."

After Roy Manifold read about Frederick Valentich's disappearance, he sent a copy of his strange photograph to Guido Valentich. He was unaware of its striking resemblance to the psychic's vision. Valentich convinced Manifold to send the negative of the photograph to a computer enhancement and analysis laboratory in the United States. Computer analysis of the UFO revealed that the object was a solid, reflective sphere, probably metallic, and approximately seventy feet in diameter. The fact that the picture was taken just minutes before Manifold heard a light aircraft suggests that the UFO in the photograph may be the craft Frederick Valentich saw just before he vanished without a trace.

If an amateur photographer looking for a snapshot of a sunset could capture this UFO, Robert Dean believes, then surely Pine Gap is hiding more and better photographs of the Valentich encounter. "I think that Frederick Valentich was grabbed out of the sky, and I believe the entire operation was probably observed. I don't think Pine Gap necessarily had a hand in what took place, but they were watching it happen. For people who tell me that UFOs and aliens are all a bunch of hooey, they are simply uninformed. They haven't taken the time to look at the evidence. Don't take my word for anything or anything anybody else might say. There's an enormous amount of evidence out there, and people have got to stop slumbering and wake up. This is real. This is not a joke."

For Guido Valentich, the reality of UFOs and alien encounters hits very close to home. He lost his son to an unknown force. Every year he returns to the site of his firstborn's disappearance and waits—for what, he's not sure. For now, all he has is a fragment of a smuggled radio transcript that may or may not represent Frederick's final words, one tantalizing photograph, rumors about a place called Pine Gap, and the memory of Frederick's smiling face turning to say, "Hey, Pa, it's going to be a beautiful day to fly."

1967, 1978

The Culture of Silence
Why Pilots Don't Talk

I didn't say anything for a long time, but when I did report it
to my boss, the reaction was rather unusual. He said, "Well,
strange things happen to people who have sightings."
— "Ted," former United Airlines pilot

According to UFO researchers, the ideal witness is a trustworthy,
credible person with a broad knowledge of aviation and aerody-
namics; someone who experiences his sighting with a critical,
learned eye—preferably from the air. In other words, the best
UFO eyewitness is a pilot. But how many pilots are there who
have seen strange craft invading their airspace, interfering with
their aircraft control systems? Skeptics and UFO debunkers are
fond of perpetuating the myth that the typical UFO eyewitness is
an intoxicated, highly suggestible hayseed (usually casting asper-
sions on bib overalls, trailer parks, and poor dental hygiene in the
process). However, UFO researchers insist that the majority of
sightings are made by sober, educated observers, tens of thousands of whom are, in fact, pilots.

Ample evidence that pilots see UFOs much more frequently
than the general public realizes can be found in a recently declas-

sified publication from the U.S. Air Force Security Service, Electronic Warfare Center. In his article about an encounter between a UFO and pilots from the Iranian Imperial Air Force, Captain Henry S. Shields makes the following statement, suggesting that pilot UFO sightings are not only possible, they are inevitable: "Sometime in his career, each pilot can expect to encounter strange, unusual happenings which will never be adequately or entirely explained by logic or subsequent investigation."

Captain Shields's statement implies that every military pilot will see a UFO, and so it seems likely that this experience would extend to commercial and civilian pilots as well. However, very few pilot sightings are ever reported in the news, because there is a code of silence among pilots that is rarely broken. For military pilots, the reason may be largely economic. According to former Air Force press chief Al Chop, "At the time I was involved with the Air Force, there was an Air Force regulation, 200-2, which said that a pilot who talked willy-nilly to the press about a sighting was subject to a $10,000 fine and loss of his commission. It was a policy to keep sightings made by Air Force personnel within the Air Force, so that they could investigate on the quiet without the press hanging around."

For commercial pilots, there are no formal regulations preventing them from speaking to the press and public, but according to several pilots, there is an unwritten rule that any pilot who speaks out about his or her UFO sighting is in serious danger of being dismissed. Former British Airways Captain Graham Sheppard is one of only a handful of pilots who has ever spoken out publicly about his airborne sightings. Sheppard recalls what happened after he recounted his personal UFO experiences on a London current affairs radio program. "I was interviewed for the *Today* program, which is very popular in the U.K., and a lot of the British Airways managers heard it. As a result, I was called in by the chief pilot to explain myself and to be advised in no uncertain terms that if I did any further media in this respect, that I would be dismissed. I was told that the pilot who becomes media friendly can endanger the airline's image. They made it quite clear that my interest in UFOs and my interest in making the in-

formation public was not compatible with the commercial position of British Airways."

In 1993, Graham Sheppard retired from British Airways and
currently flies on an as-needed basis with several carriers, including Alitalia. He feels that he can speak more freely about his UFO
encounters now that he is not beholden to one particular airline.
"I'm in a different position now," Sheppard says. "I'm basically a
freelance pilot, so as such I'm not constrained by the corporate
culture as I was in the past. My hands are untied." But Sheppard's
outspokenness has not come without a price, and he sees this as
the main reason why more retired or freelance pilots like himself
don't choose to come forward with their UFO sightings. Sheppard says, "I've been accused of hallucinating, being under-
trained, of not understanding meteorological phenomena—all
kinds of attacks have come my way. There are hazards in going
public. Being a cautious bunch, I know that many pilots look at
the road ahead and decide that it's not worth being public on the
issue of UFOs. It involves quite a lot of unwelcome attention."

Graham Sheppard has been a commercial pilot for more than
thirty years, with a sterling record as a first officer and later a captain. He admits to having seen many strange things in the night
sky, nearly all of which he was able to positively identify or make
an educated guess about. "Flying over England one night, there
was a spectacular display of light, and a lot of pilots came on the
air and said, 'Did you see that? What was that?' We quickly
learned that a satellite rig had broken up and reentered the
atmosphere," Sheppard recalls. "I've seen many odd things in the
sky, but none of them would be in the same category as my two
airborne UFO sightings."

Sheppard's first UFO sighting occurred on March 22, 1967.
He was the first officer on a British European Airlines turboprop
en route from Gibraltar to London's Heathrow Airport. Here is
Sheppard's personal account of the UFO encounter: "It was a
very clear night. We left the north coast of Spain and were over
the Bay of Biscay cruising at about 24,000 feet. Straight ahead of
us was a bright star. If you can recall Venus at its best, this star was
at least double full Venus in magnitude. There was no shape to it.

It was just a brilliant light, quite startling. We watched it for several minutes, discussing what it might be. The other first officer had a star chart and used it to try and identify what we were seeing. It wasn't on the star chart.

"Then it started to move from the twelve o'clock position straight ahead to our left, moving slowly and descending. At the same time, it was changing colors, very bright iridescent colors. When it was in a position of about ten-thirty on our relative position, it started doing aerobatics at a phenomenal rate—the sort of aerobatics which are completely beyond known aerodynamic parameters. And then from nowhere, another one joined it, and the two continued to do this amazing aerobatic display.

"These maneuvers were at an extreme high speed, which was, in my opinion, beyond anything around at the time. It was as if they were tethered on a string being spun around like a Catherine wheel firework with changing colors. The speed must have been hundreds of miles an hour, remaining constant as the lights were moving around in this looping maneuver. This suggests angular accelerations and g-forces, which I can't imagine would be sustainable by any craft which we have even now. It was an amazing aerial gavotte.

"As we flew north, the display pair moved to our left-hand side out to the west over the Bay of Biscay. I called Bordeaux radar, their military organization at that time, and they confirmed that they had unidentified traffic ten miles to the west of us, which was precisely where we thought this display team was. As far as I'm concerned this was a very good sighting, backed up by military radar."

As a young pilot, Graham Sheppard remembers his enthusiasm and his desire to talk to other pilots to see if anyone else had witnessed the bizarre UFOs. His youthful exuberance was quickly squelched. "We sat in the crew room at London Heathrow Airport, and the senior captain, who was a World War II veteran, advised us that it would be in our interest not to report it and that it would possibly compromise our career progress if we made an issue of the sighting. He was well aware of the culture of silence. So for many years I only talked to close family about it—until twenty-six years later, when I didn't have anything to fear from the point of view of my progress in the airline, because I'd just about done my time."

Sheppard's second sighting occurred during daylight hours later that same year. "It was a routine flight from Scotland back to London," Sheppard recalls, "and we were in a Vanguard cruising around 25,000 feet. We were just chatting, not doing much, when suddenly Preston radar, the controller at that time for the Manchester area, gave us quite a clear alert call, which was most unusual. The radar controller said, 'You have unidentified traffic in the airway, fast-moving, opposite direction.'

"So of course we looked out straightaway, and almost immediately a disc-shaped craft came into sight slightly below us, just off our right-hand side. It was going very, very quickly, brightly lit in the sunshine. And we all saw it. It was a beautiful sunlit day with fair-weather cumulus clouds below us—so I had excellent depth reference looking at this disc as it came toward us. Within seconds it was only 200 or 300 feet directly below us. I was looking down at a disc-shaped craft, like a hubcap shining in the sunlight with a raised center. I thought it was about thirty feet across, not very big, metallic and circular, flying on rules other than ours. My guess is that it was moving at 1,000 mph or more.

"It was on a reciprocal track, which means that it was going the opposite direction and missed us by a very small margin. It was close enough to have actually been tailing a sonic shock wave. Now, I've experienced a shock wave from a supersonic aircraft, and it is quite distinctive. It's not hazardous at all, but it's distinctive and unmistakable. But this craft going very fast, very close to us, gave no shock wave at all. That is quite unusual to say the least."

As with the first sighting, Sheppard chose not to discuss his experience with anyone outside his family or the other members of the crew. "Pilots will talk to each other in verbal confidence, but very, very rarely will they commit anything to paper. In a highly competitive, commercial environment, the last thing the airlines want is a pilot allied with a fringe subject. The airlines, with an eye to the bottom line, want absolutely no compromise for their commercial position. I understood this, and quite honestly, if I were running an airline, I would require my pilots to be circumspect about anything they saw which was not usual."

Graham Sheppard is a rare exception, a pilot willing to give his real name and his airline affiliations. In fact, he is the only pilot interviewed by *Sightings* who appeared on camera without any electronic alteration to his face or his voice. Much more typical are commercial pilots like "Ted," who agreed to discuss his UFO encounter only if *Sightings* promised to use a pseudonym and conceal his physical identity. Ted flew for United Airlines for more than thirty-five years, most of that time as a captain. In 1978, he encountered a startling UFO that appeared to gain physical control over his aircraft. It was a puzzling and frightening experience that Ted is certain he will never forget. But although Ted is now retired and no longer flies professionally, he is still not willing to reveal his identity to the public. "Many, many pilots have sightings," Ted reveals, "but have kept quiet about it because of the attitude of their fellow pilots and the general public that they're just a little bit off-center. I kept quiet but I'm still getting some static from the few people I told, who think that I was a little bit nuts at the time."

Ted describes his one and only encounter with a UFO: "I've been flying airplanes for sixty years, thirty-five of them with United. I've spent quite a bit of time up in the air and in all those 30,000 hours, this was the only sighting I had. In 1978, I was flying a DC-10 from San Francisco to JFK [John F. Kennedy Airport in Jamaica, New York]. It was night, and about halfway between Buffalo and Albany, New York, at 37,000 feet, the airplane starting turning to the left." The aircraft was on autopilot at the time and should have stayed on course even in rough turbulence. On the night of the sighting, there was no turbulence and no explanation for the DC-10's sudden turn.

"When the airplane turned," Ted continues, "of course I looked out the window immediately to see what was going on, and there was this very, very bright light just off the wing tip. The whole crew saw this. It was there for probably three to four minutes. It was disrupting the compasses on the aircraft, causing the airplane to turn left. Air traffic control immediately said, 'Uh,

1. String of bluish-white lights that appeared over Tremonton, Utah, on
July 2, 1952.

2. Sensational headline generated by the 1952 sightings of UFOs over Washington, D.C.

3. Kenneth Arnold with a rendering of his June 24, 1947, sighting—the first officially documented report of a "flying saucer."

4. One of the only two prototypes of the Navy's XF5U-1, known as the "Flying Pancake."

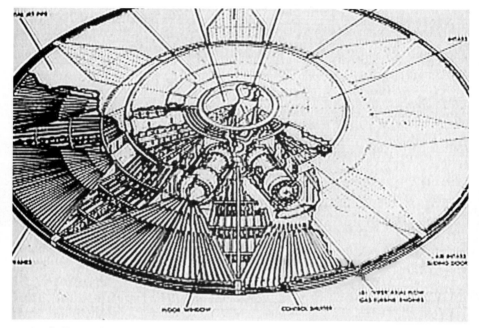

5. Recently declassified blueprint of a U.S. flying saucer project, code-named Silverbug.

6. The public unveiling of Dr. Richard Miethe's Avrocar. The craft was an unmitigated flop rumored to be a cover-up for more sophisticated designs.

7. Jack Pickett with his sketch of a flying saucer he saw while stationed at MacDill Air Force Base in 1967.

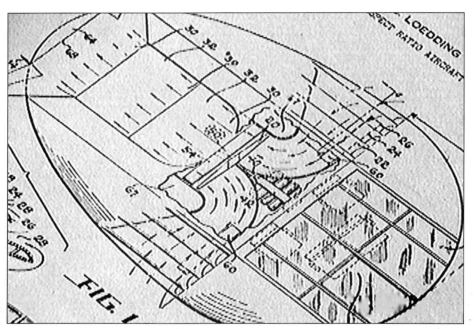

8. After leaving Wright-Patterson Air Force Base, civilian engineer Alfred Ledding was granted a government patent for this flying saucer design.

RIL 1

3,11,56

LEICHTE BEWAFFNETE FLUGSCHEIBE (JÄGER) TYPE „VRIL"
(Schumann-Gruppe)

Durchmesser: 11,50 Meter
Antrieb: Schumann-Levitator (gepanzert)
Steuerung: Mag-Feld-Impulser Jo
Geschwindigkeit: 2900 Kilometer p.Stunde
Reichweite (in Flugdauer): 5 1/2 Stunden
Hausehü aus vied erprobt))
Bewaffnung: 1 Bon KSK, fernsteuerbar, unten, + 2 x MK 108 u.
Außenpanzerung: Doppel-Viktalen

9. Instructions for building the *Vril 1* flying saucer were supposedly received by members of the Vril Society through a series of seances with "gods."

10. U.S. Air Force Area 51 in Nevada—the site of many top-secret military flight projects. *(courtesy Jim Goodall and John Lear)*

11. USAF Lt. Robert Jacobs at the time of the BU telescope project.

12. BU telescope installed at Anderson Peak in Big Sur, California.

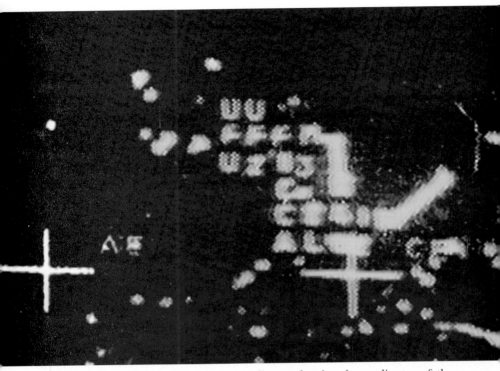

13. Recently declassified radar reading and painted coordinates of the UFO encounter at Edwards Air Force Base.

From
(1) Involvement: Witness

TO:
(2) Name: MURRAY, Alexander S. , JR.

(3) Grade: E-5

(4) SSN: 370-58-0744

(5) Race/Nationality/Ethnic Gp: Cau

(6) Position: Military Poice Desk Sergeant

(7) Security Clearance:

(8) Unit/Station of Assignment: 2nd PLT, 298th MP Compny,

Hunter Army Airfield, Ga.

(9) Duty Status: On duty

8. Publicity: Widespread publicity, including national
news agencies has occurred

9. Summary of Incident: At approximately 0220 hrs, 8 Sep 73,
an unidentified flying object was sighted by two military policeman,
SP4 BURNS and SP4 SHADE at Hunter Army Airfield while in the course
of a routihe patrol of the installation perimeter. When in the vicinity
of Cobra Hall they noticed an "object" traveling at what appeared to them
to be a high rate of speed traveling east to west at approximately
2000 feet altitude and crossing the post perimeter. Approximately ten
(10) minutes later they resighted the "object" when it appeared at
"treetop" level and made an apparent dive at their vehicle seemingly
just missing the vehicle. There was no damage to the vehicle.

1. TYPED NAME, TITLE, OFFICE SYMBOL AND PHONE
2.
3.
4. SIGNAT...

14. Copy of an official Army SIR (Serious Incident Report) concerning the
UFO encounter at Hunter Army Airfield.

15. Newspaper photo of eighteen-year-old Norman Muscarello with officer David Hunt, taken after both witnessed a UFO over Exeter, New Hampshire.

16. Ancient inscription (c. 2000 B.C.E.) from Jordan depicting three "alien" heads.

17. The image burned in the sand in Shikmona, Israel, has been described by observers as an astronaut in front of a cockpit dashboard.

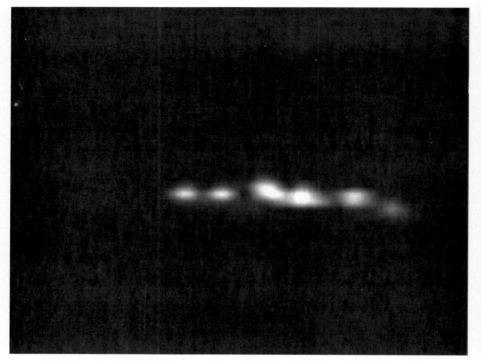

18. Menachem Kalfon's home video of a UFO, sighted over Haifa, Israel, in February 1988.

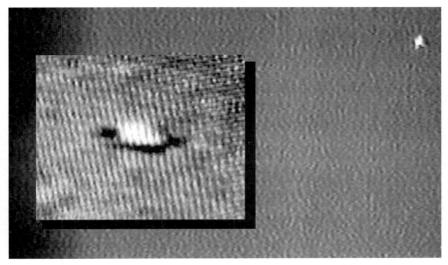

19. Eli Cohen's home video of a UFO over his Kadima, Israel, home. Inset: footage enlarged to show the UFO's saucer shape.

20. Grass circle in the backyard of Ziporet Carmel's Kadima, Israel, home. Insets: a hand stained with unidentified residue *(left)* and pieces of unnaturally pure silicon *(right)*, both found at the site.

21. UFO sighted over Tel Aviv, Israel, on April 25, 1996. *(Yossi Aloni, courtesy Maariv Daily)*

22. Close-up of the UFO seen over a Nellis Air Force Base test range during daylight hours in September 1994.

23. Chuck DeCaro (a former member of U.S. Special Forces) and "Steve" (a government subcontractor) view Nellis UFO footage.

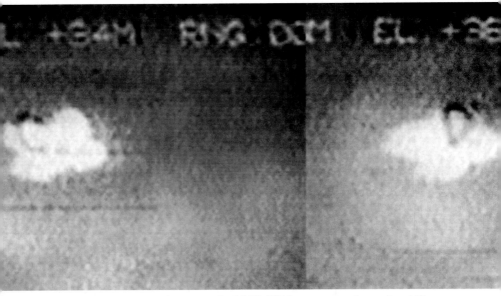

24. In split-screen close-ups, the Nellis UFO appears to have the ability to change shape.

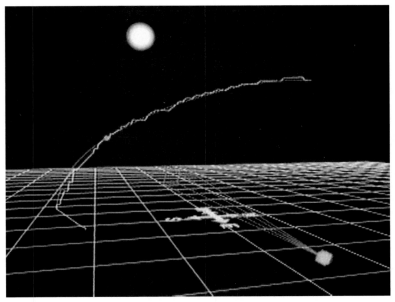

25. Graphic of the Nellis UFO's flight path. *(courtesy Chip Pedersen)*

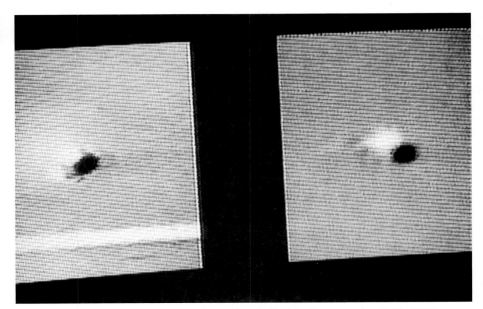

26. Side-by-side comparison shows the similarities between the Nellis UFO *(left)* and the Mexico City UFO *(right)*.

27, 28, 29. Three individual children's drawings illustrate what they witnessed during a UFO encounter outside their Zimbabwe school.

30. Frederick Valentich in his Australian Air Training Corps uniform, before his October 21, 1978, disappearance.

31. Top-secret Pine Gap surveillance facility in the Australian desert.

32. Roy Manifold captured more than just a sunset in this picture taken minutes before Frederick Valentich's disappearance.

33. "Judy" next to one of the mysterious grass rings that began appearing in her yard after her first abduction experience.

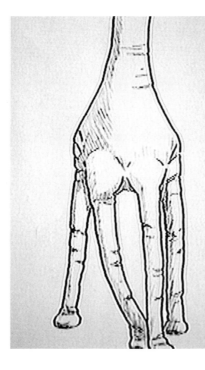

TECH'S HAND,
MOUSE BROWN SKIN,
NO PORES OR BLOOD
VESSELS.

HAND RESTED ON MY
SHOULDER FOR SEVERAL
MINUTES, FELT COOL
AND DRY - NO PULSE.

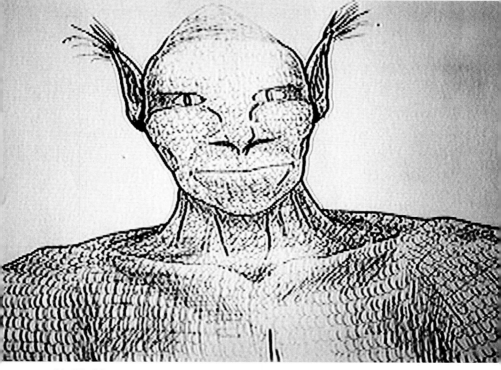

34, 35, 36. OPPOSITE PAGE AND ABOVE: Clare Holcomb's renderings of an alien hand and two alien faces, drawn after an early abduction experience.

37. Shannon and Zachary Hernandez *(left)* and Debbie Magill *(center)* are family members who claim to have experienced intergenerational abduction.

38. The archetypal image of the Men In Black. *(courtesy Stephen Crisp)*

39. George and Shirley Coyne's home video of an unmarked "MIB" helicopter, which they believe followed them for more than four years.

40. UFO over Scranton, Pennsylvania, that may have triggered a MIB sighting.

41. Martian meteorite found in Antarctica. Inset: the rock's carbon-containing compounds resembling fossil bacteria.

42. Percival Lowell and one of his 1894 Mars Canal sketches.

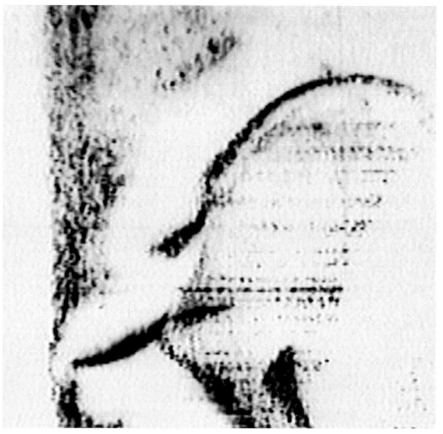

43. "Face" image captured by Dr. David Todd during his 1924 recording of radio waves coming from Mars.

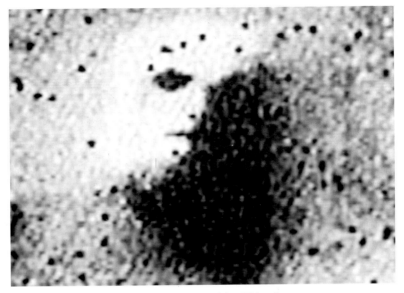

44. The "face" on Mars as photographed by *Viking I.*

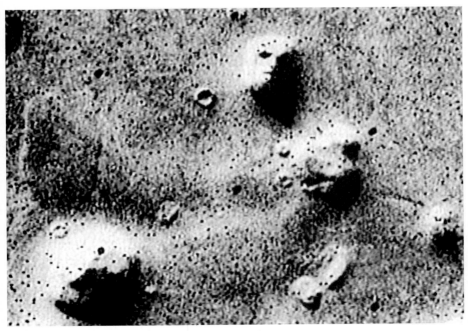

45. The so-called Mars complex of Cydonia.

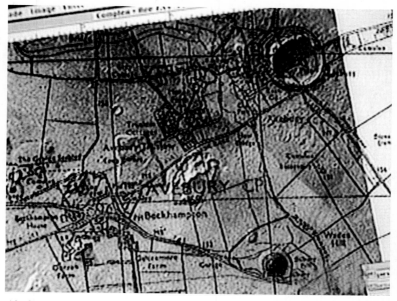

46. Survey of Avebury area, superimposed with its corresponding Mars terrain, indicating a near-perfect match.

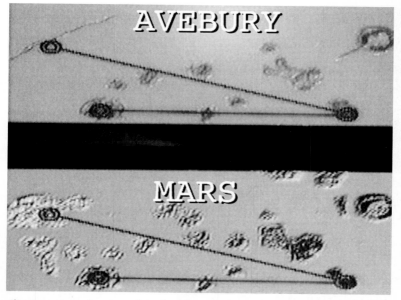

47. Computer drawing of Avebury's and Mars's corresponding geological structures with their matching 19.5 degree angle. *(courtesy Brad Grossman and Debra Matlock)*

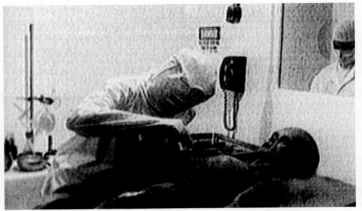

48, 49, 50. The "Roswell Autopsy" photos as originally broadcast on *Sightings*.

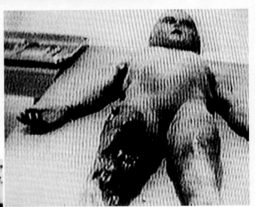

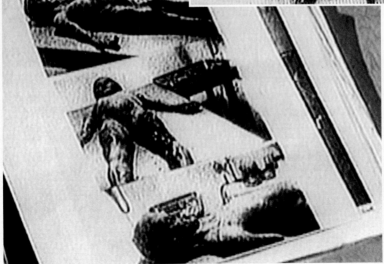

United, where do you think you're going?' and I said, 'Well, we'll let you know when we figure it out.' We turned the autopilot off and proceeded back on course toward Albany. When this thing decided to leave, it left in a hurry, flying faster than anything we have in the air."

As in the Graham Sheppard case, Ted discussed the sighting with the other crew members and they mutually agreed to let the incident go unreported. "Over Boston, we decided not to report this, because we'd end up answering questions all night long," Ted explains. "So we just let it go at that. The other crew members never have come forward. I've talked to them on the phone several times, and they've decided they don't want any part of it. I didn't say anything for a long time, but when I did report it to my boss, the reaction was rather unusual. He said, 'Well, strange things happen to people who have sightings, and I'm sorry it's happened to you.' I asked, 'What strange things happen?' and he said, 'Well, I don't really know,' and that was that."

Richard Haines is a research scientist and aviation expert who has studied pilot sightings of UFOs for more than thirty years. He has found that Ted's experience—the loss of control over his aircraft—is quite common among the pilots he has interviewed. "It's a finding that's consistent across airlines, countries, times of day, weather, and so forth," Dr. Haines explains. "The phenomenon shows focused attention on the airplane, not the other way around. The airplane is usually piloted in a constant direction to get a job done, carrying passengers or cargo. It is the UFO that approaches the airplane, perhaps flying around it or maintaining station off one wing—and then it goes away. This is reported over and over again. What it suggests to me is an interest factor, that the airplane is the focus of interest for the phenomenon. If it were simply a natural occurrence like lightning or a plasma phenomenon of some sort, I don't think that focus of attention would occur."

Dr. Haines's interest in pilot sightings of UFOs began as a hobby in the early 1960s. "I got involved when I was working as a research scientist at NASA. It was not part of my official work, but I had an opportunity to meet many pilots in that job, and I would ask them to describe their encounters. So far, I've investigated well over 3,000 high-quality pilot cases. It is perhaps the largest collection of pilot cases in the world." Dr. Haines has been able to gather such an extensive collection of reports because he has always guaranteed the anonymity of the witnesses. He has come to understand just how entrenched the culture of silence is among pilots. "Among airlines there are many procedures that are never written down, among them that in regard to UFOs, do not say anything. You can talk about it among your crew, take notes on it, put it in your flight log, but don't talk about it outside. And it's my understanding that even when no such rules are enforced, many pilots don't report sightings because of the paperwork. It's just too much bureaucracy and too time-consuming."

The lack of open communication between researchers and pilots and the public is particularly frustrating to UFO researchers like Dr. Haines, because pilots hold the key to many potential breakthroughs in our understanding of UFOs. "Pilots are particularly good reporters because of their education, their experience, their motivation, and their unique vantage point. Being in the air, they could maneuver their airplane around an object, reconstruct its flight path, gather details from the cockpit. Also, modern aircraft have a broad array of electromagnetic energy sensors on board. There are magnetic compasses, gyrocompasses, radios, radar, direction finders, transponders and each of these responds to a slightly different spectrum of energy, power level, and frequency. How each of these factors is affected by the UFO tells us a little bit more about the phenomenon, and what we're trying to do is systematically look at the unique thumbprint each UFO leaves behind."

Graham Sheppard believes that until the culture of silence changes, significant breakthroughs are highly unlikely. "Unfortunately, it's a fact of life that any alliance with a UFO sighting by any member of a particular airline will downgrade the potential of that airline to earn maximum profits, so for anybody who wants the subject debunked or kept quiet, it's very convenient," Sheppard says, explaining that he is coming forward so other pilots will be encouraged to do the same. "Come the day when pilots feel that UFOs are no longer on the fringe, then it's my view that large numbers of pilots will make a considerable difference in the whole subject."

Ted also describes his desire for more openness among members of the aviation community. "There are forces being used that we don't understand." Ted says. "When I saw that UFO, it had the capability to perform far beyond anything we could ever dream about doing. I'd like to know someday just exactly what it was. I'm interested because I have an open mind, and I'd hate to believe that we're the ultimate entities in the whole universe."

"We're getting down to the hard stuff now," Dr. Haines cautions. "The phenomena are real, there's no doubt about that. I've gone from a skeptical position to one hundred percent sure. I've talked to too many people who've convinced me of that. The question is, What is it? Pilot experiences suggest an advanced technology, but that's all I can say at this point."

Graham Sheppard sums up the feelings of many pilots: "It seems quite clear that we're sharing the planet's airspace with possibly another species. I've been brought up in a logical environment; my whole profession works on a foundation of logic. And as far as I'm concerned, one only has to go outside at night and count. Given the numbers involved, there may very well be an intelligent species out there who is well ahead of us." Finally, Sheppard holds out hope for the future. "I hope that what I have to say provides a small platform for other pilots to start from. What I think will happen, given the inevitable progress of the human species into space, is the realization of communication with some kind of extraterrestrial life."

1995

Encounter at 39,000 Feet
Cockpit Transmissions Tell an Eerie Tale

> It's right out of *The X-Files*. I mean, it's a definite UFO or
> something like that.
>   —Controller, Albuquerque Air Route Traffic Control Center

The message left on the *Sightings* hotline was short and straight-forward. "I work as an air traffic controller. A pilot from America West has seen an object 300 to 400 feet long." It was a tantalizing bit of information, implying that a UFO encounter had just occurred. But the caller left no details. Who was he? Where did the sighting occur? Was the "object" a UFO, a weather balloon, or an experimental aircraft? And, of course, the question *Sightings* must ask: Was it a hoax?

The call came in on June 9, 1995, but without any details, it was impossible to follow up on the intriguing phone message. Then, on June 20, 1995, *Sightings* received another hotline message from a different air traffic controller. He, too, mentioned a UFO sighting by an America West crew and gave several details about the airplane's location and the controller's role in the sighting. He did leave his name and phone number, and *Sightings* contacted him immediately.

The controller worked at the Albuquerque Air Route Traffic Control Center (ATC) and was able to describe the incident in detail. He said that an America West pilot had spotted an unidentified flying object over Tucumcari, New Mexico (200 miles east of Albuquerque), on May 26, 1995, and radioed the control center to try to identify the craft. The controller was not tracking the object on radar and had no information about military activity in the area. The pilot described the UFO as cylindrical, cigar-shaped, 300 to 400 feet in length, with a multicolored strobe moving counterclockwise around the craft.

Sightings was eager to investigate the UFO encounter further, but our researchers immediately ran into a snag common among pilot sightings. None of the witnesses would agree to talk on camera, even when we offered them anonymity and the electronic alteration of their faces and voices. Neither the controllers who contacted the *Sightings* hotline nor the pilot and crew of the flight wanted to go public, and they even turned down our requests for phone interviews on the record. It seemed that this was one important story that could not be told. The culture of silence had beaten *Sightings* to the punch.

In the weeks following the initial UFO reports to the hotline, *Sightings* was able to obtain a detailed account of the America West UFO encounter recorded in the pilot's and controller's own words. Through a Freedom of Information Act request to the Federal Aviation Administration, *Sightings* was able to obtain the actual radio transmissions between America West Flight 564 and Albuquerque ATC. Their words are a chilling reminder that UFO sightings can and do occur at any time, to anyone. The following transcripts offer a rare opportunity to sit in the cockpit of a Boeing 757 and experience an actual UFO sighting.

I

In the first transmission, America West Flight 564 (using the call sign Cactus 564), traveling westbound over eastern New Mexico, radios Albuquerque Air Route Traffic Control Center with the initial sighting. The tone is calm and professional. It is 10:00 P.M.

AMERICA WEST: Albuquerque Center. Cactus 564.

ALBUQUERQUE: Cactus 564, go ahead.

AMERICA WEST: Yeah, off to our, uh, three o'clock. Got some strobes out there. Could you tell us what it is?

ALBUQUERQUE: I'll tell you what. That's some, uh, right now I don't know what it is. There is a restricted area that's used by the military out there in the daytime.

AMERICA WEST: Yes, it's pretty odd.

ALBUQUERQUE: Hold on. Let me see if anybody else knows around here.

II

After a break in the audio, presumably to check with other controllers, Albuquerque radios America West that the only report in the area refers to slight air turbulence (called "chop").

ALBUQUERQUE: Fort Worth Center reporting nothing more an occasional light chop in that area.

AMERICA WEST: 564. Did you tape that object at all from your radar?

ALBUQUERQUE: Cactus 564, no, I don't and talking to the three or four guys around here, no one knows what that is. Never heard about that.

AMERICA WEST: But nobody's painting it [picking it up on radar] at all?

ALBUQUERQUE: Hey, Cactus 564, say again.

AMERICA WEST: There's nothing on their radar on the other centers at all? On that particular area, that object that's up there?

ALBUQUERQUE: It's up in the air?

AMERICA WEST: Affirmative.

ALBUQUERQUE: No. No one knows anything about it. What's the altitude about?

AMERICA WEST: I don't know. Probably right around 30,000 or so, and it's, uh, the strobe, it starts going counterclockwise and the length is unbelievable.

III

There is another break in the audio. It is not known if or why the tape has been edited. The next transmission is between Albuquerque ATC and Cannon Air Force Base, the military installation closest to the 757's position. The "Taiban" referred to here is a small town on Highway 84, forty miles west of Cannon AFB and eighty-five miles north of Roswell, New Mexico.

ALBUQUERQUE: Cannon 21.

CANNON AFB: Cannon. Go ahead.

ALBUQUERQUE: Hey, do you guys know if there was anything like a tethered balloon or anything released that should be above Taiban?

CANNON AFB: No, we haven't heard nothing about it.

ALBUQUERQUE: Okay. [*Nervous laugh*] Guy at 39,000 says he sees something at 30,000 that, uh, the length is unbelievable and it has a strobe on it. This is not good. [*Nervous laugh*]

CANNON AFB: What does that mean?

ALBUQUERQUE: I don't know. It's a UFO or something. It's that Roswell crap again.

CANNON AFB: Where's it at right now?

ALBUQUERQUE: He says it's right in Taiban.

CANNON AFB: He's right . . . it's right in Taiban?

ALBUQUERQUE: Yeah.

CANNON AFB: No, we haven't seen nothing like that.

ALBUQUERQUE: Okay. Keep your eyes open.

IV

It's clear that interest is beginning to grow in the air traffic control center. America West 564 is apparently at 39,000 feet looking down at a slight angle to the unknown object at an estimated altitude of 30,000 feet over Taiban, New Mexico. Cannon AFB knows of no military craft in the area. The controller's reference to "Roswell crap again" is oblique. Is he simply a skeptic, or have there been other bothersome UFO sightings in the area that have gone unconfirmed? On this night, there are thunderstorms

in northern New Mexico. America West 564 is skirting the storm
and reports that the UFO appeared between the 757 and the
cloud bank, backlit by lightning strikes.

> ALBUQUERQUE: Cactus 564, we checked with Cannon. They don't have any weather balloons or anything up tonight. Nobody up front knows any idea about that. Can you still see it?
>
> AMERICA WEST: Negative. Back where we initially spotted it, it was between the weather and us. When the lightning hit, you could see a dark object and, uh, it was pretty eerie-looking. There's aircraft off to the right here going east-bound. Maybe he'll see it.
>
> ALBUQUERQUE: Okay.
>
> AMERICA WEST: First time in fifteen years I've ever seen anything like it.

V

Albuquerque does make contact with the aircraft traveling eastbound, toward the site of America West's UFO encounter. The
second airplane's type or airline affiliation is not discernible from
the tape. America West 564 listens in as the aircraft (call sign
Hawk 85) attempts to confirm the original sighting. Note that Albuquerque is telling Hawk 85 to look in the wrong direction and
that the airplane is approximately 3,000 feet *below* the UFO.

> ALBUQUERQUE: Okay. Go ahead.
>
> HAWK 85: What was that Cactus guy talking about he saw?
>
> ALBUQUERQUE: I don't know. Off your right wing about fifteen, twenty miles he's saying he saw a large object with a strobe that looked like it was at 30,000 feet.
>
> HAWK 85: It's secret stuff?
>
> AMERICA WEST: Cactus 564.
>
> ALBUQUERQUE: Oh, Cactus 564, go ahead.

AMERICA WEST: Yes, sir. That aircraft that passed us earlier on the right side. He'll be in that area in a few minutes. Is that correct?

ALBUQUERQUE: Yeah, he'll be there in about three or four minutes at twenty-seven [thousand feet]. I'll ask him what he sees.

AMERICA WEST: Yes, his left-hand side looking into that thunderstorm. Thanks a lot, we'll just monitor and listen.

ALBUQUERQUE: Okay.

AMERICA WEST: Three of us up here saw it.

ALBUQUERQUE: [*Amused*] Okay. Hawk 85, in the next about two to three minutes, be looking off to your right side. If you see anything about 30,000 feet. One aircraft reported something. It wasn't a weather balloon or anything. It was a long, uh, white-looking thing with a strobe on it. Let me know if you see anything out there.

HAWK 85: Will do.

ALBUQUERQUE: Cactus 564, are you still up?

AMERICA WEST: Affirmative. 564.

ALBUQUERQUE: And that was south of your position?

AMERICA WEST: It was north.

ALBUQUERQUE: Hawk 85, uh, let's make it out the left window now.

HAWK 85: Are you seeing any traffic off my left wing right now?

ALBUQUERQUE: Only thing I have is [Flight] 31 traffic to the north of you.

AMERICA WEST: Albuquerque, if we get a chance. Cactus 564.

ALBUQUERQUE: Yes, sir. Go ahead.

AMERICA WEST: You know, we're all up here huddled up and talking about it. When it lightninged, you could see a dark object. It was like a cigar shape from the outlook that we could see it. And the length is what got us sort of con-

fused because it looked like it was about 300
to 400 feet long. So I don't know if it's a wire
with a strobe on it, but the strobe starts from
left and goes right, counterclockwise. And it
was a pretty eerie-looking sight. But, uh—

VI

At this point, the tape cuts off. Then, after several minutes of un-
intelligible transmissions, Albuquerque is heard relaying the
story to an unidentified controller, who responds, "No, we don't
have any published highballs today," meaning no known high-
altitude military or civil aircraft were in the air on May 26, 1995.
America West Flight 564 is then heard asking for the Albuquerque controller's call sign, and then there is a final exchange.

AMERICA WEST: Albuquerque, 564. It's the last time. Just for
                  our notes so we can take a message. Was that
                  in a restricted area that was just basically
                  south of Tucumcari when we reported it?
ALBUQUERQUE: Okay, uh, the way you went through, the only
                  restricted area is on your south side. Nothing
                  to the north side.
AMERICA WEST: [*Surprised*] Huh.
ALBUQUERQUE: And those areas are inactive. There
                  shouldn't be anything going on.

There are no further transmissions from America West Flight
564. *Sightings* played the FAA tapes for UFO researcher and aviation expert Dr. Richard Haines. He pointed out several key elements in the transcripts that increase the significance of this pilot
sighting. "The pilot records seeing a strobe of some sort," Dr.
Haines explains, "and he uses the term 'counterclockwise.' This
suggests something I've heard from other pilots, that the UFO
has a series of lights like a theater marquee that are strobing from
left to right along the side or the edge of the object. Also, the pilot uses the word 'eerie,' which I think is important. Now, pilots
tend to be conservative. They have to be. They have to make

good judgments under stressful conditions, and so to use a word like that suggests he really could not identify it. And he was courageous enough to make a call to the authorities on the ground and ask for assistance."

Dr. Haines has investigated over 3,000 pilot sightings, for some of which he was able to find earthbound explanations. This is not the case with the America West sighting. "If we check flight charts for this area," Dr. Haines says, "there are a number of military restricted airspaces. However, most of them are not operating after dark, which would eliminate air intercepts or advanced tests of some sort in the region."

Veteran commercial airline captain Graham Sheppard also listened to the tape and gave his assessment to *Sightings:* "I have absolutely no doubt that the tape is real. There are parts of it that are difficult to understand, and some editing has gone on, but the language is heavily laced with jargon particular to air traffic controller and pilot dialog." Sheppard was struck especially by the pilot's description of the UFO illuminated by lightning. "It's quite practical to fly along thunderstorms, because they have very discreet boundaries provided you stay at a distance of about ten miles. At 39,000 feet, they're very pretty. Lightning discharges light up the whole thundercloud like an illuminated globe. It would provide a very good backdrop for anything that was between the airplane and the cloud itself."

Both Haines and Sheppard were struck by the size of the UFO, claiming that there is no aircraft in the current military inventory that is 400 feet long (nearly twice as large as a Boeing 747 jumbo jet). But despite the significance this event has to UFO researchers, the Albuquerque controller at the time of the incident appeared detached, almost cavalier, about the incident. There is laughter seemingly at the pilot's expense, and he gives the eastbound pilot flying into the UFO area misinformation about the object's location and its description. Yet it is this same controller who, after signing off with America West Flight 564, chooses to follow up on the UFO sighting. The final exchanges on the FAA tape begin with the controller's call to NORAD, the North American Air Defense Command.

VII

"Bigfoot" is the call sign for NORAD. After Albuquerque describes the shape and location of the unknown craft, the two controllers begin hypothesizing about what the UFO might be. There is a reference to the possibility that the UFO is an aerostat. Aerostats are tethered surveillance balloons used by the military. According to Graham Sheppard, "Aerostats are about one hundred feet long, shaped like a balloon with fins. They generally carry a platform either internally or externally, which can carry sophisticated radar. To my knowledge, they only go up as much as 15,000 feet and always fly in a restricted area that would be on an aeronautical map and known to air traffic control." One of the most significant parts of the tape is right at the beginning, when Albuquerque states that "a couple of aircraft" have seen the UFO. This is the only time reference is made to eyewitnesses other than America West Flight 564.

ALBUQUERQUE:	Bigfoot. Albuquerque Sector 87.
NORAD:	Bigfoot's on.
ALBUQUERQUE:	Yeah, I've got, uh, something unusual, and I was wanting to know if you all happen to know of anything going on out here around Tucumcari, New Mexico, north of Cannon. I had a couple of aircraft report something 300 to 400 foot long, cylindrical in shape, with a strobe flashing off to the end of it. At 30,000 feet.
NORAD:	Okay. Hang on a second
ALBUQUERQUE:	Yeah, I didn't know if you happened to know of anything going on out there. No balloons in the area? Nothing reported?
NORAD:	Okay. Where is this at again?
ALBUQUERQUE:	It's in Tucumcari, New Mexico. That's about 150 miles to the east of Albuquerque.
NORAD:	Okay. How far from Holloman [Air Force Base]?
ALBUQUERQUE:	Holloman. It looks like it's off to 030 of Holloman for about 220 miles.

NORAD:	Okay. It's kind of hard for us to see here. 030 for about 200. Um, we don't have anything going on up there that I know of.
ALBUQUERQUE:	Yeah, I didn't know if—we tried everybody else and nobody else is—this guy definitely saw it run all the way down the side of the airplane. Said it was a pretty interesting thing out there.
NORAD:	Okay. It was at 30,000 feet. Do you know what the shape—
ALBUQUERQUE:	It's right out of *The X-Files*. I mean, it's a definite UFO or something like that. But, I mean—
NORAD:	Oooh. You all are serious about this? [*Laughs*]
ALBUQUERQUE:	Yeah. He's real serious about it, too, and he looked at it, saw it. No balloons are reported tonight? Nothing in the area?
NORAD:	And it was strobing out the front, he said?
ALBUQUERQUE:	I think the strobe is off the tail end of it. He said it was kind of—well, it was dark, but—
NORAD:	How long did he think it was?
ALBUQUERQUE:	He said it was 300 to 400 foot long.
NORAD:	Holy smokes!
ALBUQUERQUE:	Yeah, and we don't have any air carriers out there that are strobing along?
NORAD:	The only thing that I can—I wonder if any of our aerostats got loose or something? 'Cause we don't have any aerostats out there.
ALBUQUERQUE:	Yeah, not that far to the north.
NORAD:	I mean, to me it would sound like an aerostat, but I don't know. I don't think ours are that big, though.
ALBUQUERQUE:	No, they're more like a blimp rather than this sounded like some sort of flying hot dog or something.
NORAD:	And did he say how big around it was?

ALBUQUERQUE: No, he didn't really have an idea of how big around it was.

NORAD: Kind of like a plane without wings?

ALBUQUERQUE: Yeah, sort of like that. We didn't know if there's a cruise missile somebody maybe fired one out here or something?

NORAD: Hmmm, let's see. White Sands missile range is to the south. Did he say how large it was or anything like that? Could he get an idea of that?

ALBUQUERQUE: Just 300 to 400 foot long, but that's it.

NORAD: Okay. Well, what we could do is kind of like maybe monitor that area. But you know we pick up everything that you all pick up.

ALBUQUERQUE: Yeah, I know. We're not seeing anything out here at all so we was just wondering if you happened to know if anything was going on.

NORAD: And did he know what the speed was?

ALBUQUERQUE: No. He didn't really give us an indication of that. He was opposite direction.

NORAD: Okay. And so this guy was up in an air—he was in a jetliner?

ALBUQUERQUE: Yeah, America West.

NORAD: It's hard for us to determine if it was a plane unless it was like at 30,000 feet and was in our radar coverage, and it disappeared or something.

ALBUQUERQUE: Right. Okay. Thanks, I appreciate it.

NORAD: Okay, then. Bye.

Suddenly, the Albuquerque controller is the one trying to convince NORAD that the UFO sighting is legitimate, and not a prank or a hoax. He almost apologizes for asking if there are any balloons or other experimental craft in the area. It is the controller at NORAD who now assumes the role of the disbelieving outsider. This exchange ends with little hope that anything more can be known about the UFO over Taiban. But then, there is one final transmission on the FAA tape.

VIII

In this startling transmission, it appears that NORAD is confirming the appearance of an unidentified flying object over northeastern New Mexico. The controller describes a vehicle on a "search only track," meaning a vehicle with no positive identification or transponder. By law, all aircraft flying in controlled air space must have a transponder, a device that emits an intermittent electronic signal for tracking and locating purposes.

NORAD: Yes, uh, we had someone call here earlier about a pilot spotting an unidentified flying object.

ALBUQUERQUE: Yep. That's us.

NORAD: Okay. Well, hey, we're tracking a search-only track kind of up where that might have been.

ALBUQUERQUE: Okay. Can you give me a radial?

NORAD: Okay. Off of Holloman, it is 038 for 283. I mean, that's about ten degrees off of what you gave me before and about eighty miles off. It's tracking about 390 knots. We've been tracking it for about three, four minutes now. I mean, to be going that fast, it's got to be up kind of high.

ALBUQUERQUE: Yeah. And we got no code on it?

NORAD: Nope. It's search only. Off of Holloman 037 for 280.

ALBUQUERQUE: Okay. I'll see whether I can look up there and see anything.

NORAD: Okay, then. Bye.

ALBUQUERQUE: Thanks.

This is the end of a historic event. Audiotape confirms that at least one highly trained flight crew witnessed an enormous UFO, an unidentified flying object confirmed on radar by the North American Air Defense Command, our government's supersecret surveillance organization. This is one encounter that cannot be dismissed as a hallucination or a hoax. Something was up there. Unfortunately, unless the eyewitnesses are willing to go public or NORAD is willing to reveal if it knows more about the search-only craft it tracked that night, the investigation must end here.

ABDUCTION

1989–Present

The Legacy of Abduction
Terror, Grass Rings, and Healing Power

> I woke up in the middle of the night and there was some-
> thing along the side of the bed. I reached out and touched
> the shoulder of a being that was probably the size of a five-
> year-old. I started to scream and as soon as I did, I was par-
> alyzed. This thing had total control of me.
>
> —"Judy"

She has asked to be known only as Judy to spare her family the
public ridicule that would be caused by the disclosure of her private nightmare. She agreed to a *Sightings* interview reluctantly,
but in the hope that her story might in some measure ease the
pain and terror of people like her, the thousands of people who
Judy believes are silent victims of the alien abduction phenomenon. Imagine spending each and every day waiting and wondering when the next episode will begin. Will I be taken tonight?
What will they do to me this time?

Judy's story came to light because of a small article in her local
southern Michigan newspaper. Reporter Holly Cogan had written a short feature piece on UFO sightings in the area and had
briefly mentioned Dr. Ron Westrum, a professor studying the

alien abduction phenomenon. Judy read the story and called the newspaper. Cogan remembers that Judy's voice was soft and shaking. Judy began to describe the terrifying encounters she was having with creatures she felt were not of this world. She wanted to get in touch with Professor Westrum. "When I spoke with Judy, she came across as very frightened, but also as a very honest person," Cogan recalls. "I had no reason to think that she was doing anything but saying what she believed. Whether I believed her or not is really not very important. I have no way of knowing, but in my judgment she seemed absolutely sincere."

Ron Westrum, Ph.D., is a professor of sociology at Eastern Michigan University who has researched the abduction phenomenon and its impact on both the abductees and society in general for nearly a decade. He first met Judy in 1992. "When I first went to her house and talked to Judy at some length, I was just trying to figure out where she was coming from. Was she off the wall? What's really going on here?" Dr. Westrum explains. "But it rapidly became clear that she was very straightforward about the experience and was genuinely puzzled. Things were going on that affected her whole family, and she did not know how to deal with it. In the beginning, my attitude was very clinical, trying to determine what was happening, what was the diagnosis, but after a while I began to act more as an adviser, helping Judy and her family cope with the constant intrusions in their lives."

Judy's memories of abduction began in 1989. Unlike many abductees, Judy has not retrieved her memories through hypnosis. "I would say 85 to 90 percent of my experiences I've been wide awake, just as awake as I am right now talking to you," Judy told a *Sightings* investigative team. She claims her conscious memories are as vivid to her now as the moment they first occurred. "My first encounters started in July of 1989," Judy says. "At first I thought they were just very intense dreams. I would wake up and remember standing outside in my pajamas looking at a cigar-shaped object hovering over the backyard. I would remember a very odd-looking person standing next to me saying, 'You will be riding in this soon.' It was almost as though he was saying, 'Ready or not, here we come,' but I didn't know at that time what was go-

ing on. I didn't know anything about alien abduction. I just
shrugged it off as a dream. But about a week later, everything
changed, when I literally woke up on a table with no clothes on,
unable to move, wide awake, and looking straight ahead at a being that was grayish in color with large black almond eyes. I was
getting a physical exam from this being. The next day at the
breakfast table I told my husband, 'This isn't a dream. This is
real.' He looked at me and said, 'I think you're losing it.' We had
no idea what was going on."

The strange encounters continued, and Judy was living with a
fear she could not share. "We had a very tough time in the beginning," Judy remembers. "We had problems with the children. My
husband and I had problems. We came close to a divorce over
this . . . until my husband woke up on a table being examined by
three grays. This is something we didn't ask for. We didn't want it
to happen. It's totally changed our lives. I have been told by the
beings that this is a privilege. I can't understand that. I don't see
it as such. It's been a struggle."

Judy does not know how many times she has been abducted,
only that the encounters are frequent and often painful. She believes that she is being used for some kind of medical testing or
genetic engineering. In each encounter, she is examined, prod-
ded, and probed. The abductions follow a pattern that has become part of Judy's established routine.

"I remember the dogs barking, and trying to get up and see
what is wrong and then finding the aliens near the couch," Judy
says of a typical encounter. "I am floated up and out through the
window on a bluish-white beam of light. I can see my house below
me, and I feel frightened, like I am going to fall. There isn't any
support under me. I have been told, 'Don't be afraid. You won't
fall.' I have felt an energy around me, the kind of energy that
makes your hair stand up. Once, I saw the ship above me, and I
expected to hit my head on a steel door in the bottom of the ship,
but I didn't. I felt an energy go through me, and it felt like I was
not whole. Then I passed right through the steel door and I was
on an examining table. I've seen different aliens. I've seen gray-
colored beings with black almond eyes. The grays are the medical

technicians. I've seen taller, tan beings with flaky skin and larger, rounder eyes. They are the ones who most often transport me. The being that does the physicals is a pasty-white, willowy-type being. I am unable to move when they are present, and we communicate telepathically."

David Jacobs is a professor of history at Temple University and a world-renowned expert on the alien abduction phenomenon. He has studied Judy's case and finds that her experiences are extraordinary, but also typical. "Even though people are describing unique and incredible experiences, the abduction phenomenon is very systematic and very routine. Judy's experiences fall directly in line with the experiences of most abductees." Dr. Jacobs has been particularly interested in Judy's description of genetic experiments. "There is a strong reproductive component to the abduction phenomenon," Dr. Jacobs explains. "Women report embryos being implanted in them and fetuses being extracted from them. Men report sperm being taken. And this is a constant, not something that we can get around or brush aside. This is something that all abductees report, all of them. This is the reason for the abduction phenomenon."

Judy believes that some of the reproductive experiments performed on her have had long-lasting physical effects. "I have experienced missing menstrual cycles, lactation, and morning sickness followed by an abduction experience in which a fetus was taken," Judy claims. This is particularly disturbing to Judy, who had a tubal ligation more than twenty years ago and should be incapable of pregnancy. "They are doing genetic experiments. I have seen hybrid babies on board the craft. I have seen them in boxes that were filled with light, and I was told they are creating these beings for two reasons. They want human emotions, and they want to reproduce as we do but they can't. I have been told these children are mine. They are very fragile, very tiny. Some have no hair and some have hair almost like a peach fuzz. They have eyes that are a cross between our eyes and the aliens' eyes. They have a little nose and a little tiny mouth. They don't cry."

One of Judy's most traumatic abduction experiences occurred when she says she was given one of the so-called hybrids to hold.

"A gray took one of the infants and put it in my arms." Judy says. "I felt anger and the sadness of having children somewhere and not knowing what is being done with them or what is going to happen to them. When I was brought back, I had what felt like labor contractions. I contacted my physician and got to his office immediately. My cervix was dilated, and he said, 'This doesn't happen unless it is a miscarriage or induced by instruments.' I had my tubes tied in 1976, and there's no way that I could have had a normal pregnancy."

Ron Westrum was able to follow up on Judy's incredible claim. "I spoke with her general practitioner, and all the things she told me are things that he confirmed," Dr. Westrum says. "In fact, he was very puzzled by these appearances and symptoms and really didn't know what to make of it. I tend to take that very seriously. And the emotional reaction Judy has had is very powerful. I remember one case when she talked about being presented with this baby and she wept. It was very disturbing to her. Here was a baby that seemed helpless and alone, and it really shook her up." This was the abduction experience that Judy's husband believes he was also a part of. "Apparently, the same evening, Judy's husband had the same kind of experience. He had seen the baby, too, and it bothered him a great deal," Westrum explains.

Judy recalls, "My husband woke up on a table, and he was completely naked. He was being given a physical exam by three gray beings: one on each side of him and one at the foot of the table. He states that he was awake, he woke up there. After that, there was absolutely no doubt in his mind or in mine that he had experienced something real." Judy's husband declined *Sightings'* request for an interview, but Judy's sister Mary (also a pseudonym) did agree to speak on camera, only if she were videotaped in silhouette and no personal details were given about her or her family.

Mary has not had abduction experiences to the degree that her sister Judy has, but several strange dreams have plagued her since Judy's abductions began in 1989. Mary recalls, "I have had memories of being on a table and having different lights shining down on my body: a triangle-shaped light over my head and my throat and a rectangle-shaped light over my stomach area. I have dreamed that I have had something attached to my head. Then I'll wake up and have a headache, and the last time, I found an indentation the size of a dime on the side of my head where I had felt something being attached. One morning I woke up, and my hair had been cut to within an inch of my scalp in certain spots all over my head. I checked my pillow and there was no hair on the pillow. Nobody had been in my bedroom the night before."

Judy's and Mary's experiences are not verifiable. However, there have been physical changes in Judy's home environment and in Judy herself that can be measured and may be linked to the family's abduction experiences. Beginning with Judy's first abduction in 1989, strange rings of grass have appeared periodically around her suburban home. (See Photo 33.) *Sightings* asked Dr. William C. Levengood, a prominent research biophysicist known for his crop circle studies, to examine the grass rings and perform an analysis.

Dr. Levengood describes the rings he has been evaluating since 1993: "These are bright lush rings, always much darker than the surrounding grass, that vary anywhere from two feet to as much as twenty feet in diameter. The width of the rings varies from eight to twelve inches and consists of extremely green grass indicating a much higher chlorophyll content than in the surrounding grass. In December of 1993, even though the grass in Judy's yard had turned brown, the rings were lush green. And in February, after heavy winter snows, the same rings were still lush green. The rings are completely out of phase with the growing season. They have a very high concentration of fungi, which suggested at first that they might be so-called fairy rings, naturally occurring rings of mushrooms. But through an extensive study I have found that this is not the case. The rings are not the result of the fungi; fungi are growing as a result of the rings.

"The program of study I have conducted involved taking samples of the lush green grass, unaffected grass at the epicenter of the ring, and normal grass at least thirty feet away. I took those samples into the laboratory and tore them apart to look at the cellular constituents. And from this I was able to tell that there was a much higher degree of respiration in the very lush grass as compared to the respiration in the normal grass. To put it in more common vernacular, the grass in the rings is simply producing more energy than the normal plant. There is some kind of energy stimulating the growth of the grass in the rings. At this point, I don't think we can say why there is more energy, but there is a definite indication that there's electromagnetic energy involved in the formation of the rings."

In addition to the grass rings, Judy and her family have experienced other strange electromagnetic effects inside their house. Judy recalls that after her first abduction experience, "Balls of light would float through the house. Balls of light that were about the size of a volleyball left a tail and sparks that were red and white. Television sets that had been unplugged for months would begin to glow. Appliances still go on by themselves, even when they're not plugged in." One of Judy's neighbors told a *Sightings* researcher that she has seen a strange haze appear over Judy's house. "I work at nights," the neighbor explained, "and sometimes when I come home I see a mist or a foggy-type appearance around Judy's property. You see it around her property, but not around anybody else's. It's almost like there's a glowing cover around everything."

Dr. Levengood has also been a witness to energy anomalies produced in Judy's home environment. "There has been quite a lot of unusual electrical activity in Judy's area since I have been investigating this case. Things happen you just can't explain," Dr. Levengood says. "Appliances turn on by themselves just unaccountably: dishwashers, smoke alarms, radios. I have direct evidence and was involved with a radio that turned on—and this was in a period of a brownout when the electricity in the whole area was on a low level, at one-third power. The radio's switch was in the off position, but it was playing. When you'd move the switch to the on position, it kept on playing but it was on a different station. I have no explanation as to what energy can do that."

Where does this anomalous energy come from? Could it be emanating from an extraterrestrial source or is it a terrestrial phenomenon that is somehow attracting alien visitors? Judy believes the anomalous power may be coming from inside her. "On November 11, 1989," Judy remembers, "there was a gray by my left side, and he was putting what appeared to be laser-type objects in my brain. He put one in each temple, one in my forehead, one in the base of my skull. I asked him what he was doing, and he said, 'This will prevent seizures when the energy comes through.' I didn't understand what he was talking about. I was told that I would have an energy and that I would be able to help people who are ill. Since then, I've worked on somewhere between 500 and 800 people."

According to David Jacobs, "Some abductees feel that after the return from an abduction event they have increased powers, either psychic powers or healing powers. This is extremely unusual and very controversial. Judy has felt that she has the ability to have a therapeutic touch, so to speak, and this might certainly be true. It's something that we can't dismiss out of hand, and it might be related to the abduction phenomenon. But this has got to be very scientifically and objectively investigated." Ron Westrum concurs. "It's difficult to evaluate Judy's therapeutic touch. I've read a lot of the testimony by people she has treated, and it's obvious that there's something there. There's something that the proximity of her hands does to people's bodies, but I don't know what that something is."

Sightings was able to talk with one woman who felt that she had been successfully healed by Judy's extraterrestrial energy. She, too, requested anonymity, more to protect Judy than herself. "Rose" was suffering from serious complications caused by shingles, a debilitating disease related to chicken pox that can last a lifetime. "I got very sick one night," Rose explains, "and the pain was so intense I passed out. I had a fever, nausea, and blisters from the center of my back through my abdomen and down my right hip."

Rose had never been to an alternative healer and was not told what type of treatment she would receive from Judy. "When I went to see her, Judy seemed to be just a normal, warm, and caring person. I was feeling very sick. The pain was intense. Judy placed her hands on me, and after about three minutes, I noticed I was beginning to feel very warm, and the areas where her hands were I felt intense heat. Then my whole body began to tingle and relax. I asked Judy, 'Am I supposed to be feeling as warm as this?' and she said, 'Yes.' Then she moved her hands down the area of the shingles, and it felt like a million pins and needles were going in me at a very rapid rate. It was very, very painful and hot.

"Within twelve hours," Rose continues, "the nausea went away. After a second treatment, the blisters diminished noticeably, and the pain would come and go. With the third treatment, there was not so much pain. And now after five months, the shingles are gone, and the pain has disappeared. I believe that Judy's energy was staying in me. I was not necessarily feeling hot all the time, but I was feeling better because this energy was healing me." Dr. Levengood has tried to find a correlation between the energy Rose is describing and the electromagnetic anomalies that surround Judy's home. "My investigation of the possible energy emanations from Judy's hands is in the very exploratory stages. I can't get into great detail, but I can say that there is an indication that during her healing sessions, she emits a high degree of electrostatic potential. Every living organism has this type of energy, but hers seems to be at a very high level."

Judy has come to believe that the terror and pain she experiences during an abduction are the price she must pay for her healing powers. "I see the peace that comes to people that are getting the treatments. I see physical ailments that are being healed, and I have decided that this is something that I should do."

Judy's abduction story presents information that is fantastic and unfathomable. Were it not for the legacy of her abduction experience—the anomalous energy, the grass rings, and her healing power—Judy's story might never have been told. The physical evidence surrounding her alleged abductions is worthy of further investigation. The things that are happening in her modest home in southern Michigan cannot be dismissed as hallucination or psychosis. Too many people have witnessed the ring, felt the energy, and shared her abduction memories. But will other serious scientists join Dr. Levengood's study?

David Jacobs is doubtful. "The scientific barrier is a very serious impediment to us. Most scientists feel that the abduction phenomenon is unworthy of any kind of study, unworthy of even being looked at. And yet we have tens of thousands, if not hundreds of thousands, of people who have seen UFOs and are claiming they have been abducted. We have a worldwide phenomenon here that the academic community thinks is unworthy of attention. It is the only subject of this kind that has ever come about that the majority of the scientific community refuses to look at."

Shared Memory Abduction

New Friends Discover a Chilling Childhood Connection

> I am a lab rat. They have a program that I'm a part of, and they have told me that I'm their property. They say they can do anything they want with me, and when I'm under their control, they do.
>
> —Diana Graves, abductee

It's an experience common to just about everyone. You meet a stranger and sense something familiar. You know each other from somewhere but just can't figure out where. Clare Holcomb and Diana Graves had that feeling of mysterious connectedness the first time they met each other. They racked their brains for more than four years, trying to puzzle out how they knew each other, and when they finally found the link in the chain that bound their lives together, it was at once terrifying and strangely comforting.

In late 1987, Clare Holcomb was looking for a change. She wanted a new job, a new hometown, a whole new lifestyle. She thought she might have found what she was looking for in a small help-wanted ad in a northern Virginia newspaper. "I had decided that I was not happy doing what I was doing. It hadn't been fulfill-

ing for me, and I felt there had to be more out there somewhere," Clare recalls. "Diana had placed an ad looking for someone to work and live on her horse ranch, and something about it
struck a chord with me. I responded to the ad and as soon as I
drove onto the property, I knew I would be there forever. This was
home." That feeling of belonging grew even deeper as soon as
Clare came face-to-face with Diana. "We had an instant recognition for one another—as if we had known each other for a lifetime," says Clare.

Diana remembers feeling that same inexplicable connection.
"I felt like, 'Hey, I know this person.' She was very comfortable
around horses, and I had a kind of instant recognition. I hired
her on the spot," Diana recalls. And Clare adds, "We felt that we
must have met somewhere before. We spent some time trying to
figure it out, asking each other where we might have met but not
finding anyplace where we would have lived at the same place at
the same time." It wasn't until late in 1991 that the pieces of the
puzzle started to fit together, when Clare had a bizarre encounter
on a country road and began to delve into the dark thoughts of
her childhood memory.

"I was on my way home early in the evening," Clare remembers. "It was a warm night for December. I saw lights in the sky
that I thought were low-flying aircraft, but I wasn't hearing any
engine noise. I was concerned that perhaps the engines of a
plane had shut down. I pulled over to the side of the road and was
blinded by these lights. I was frozen to the spot, and I didn't know
what was happening. I couldn't see because the light was so
bright. Then I blinked. That's all I did. I blinked. And when I
opened my eyes again in what seemed to me to be less than a split
second, I was back in my car, some four miles away driving at
breakneck speed. I had lost about an hour in the blink of an eye.
I was sick to my stomach, disoriented, scared. I had no idea what
might have happened. When I got home the first thing I noticed
was that my contact lenses were missing from my eyes—and I certainly had them in when I was driving."

Diana remembers that Clare was in a panic. "Clare came home
that night," Diana recounts, "and she was very, very distraught. I

think both of us thought she was going crazy. Maybe she had too much stress, or maybe she had a blackout. We couldn't explain the missing time. We didn't know what it was." Diana encouraged Clare to put the unsettling events behind her, suggesting that it was an isolated incident and nothing a little more rest couldn't cure. But less than two weeks later, Clare had another bizarre encounter.

"Again I was driving home during the early evening," Clare explains. "And again I saw lights coming toward me. Instinctively, from somewhere very deep inside, I recognized that something was happening that I should know about. The inside of my car lit up so bright I couldn't see outside. It was a blinding white light. I had no memory of what happened next. Again, there was an hour or more missing that I could not account for. When I gained my memory back, as with the first event, I was just tearing down the road. It was as if the car was driving itself, and I didn't seem to be able to get my control back until several seconds into this. When I arrived home my earrings were in backwards. I couldn't have gotten them in that way if I tried. My earlobes were raw and bleeding."

Clare and Diana began to search for an answer to what was no longer one isolated event. "The first thing I did was to try to find out if I had experienced something unique or if other people might have reported the same thing," Clare says. "I did not seem to be under stress or have any other kinds of emotional problems that might cause a blackout. I was very levelheaded." Diana echoes Clare's assessment of her mental state at that time. "After the second incident," Diana says, "I got the feeling that there was something more going on than Clare going crazy or having a nervous breakdown. She was reporting to me that she had seen lights. She told me that she had seen some strange things, including memories of a weird hand that she drew for me. [See Photos 34–36.] I knew we needed help. I knew I could no longer handle it."

Because Clare had reported seeing strange lights and figures, Diana contacted the Fund for UFO Research, an organization that investigates extraterrestrial events in an attempt to separate fact from fiction. "I just looked up UFO in the phone book," Diana recalls with a laugh. "That's how much I knew about the subject at the time." Initially, she was looking for other eyewitnesses to the lights that Clare had seen during her two encounters. "When we contacted the Fund for UFO Research," Clare says, "it was a way of eliminating explanations. We were sure that the organization would tell us that this had never happened to anyone else, and then we could move on and look into other possibilities."

But Richard Swiatek, the Fund for UFO Research investigator who took Diana's call, didn't tell her that this had never happened to anyone. He felt that Clare was exhibiting some of the classic signs of an alien abduction experience and arranged a meeting with Diana and Clare. "I was quite familiar with abduction cases. We had a pilot study going on at the time in the Washington, D.C., metropolitan area, and I had already had extensive contact with many abductees," Swiatek explains. I had done a lot of reading and a lot of research, and many of the things that Clare said— while not completely unique—were disturbing things that I had only read about before. I had no reason to think that she was making things up or that her story was fabricated in any way."

"It frightened us when we had our first consultation with Richard," Clare recalls. "We found out that similar things had been reported by others, and it was startling to discover that anybody could possibly have experienced these things and we'd never heard about it." Swiatek was careful not to give the women any specific details about what other abductees had reported. He did not want to influence the women or give them information that a debunker could later claim he had planted.

"As time passed, we began to look into and sort of accept the possibility of alien abduction as a way of explaining what had happened to me," Clare explains. Diana then took over the researcher role. She was fascinated by the phenomenon but a little frightened by it. She wanted to help me, and she was giving everything she had to support me. But in the process of trying to figure out what had happened to me, we began to discuss memories from our childhood. There were strange things that bothered us, and in the process of having those discussions, we realized that we had a lot of nearly identical childhood memories." Diana adds, "First, I realized that I had a lot of memories from my childhood that I couldn't explain. As I grew up, I had just put them in the back of my mind, but I still had this whole storehouse of things that didn't quite make sense."

"Diana was beginning to believe that she may be involved in the abduction phenomenon herself, and she didn't want to be involved any more than I did," Clare continues. "I think it frightened her when she began to doubt that she was just an impartial observer. Normal people don't have these experiences. Crazy people have these experiences, not us."

In a strange twist of fate, it was a chance meeting with a skeptical psychologist that ultimately led Clare and Diana to conclude that they were both abductees. "The clincher for me," Diana explains, "came when I met a hypnotherapist at the wedding of a mutual friend of ours. I told her what had been going on and what Clare and I thought it might be, and this therapist was completely aghast. She was certain it was not abduction, and in fact, she was very skeptical about the whole phenomenon. She had dealt with multiple personalities and childhood abuse and told me that this was what we were most likely dealing with." Diana made an appointment with the therapist and agreed to undergo hypnosis.

"I did the session with her," Diana recalls, "and sure enough, the first memory I had I was screaming because I saw alien eyes right in front of my face and I couldn't get away from them. That convinced me that I really had been abducted, because this therapist didn't even believe in the phenomenon and there was no way she could be planting this information in my head, and yet I was having the same memories that other people were having under hypnosis."

Through continued therapy, Diana began to piece together horrifying memories of experimentation, torture, and forced reproduction. "Through hypnosis I was able to drop back to a time when I was out in the back fields of the farm, and I had been pulling weeds. I remembered being approached by four grays, and I was taken to where a spaceship was waiting, a small one only twenty or thirty feet in diameter. I was taken aboard that spaceship and artificially inseminated. They used a very long tube to take an egg from me, which I assume they then fertilized, because then they used another tube to place it back in my body. It was a very disturbing experience for me," Diana remembers with difficulty. "During a later regression," she continues, "I remember I was on a table, and I was in great pain. I had a lot of cramping in my stomach. It was very, very intense. Then all of a sudden the pain was gone, and I was shown this thing about the size of a pear that had come from my body. It was a fetus. After they showed it to me, they took it away."

Clinical hypnotherapist Marilyn Carlson is convinced that Diana is recalling real events, which have been deeply buried in her subconscious. "After my first session with Diana, I knew that she had experienced something significant," explains Carlson. She took over Diana's case from the original psychologist, who felt she was not treating Diana effectively. "I knew by the way she went through the regression—her body animation, her emotions, and the fear that was coming through. She had truly experienced something during her missing time, and we explored what it was that had happened." Carlson also hypnotized Clare. She was careful to keep the two women separated during their sessions and asked them not to reveal details of their regressions to each other. In one of her early sessions, Clare tried to fill in an episode of missing time that had left her with demonstrable physical effects: gaping sores on the bottom of her feet.

"I was abducted from my bedroom," Clare recalled under hypnosis. "I had on a nightgown and no shoes. Naturally, I didn't sleep in my shoes. And when I was brought back, the aliens made a mistake. Instead of putting me back in the house, they left me outside. We'd had severe ice storms, and it was bitter cold. I couldn't get in the house. The doors were locked. The garage door was frozen shut, and I couldn't get it open. I was standing on frozen gravel with about an inch of ice on it, and my feet adhered to the ice. I thought I was going to die because they wouldn't find me until morning. When I started thinking about death, the aliens came back, picked me up and put me back in the house. The next morning, all the skin on the bottom of my feet had been burned off from sticking to the ice."

Regression was and continues to be very traumatic for both

women. "It's painful for Diana," Carlson says. "She cries. She tells them, 'No, you're hurting me.' There are times when she is made to drink something or they inject something, and in the hypnotic state she begins to gag and feel nauseated. Clare is extremely stressed. She has feelings of not being able to escape it. She's highly agitated, extremely nervous. When I visit her in her home there are times when she says, 'I don't want to be in this room. I have to go outside.' She wants to be able to say, 'No more,' but she can't."

In an effort to cope with the relentless fear and anxiety, Diana and Clare sought out world-renowned abduction researcher Budd Hopkins. "They were extremely impressive, obviously filled with a lot of emotion about their experiences, a lot of anger, a lot of fear," Hopkins says. "And in terms of credibility, these are two of the most believable people I've ever worked with. They are extremely intelligent, open to exploring difficult experiences—and they're very brave. They are extremely credible, and they have gained nothing by going public."

It was during a hypnosis session after their initial meeting with Hopkins that Diana and Clare made a dramatic discovery. They believe not only that they have both been abducted, but also that they have been repeatedly abducted together, stretching back in time to before they met in 1987. It was Clare who had the first memory of a shared abduction. "We were both in a large room. Scenes were being projected against the walls, very disturbing scenes of devastation: tornadoes, hurricanes, floods, blizzards, every kind of natural disaster. It was very upsetting. We were told to watch it and to learn from it and to understand that these things were going to happen and we must be prepared. We were holding each other's hand. We didn't want to look, but we were forced to look."

Was Clare simply projecting her experience onto Diana? Were the women being unduly influenced by each other or by their hypnotherapist? "Clare recalled being in the same room with Diana," Carlson explains, "and the positions that she said Diana was in coincided with the positions that Diana later said she was in. We separated them during their regression work so there would be no outside influence, and still there were many similarities in their experiences—which leads me to believe that, yes, they are definitely recalling a shared abduction experience."

According to Budd Hopkins, Diana and Clare are definitely not the first and surely won't be the last people to recall a shared abduction experience. Hopkins says, "The issue of shared abductions is something we should sort out here. Many, many, many people are abducted with other abductees. That's typical. It's a kind of myth that this only happens to one person at a time. The very first abduction case that the world heard about was the Betty and Barney Hill case, which was the joint abduction of two people. But the thing that makes Clare and Diana's situation different and extremely interesting is the fact that they were apparently abducted separately and brought together from childhood on."

Diana and Clare believe there is one particular incident from their collective past that proves that they have been abducted together since childhood. "When I was about twelve years old, I went on a picnic with some friends from school," Clare recalls. "I'd moved off by myself to sit on a bench for some reason. I saw a little girl about nine years old coming toward me who I didn't recognize. She had long blond hair and was wearing a blue uniform. She walked over and said hello. She had some kind of an accent that I thought might be British. Without stopping to think or discuss why we were doing this, we both meandered away from the picnic area into the woods. We reached a clearing and from there we were abducted. Once we were on board the ship, I knew who she was and that I had seen her many times before."

"The girl Clare was describing," Diana says, "sounded like me when I was about that age." Clare picks up the story: "Diana described to me how she was going to school in England at that time and she described to me how she used to dress."

"When Clare described to me what this little English girl was wearing," Diana continues, "I went up to my storage closet and pulled out a school uniform jacket from when I was nine years old that exactly matched her description. I was that other child."

"I didn't want to believe that she was the other little girl," Clare says. "I wanted her to tell me she didn't know what I was talking about, that she had never been in England or worn that kind of uniform. It scared me, and I didn't want to believe it. But then Diana gathered together some pictures of herself as a child at about that age and I gathered pictures from my family, pictures I hadn't seen in years, and we both recognized those children as ourselves and having seen each other on board some kind of craft with these aliens." Budd Hopkins has found this and other shared childhood memories compelling evidence of the alien reality. "We have found a pattern," Budd Hopkins explains, "that Clare and Diana have been abducted since childhood separately, then brought together and made to interact as if the aliens were interested in studying human relationships and human friendships."

Trying to answer charges that these so-called shared memories are more than fantasy, or at worst collusion, has been difficult for Clare and Diana. Clare says, "As we began to look into these memories of childhood experience through the use of regression and hypnosis, we started testing each other. I remember one instance where we both recalled playing games on board the spaceship when we were children. Separately, we each wrote down identical descriptions of how the games were played, even though we had never discussed them before. One of the games we remembered being forced to play we both called 'the game with the burning stick.' We were placed equidistant from one of the grays. He would toss a stick to us and when we tried to catch it, when we touched it at all, it burned. We didn't know what we were supposed to do, but after several painful burns and then refusing to catch it, we realized that the being never had to touch it. He could move it by simply looking at it. So the next time he threw it, we both concentrated on the stick, and it turned in midair and went right back to the gray."

Uncovering what Diana and Clare believe are shared memories of recurring abduction has done little to ease their anxiety. While they do take comfort in knowing they're not alone, terror is still the most vivid legacy of their abduction experiences. "I can't pick up the phone and call 911 and say, 'Come here quick, I'm being abducted,'" Clare says. "I can't take a pill or go have a treatment and make it go away. I wish escape were possible. It's not that we haven't tried. We have attempted to get away. We've thought about just never being in the same place at the same time, but we've been abducted together even when we've been separated by several states and hundreds of miles. I don't know how to get away from them. If I knew how to get away I would have done it already."

Diana takes an even more sinister tone: "I am a lab rat. They have a program that I'm a part of, and they have told me that I'm their property. They say they can do anything they want with me, and when I'm under their control, they do. I'm convinced that they planned my meeting with Clare. They brought us together all through our lives, and I can't help but believe that Clare's coming to this farm was not a coincidence. They arranged it. I don't understand their plan, but I'm glad Clare and I met."

Clare and Diana continue to share abduction memories to this day, and Budd Hopkins continues to search for more solid evidence of the shared abduction phenomenon. As Hopkins puts it, "One of the most tantalizing questions that this story raises is, Are the aliens manipulating circumstances to bring people together in the real world? I've looked at six cases where I've been able to look into both individuals, six pairs of people who finally met in the real world and remembered each other from prior joint abduction experiences starting in childhood. Is the pattern very widespread? Are aliens arranging things so that certain people meet each other and form relationships? We don't know, but it's a very tantalizing question."

Intergenerational Abduction

Three Generations Share
Extraterrestrial Contact

The advantage of the whole family being experiencers is
that we can talk about it openly. You don't have to start at
square one explaining the whole concept. And you don't
have to prove to anyone what everybody in the family already knows.

—Debbie Magill

It's happening to a lot of families out there. They just don't
know it yet.

—Shannon Hernandez

Debbie Magill and Shannon Hernandez are mother and daughter. They both claim that they have had repeated contact with extraterrestrial visitors since childhood. And they are not alone in
this belief. "My mom, my dad, my sister, her daughter, my oldest
son, and possibly my youngest son—we're not sure yet, he's only
one—and even my husband have all had experience with the extraterrestrials, the ETs we call them," says Shannon Hernandez.
(See Photo 37.) Her family is part of a growing paranormal phenomenon known as Intergenerational Abduction, also called In-

tergenerational Encounters by those who see the phenomenon in a more positive light.

"Intergenerational Encounters is defined as a series of contacts between extraterrestrials and more than one family member. The most common form is between parent and child, and sometimes we see three or even four sequential generations who have all experienced extraterrestrial contact," explains Richard Boylan, Ph.D., a clinical psychologist whose work with abductees, or "experiencers," has been controversial, even within the UFO community. "ETs have indicated [to his clients] that they follow certain people over time, both to become acquainted with them in a very thorough way and also because there seems to be some kind of education and physical program going on to prepare the experiencers for future events. As a result of this long-term exposure, life goes on, people have kids, and the ETs begin to bring the children into the experience, getting them used to the idea of extraterrestrial contact.

"The experience of the Magill-Hernandez family is a classic case of a three-generation extraterrestrial encounter," Dr. Boylan continues. "Debbie, the mother, originally had some contacts earlier in her life, and they have continued and become more numerous at present. Her daughter Shannon has had contact starting at about age three and becoming progressively more frequent. And now Shannon's son Zachary, at five years old, is having many extraterrestrial contacts as well."

Unlike a majority of self-proclaimed alien abductees, the Magill and Hernandez families believe their extraterrestrial contact has been positive and enriching. For that reason, they abhor the term "abductee" and prefer to be known as "experiencers." "'Abductee' has a negative connotation to it. It means stolen," Debbie Magill explains. "I consider myself an experiencer, because I go willingly. It's like being called on a telephone. I can answer the phone or not. It's my choice. There's a big difference when you go by force. When you go because you're okay with it and it's your choice, then you don't feel powerless."

Debbie Magill believes her first extraterrestrial encounter probably occurred around the age of eleven. Although she has no memory of her first encounter, she believes she bears a physical scar from that experience. "I have little marks on my left thumb, little scooped out spots that appear after ET contact. The first one appeared when I was in the fifth grade. I didn't think much about it at the time, thought I did it maybe eyeing potatoes—only thing was, I'm left-handed. Years later, after I started recalling other contacts, it dawned on me that this scoop mark came from an ET experience."

Debbie's first conscious memory of an extraterrestrial encounter occurred in 1972, when she was a young mother with two small children. "We were living in Walnut Creek, California, at the time. It was about five-thirty, quarter to six—rush-hour traffic time—and I was coming home from beauty school with the kids; Shannon was about two and a half, Brynna was just a baby. It was summer. It was very well lit outside. When I pulled into our carport, I saw this huge ship with no windows and no markings just sitting in the yard not making a sound. The hair on the back of my neck stood up, and I grabbed the kids and ran into the house," Debbie remembers. What Debbie doesn't remember is what happened next, but recent hypnotherapy sessions have led her to conclude that she and her children were all abducted at that time and taken aboard an extraterrestrial spacecraft.

After her UFO encounter in 1972, Debbie Magill began to have a growing sense that she was being contacted by extraterrestrial forces. She explains, "I don't remember how I would get from my room into the ship. It was more on a telepathic level, a feeling that 'tonight's the night that they're coming for me.' I also had the sense that the whole family was going, but I have no specific memory of one person on this bed, and another person on that bed, like some people do. I do recall seeing the same ETs over and over again, like they are the teachers and I am in school. One I remember in particular is part gray and part reptilian. He is very tall, close to seven feet; very dark and very kind. I feel no fear or animosity toward him. I feel very, very connected to him, like he is a part of myself. I feel he is there to teach me things. His name is Thigma."

Unlike many alien abductees, Debbie does not feel any trepidation during her extraterrestrial contact. "The only time I experienced any fear was in 1972," Debbie explains. "It was fear of the unknown, and I think that's why a lot of people are afraid—because of the unknown and because they don't remember ever agreeing to go. I don't feel that way. I feel that they have something to teach us, a message they want to get out. They're not negative, they're positive. They're more intellectual than we are. They've developed the mental part of their personality and done away with the emotional aspects. They're surprised when people are afraid of them. They don't understand our emotional reactions to things."

Debbie did not share her experiences with her family for more than twenty years. Dr. Boylan has found in the 150 cases he has researched that reticence like Debbie's is common. "It's usually the child who comes to terms with their own contact first and then talks to a parent. This is when the child finds out their parent has been secretly harboring a contact experience in his or her own life," Dr. Boylan explains. And, in fact, it was Debbie's daughter Shannon who was the first to discuss openly with the family her own alien contact experience.

"I knew Shannon and Brynna were being contacted," Debbie says, "but they didn't seem to have any awareness. It's just you can't know something until you're ready to know it. One day, I kind of mentioned ET contact to Shannon—feeling her out—but she was afraid, so I just dropped it. And that's been my perspective, too, that a lot of people are being contacted, and it's just a matter of not being open to accepting it until you're ready." Shannon, too, remembers that first conversation with her mother. "My mother asked me if I was having any unusual experiences, and I said, 'Not me, no way,'" Shannon recalls. "I guess I just had to grow into a certain state of mind where I could accept what was happening to me. When my mom saw that I wasn't ready to hear about it, she just backed off and waited."

Several years later, in 1995, when Shannon was twenty-five and a mother herself, she told Debbie about a strange dream. "I was being pulled by what everybody calls 'grays,'" Shannon told her mother. "I had grays on my lower arms and my upper arms, and they were pulling me up into a UFO. There were ETs all around me, and I woke up terrified. I didn't know what was going on. The images were familiar to Debbie, whose own contact experiences had been almost identical to Shannon's "dream." Then, right after the first dream, Shannon had an eerie experience while she was awake that mirrored many of her mother's own experiences. "I was sleeping over at my uncle's house," Shannon explains. "I'd just gotten up in the night to give the baby a bottle and had fallen back asleep. The next thing I know, I'm awake and I'm hearing really strange noises outside and footsteps in the hallway—very light footsteps. I hear a weird hum. It's pitch dark and I feel somebody staring at me. Then it just stopped, the hum, the footsteps, everything. That was strange."

When Shannon told her mother about her bizarre experience, Debbie felt the time was right to broach the subject of extraterrestrial contact once again. She gave Shannon Dr. Boylan's book, *Close Extraterrestrial Encounters.* "I took the book on vacation with me," Shannon says, "and when I got back, I talked to my mom, and since then we've all been in a kind of ET whirlpool. They're out there. This is happening to us. And the family is very open to it. We're all very open and understanding with one another, and I think that's a lot different from a lot of other families. We don't keep secrets. Everything's out in the open and real honest." Debbie agrees with her daughter: "The advantage of the whole family being experiencers is that we can talk about it openly. You don't have to start at square one explaining the whole concept. And you don't have to prove to anyone what everybody in the family already knows."

Debbie and Shannon were the first family members to try to recover memories of past extraterrestrial contact. They contacted Dr. Boylan and began to work with him in a series of hypnotherapy sessions. The controversial use of hypnosis to recover deeply buried memories is not exclusive to the UFO community. A number of prominent researchers question the use of hypnosis as a valid method for recovering memories of, in particular, Satanic ritual abuse and alien abduction. It has been suggested that books, television, movies, and the therapists themselves are subconsciously fueling the experiencer's imagination, creating false memories. However, many clinicians who specialize in the abduction phenomenon strongly oppose the charge that they are inducing false memories. "Hypnosis is a special state of mind where the unconscious and conscious minds are both available to the person at the same time," according to Dr. Boylan. "A memory of an experience that has been partially pushed into the unconscious mind can be accessed through hypnosis." The clients themselves, including Debbie Magill and Shannon Hernandez, insist that hypnosis is the only way to remember their entire encounter. "It's really hard to remember," Shannon explains, "because they can really block it out of you. The ETs don't want us to know too much too quick. They are easing us into this." For Shannon, Debbie, and many others, extraterrestrial contact remembered through hypnosis is not hallucination or imagination; it is objective reality.

"For a couple of weeks, as I started to remember more about what had happened to me, I was real scared. It was a real adjustment," Shannon says of the first few weeks of hypnotherapy. "My main fear was the eyes. I was really scared of the big, black eyes. But the more I was hypnotized, the more I lost the fear and realized that when you look into the ET's eyes there's just so much love. It's like an old friend, just a wonderful feeling." Among the first memories that she recovered involved the incident at her uncle's house in which she had heard a weird hum and light footsteps. "Through hypnosis I remember being up in a spaceship. I remember looking at the earth. We were really zooming past stuff, seeing planets, different star systems, and I remember a comet burning past us. I was being told to hurry up by what I now know is my main ET. His name is Timmon. I know now that he is the one who has been with me since I was young. He was the one who brought me back to my uncle's house. He kind of waved as he left and then just went off. I realized those were the footsteps I was hearing. It was him going down the hall."

Like her mother, Shannon is not aware of how she is transported between her home and the extraterrestrial spacecraft. She does have the same telepathic sense that Debbie has about an impending experience and also occasionally feels her bed shake just before and just after an alien encounter. "I also sometimes get a ringing in my ears," Shannon explains. "They shake my bed, and then I'm gone. One time they went all out. The bed started shaking, a light came in through the window, and I saw one of them in my room. He was telling me, 'We're here. It's time to go.' At that time I wasn't as open to it as I am now, and I said, 'No! Wait until I'm asleep!' It all stopped, and I instantly fell asleep, fell hard from full consciousness to out like a light. I woke up a few hours later with a pounding heart and the bed still shaking."

That was Shannon's conscious memory of the event. After several hypnosis sessions, she felt that she had filled in the details, the missing time, of her encounter. Shannon believes it is typical of hundreds of encounters she has been having since early childhood. "When I first realized that they were coming, it was scary. But I have grown to realize that they're not out there just doing all this physical stuff to us. They're teaching us things. They're trying to help us. The dentist-type chair that so many people describe being in as they are being examined and worked on—they say they are petrified. Well, I've been in that chair willingly and I remember the experience as being just fine. They have done different procedures on me, and I have given my consent. I don't do anything I don't want to do, and they are not sitting there forcing me. They have put something in the base of my head to enhance my listening skills with them, to enhance our telepathy so we can communicate. I don't consider that negative. If it makes me better, then I'm up for it."

Although Shannon and Debbie shared their experiences with the rest of the family, they were careful not to discuss their extraterrestrial contact with Shannon's five-year-old son, Zachary, for fear of alarming him. They needn't have worried. "One day Zachary told me how the aliens had landed in the backyard. He showed me where they had parked," Shannon explains. "He said, 'They take me up into the spaceship, and we play and have fun.' I just stood there with my mouth wide open and thought, 'Whoa! This can't be happening.' But it was. So we had an open discussion about it, and he's been fine with it. Since then, there've been several nights when I know he's gone. I hear him walking around and then going. Some people ask me, 'Aren't you afraid to let your son do this?' But I don't have a problem with it. I have explained it to him so he can see the good in this—and the love—and he has fun. He likes it."

Dr. Boylan has found that children do in fact have the most positive encounters. "From my research, kids seem very much more comfortable, natural, and positive from the get-go with ET encounters than adults do. Children are already in the imaginary world. For them it's not that unusual that a strange-looking person pops up and communicates with them. They're used to new things happening in their lives all the time. They don't know what the boundaries of reality are, so when they're asked to go up a beam of light into a spaceship, they're ready to go with it."

At five, Zachary is a bright, precocious child who repeatedly told a *Sightings* investigative team that he likes having fun with the ETs, although he admitted being very frightened at first. "They came into my room. They freaked me out. I yelled and they ran away. Then I said, 'Come back, come back,'" Zachary says of his first encounter. "Now they visit me, and we all have a party. We go into space. They let me take books out of a special library up on outer space. We play for a little bit with toys, and there are games called Finko and Wanwan Sing-a-long where you sing what they sing, and then you do what they do."

Dr. Boylan; Zachary's mother, Shannon; and Zachary's grandmother, Debbie, do not believe that this is just a child with an overactive imagination. They believe he is experiencing extraterrestrial contact, and Debbie and Shannon have seen physical effects from this contact. "Zachary has had bruises on him," Debbie says. "Like finger-mark bruises on his arms and on his leg, and I think that's from the ETs trying to lead him through. They don't hurt intentionally. They're just a little stronger than they realize." Debbie feels that overall Zachary's ET experiences do much more good than harm. "One night he had a nightmare," Debbie remembers, "and he was talking about this toy coming to get him—and it was in the closet, and it was going to come out of the closet and get him. Well, we calmed him down and he went back to sleep. And in the morning he told Shannon that the ETs came and told him they wouldn't let anything come out of the closet and get him, and they were there to protect him. So Zachary felt better, and I'm not worried at all. He's much safer with them than he would be playing out on the street here."

While Dr. Boylan agrees that Zachary's experiences are positive, he does note an underlying trend among children who are part of the Intergenerational Encounters phenomenon. "Based on my observations of Zachary," says Dr. Boylan, "he certainly seems to be above average in poise and verbal skills for his age group, and there seems to be a statistical trend with kids who've had ET contact that they seem to be at a performance level a bit above average. You wouldn't expect that to hold true as much as it does if it was just a fluke. We know that the ETs manipulate metabolism and possibly even the genes of the experiencers, and it may be that some of these children are the product of some genetic engineering."

In 1995, when *Sightings* first interviewed the Magill-Hernandez family, an investigative team was invited to attend a hypnotherapy session with Debbie, Shannon, and Dr. Boylan. Both Debbie and Shannon were interested in uncovering memories of a recent encounter they had each had separately and which had left them with a strange feeling of urgency. Under hypnosis, the mother and daughter revealed strikingly similar details. Each session began with a long process of gradual relaxation into a hypnotic state. Then Dr. Boylan began to ask simple questions, which he claimed would not suggest or influence the women's answers. Here is an excerpt from Shannon's hypnosis session. She is recalling the appearance of a kind of television inside the spacecraft in which she believes she is traveling:

DR. BOYLAN: Do you notice anything around you?
SHANNON: Pictures.
DR. BOYLAN: Where are the pictures?
SHANNON: In front on a screen.
DR. BOYLAN: What are the pictures of?
SHANNON: Not sure.

DR. BOYLAN: Is there one picture that you can describe?

SHANNON: Too many pictures.

DR. BOYLAN: Do the pictures stay on the screen for a while?

SHANNON: No.

DR. BOYLAN: Do they come fast?

SHANNON: Yes.

DR. BOYLAN: Do you know why you're seeing these pictures?

SHANNON: To learn.

DR. BOYLAN: Who wants you to learn?

SHANNON: ETs.

DR. BOYLAN: Is there anybody else around where you're watching these pictures?

SHANNON: To the right.

DR. BOYLAN: Is that somebody human?

SHANNON: No.

DR. BOYLAN: Is that somebody an ET?

SHANNON: Yes.

DR. BOYLAN: Do you know the ET's name?

SHANNON: No.

DR. BOYLAN: Is it male or female?

SHANNON: Male.

DR. BOYLAN: Shannon, I would like you to move ahead to a point where the next thing happens and notice what's going on.

SHANNON: Not sure.

DR. BOYLAN: Are the pictures still showing?

SHANNON: Yes.

DR. BOYLAN: Are these pictures familiar?

SHANNON: Some.

DR. BOYLAN: Do they include pictures of people?

SHANNON: No.

DR. BOYLAN: Do they include pictures of Earth?

SHANNON: Lots.

DR. BOYLAN: Are they pictures of things going on now?

SHANNON: No.

DR. BOYLAN: Is it about the past time of the earth?

SHANNON: No.

DR. BOYLAN: Is it about the future of the earth?

SHANNON: Yes.

DR. BOYLAN: Do the pictures show a good future for the earth?

SHANNON: Not sure.

After nearly an hour under hypnosis, Shannon was gradually brought back into full consciousness. Once she was fully awake, Shannon began to reveal a much more detailed account of what she had experienced. Dr. Boylan, and many other hypnotherapists specializing in ET contact cases, have found that typically it is the information gathered just after the hypnosis session that is the most valuable for their research. Here is part of Shannon's posthypnosis interview with Dr. Boylan:

DR. BOYLAN: Where were you?

SHANNON: I was most definitely in a spacecraft.

DR. BOYLAN: What was it that told you that it was a spacecraft?

SHANNON: The fact that we were in space. Planets were whizzing by us. The planets were like little peas that just kind of flicked past.

DR. BOYLAN: . . . And you said there's an ET next to your right?

SHANNON: The one next to me was the praying mantis type with real long skinny arms and a really tall, skinny body. He had his hand on my shoulder.

DR. BOYLAN: What's the hand like?

SHANNON: I think there were three fingers. I didn't look to see but I could feel them on my shoulder.

DR. BOYLAN: What was the touch like?

SHANNON: It was very soft and warm, very loving. He was kind of calming me.

DR. BOYLAN: What about the eyes?

SHANNON: Kind of like watermelon seed–type eyes in the dark. Every now and then he would point to the pictures. Some of them were symbols that I didn't quite understand.

DR. BOYLAN: Were they strange symbols, or have you seen them in magazines and things?

SHANNON: No, it wasn't like a pound sign or anything that
                I'm familiar with. I don't even think the symbols I
                was seeing were from Earth. They were different
                and strange.

DR. BOYLAN: . . . You said you spent most of your time sitting
                and looking at a rapid, changing series of pic-
                tures. Can you tell me what the pictures are
                about?

SHANNON: We're going to go through some major geological
                changes. I saw mountain ranges like on the Pacific
                coast falling off into the ocean and the ocean
                coming up, and part of the mountain range falls
                into the ocean, literally splitting in half. Not like
                an earthquake, bigger than anything we could
                ever imagine. I saw islands being swallowed up by
                the ocean. But I got the message from the ETs
                that even though the earth is getting readjusted,
                still things will be okay because it's all for the best.

In a separate hypnosis session, Shannon's mother, Debbie, also
recalled being shown a flashing video screen. She, too, saw pictures of frightening geological changes. While still under hypnosis, in a state of deep relaxation, Debbie described the earth
changes she was shown by her extraterrestrial "teachers":

DR. BOYLAN: What is one of the places you've been shown that
                you recognize?

DEBBIE: Florida.

DR. BOYLAN: What does the picture there show?

DEBBIE: Changes.

DR. BOYLAN: Changes?

DEBBIE: Changes in the earth.

DR. BOYLAN: Are the changes inland or near the coast?

DEBBIE: Coast.

DR. BOYLAN: What is the change in the coastline?

DEBBIE: Moves.

DR. BOYLAN:	When it moves, is there more coastline exposed or less?
DEBBIE:	Less.
DR. BOYLAN:	In other words, water moving in over land?
DEBBIE:	Ocean water.
DR. BOYLAN:	How far in? A block or a mile?
DEBBIE:	More.
DR. BOYLAN:	Is this now?
DEBBIE:	No.
DR. BOYLAN:	Is it in the past?
DEBBIE:	No.
DR. BOYLAN:	In the future?
DEBBIE:	Yes.
DR. BOYLAN:	Very far in the future?
DEBBIE:	No.
DR. BOYLAN:	In the next year?
DEBBIE:	I don't know.
DR. BOYLAN:	In the next five years?
DEBBIE:	Yes.

Since this session and others that have followed, both Debbie and Shannon have felt an inexplicable need to move from their homes in northern California to Santa Fe, New Mexico. Shannon describes the feeling as very much like what was experienced by Richard Dreyfuss's character in the movie *Close Encounters of the Third Kind*. "The drive that Richard Dreyfuss had in that movie is like me," Shannon feels. "I have this immense drive to go. I need to go to a place I've never been or even seen a picture of. I have an urgency to go to Santa Fe, because there's something we're supposed to do. I don't know what. I suppose we'll find out more when we get there." Debbie has had the same inexplicable desire. "I just got up one day and said, 'I've got to move to New Mexico.' I mean, I just knew. So I thought, well, I better look at a map and see where it is and how big it is. We knew nothing of the area."

Several months after their *Sightings* interview, The Magill-Hernandez family did pack up everything they owned, sold their house, and moved to New Mexico. They believe that they are part of a new wave of experiencers who must prepare other people for the inevitable: massive geological changes and more widespread contact with extraterrestrial visitors. "People need to have a very open mind," Shannon says. "They need to be very open to this, because it's all coming true; different species of souls, you might say, all coming together for a good purpose—and that's to help one another. I think people need to evoke the more positive sides of the ETs, so there will be less fear. The ETs really just want to help us. They feel so desperate because we are resisting."

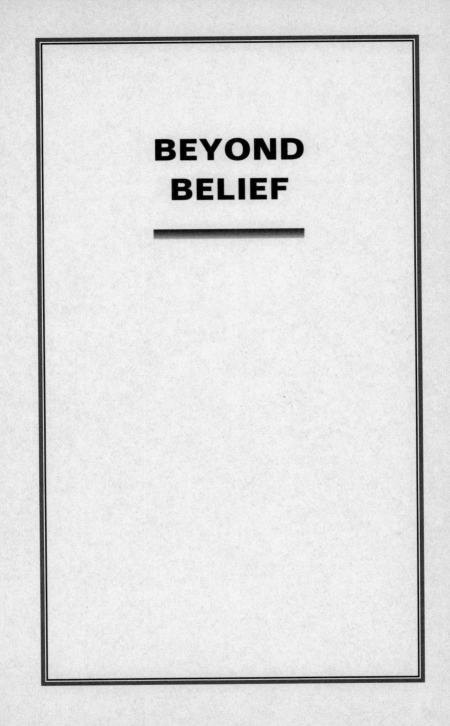

BEYOND
BELIEF

Men In Black

Are Extraterrestrial Thugs Harassing UFO Witnesses?

> I certainly believe that we are being pursued by aliens, and I think what has happened is that they've left their black Cadillacs behind and have taken to using black helicopters.
> —Shirley Coyne, former UFO investigator

UFO insiders call them MIBs, mysterious Men In Black who appear seemingly out of the blue to harass and even threaten UFO eyewitnesses. The MIBs often claim to be working for the FBI or local law enforcement and show credentials that look authentic. But witnesses consistently describe the MIBs as having an odd aura, a kind of awkwardness in speech and appearance that makes them seem strangely out of place. Their reportedly robotlike movements, ill-fitting clothing, and unfamiliarity with local customs has led many UFO researchers to hypothesize that MIBs are poorly disguised extraterrestrials posing as government officials.

Their mission? To find out what the UFO eyewitnesses know and to intimidate them into keeping quiet about what they've seen. While most debunkers insist that MIBs are figments of overactive and paranoid imaginations, there have been just too many sightings of and encounters with these Men In Black for ufologists to accept the idea that the phenomenon begins and ends with mass hallucination. Taken singly, stories of MIB encounters sound absurd, researchers concede; taken all together, however, MIB stories from around the world are worthy of serious investigation.

The MIB phenomenon officially began on June 21, 1947, when Harold A. Dahl, an ocean salvage operator, claimed that he and his small crew had witnessed a UFO rendezvous near Maury Island, Washington. Further, Dahl said that he had collected metal debris and rocks that shot out from one of the alien spacecraft. The next day, the *Tacoma Times* would later report, Dahl met a mysterious stranger wearing a black suit and driving a black sedan. The stranger warned him not to talk about what he had seen and to hand over the debris he had collected, "if he loved his family and didn't want anything to happen." At the end of July 1947, Dahl was also visited by bona fide Army intelligence officers, who took a full report on the UFO incident and also collected some alleged extraterrestrial debris. The officers determined that Dahl's story was a hoax, and not a very good one at that.

The day after their interview with Dahl, both intelligence officers were killed when their B-25 crashed near Kelso, Washington. The *Tacoma Times* carried the headline: SABOTAGE HINTED IN CRASH OF ARMY BOMBER AT KELSO. The article reported that the plane had been sabotaged or shot down to prevent the shipment of "flying disk fragments" and classified material. In the days and weeks that followed, additional reports came out about UFO investigators' hotel rooms being bugged, their phones tapped, and at least one more "confirmed" appearance of the mysterious Man In Black. Whether or not Dahl's original UFO story was a hoax, the fallout from his disclosures opened a brand-new chapter in the UFO experience. By the early 1950s MIBs were popping up all over.

In 1956, Gray Barker wrote *They Knew Too Much About Flying Saucers,* the first nonfiction work about the MIB phenomenon. Barker recounted the story of Albert K. Bender, founder of the International Flying Saucer Bureau, an early UFO research organization. Bender's 1953 experience with a menacing Man In

Black is generally considered to be the first verifiable MIB encounter. "Bender experienced terror after having a visit from a man who dressed in black clothing, an outdated double-breasted suit from the 1940s," explains UFO researcher and writer Larry Fenwick. "Bender said the man was rather pale-looking. You could almost see through his skin. He moved almost like a robot and asked a number of questions about Bender's interest in UFOs. The Man In Black warned him not to continue his investigation, and actually after this encounter, Albert Bender quit the UFO business entirely."

Throughout the 1950s, '60s, and '70s, MIBs continued to make random appearances at the doors of UFO eyewitnesses. Reports of these encounters show many common themes in the MIBs' appearance and purpose. (See Photo 38.) In general, MIBs appear in pairs, although sometimes a third MIB will be waiting outside in a black four-door sedan, usually a Cadillac or a Buick. The car is often described as having a purplish glow emanating from inside. When the car's license plate numbers are checked, they invariably turn out to be unissued numbers, providing no clue to the drivers' identities. The MIBs are dressed all in black, usually with a black fedora, and are most often described as looking like G-men from a B movie. They are physically awkward and talk in stilted slang, sometimes talking backward or breaking their sentences in odd places.

"They give false names and don't seem to know much about our manners or customs. For example, there was one report where a MIB tried to eat soup with a fork," Fenwick recalls from his research. "I know of one incident in which an eyewitness stated that he saw some sort of a cord, like an electrical cord sticking out of the trouser leg of a MIB. And in many instances, the MIBs say that their energy is fading, or that they must leave quickly—and as they say this, their voice slows down as if it's a recording or a tape being played."

"The Men In Black come in a variety of sizes and shapes," says Don Ecker, UFO investigator, radio host, and editor of *UFO Magazine*. "In many cases, they are tall, almost cadaver-looking individuals with a lack of hair and deep, piercing eyes. In other cases, they're small and Asian-looking, standing anywhere from four feet nine to five feet three inches tall. There have also been cases of MIBs that were android types, and witnesses have described seeing wires running out of their bodies. In most cases, they have a paranormal quality about them, arriving seemingly from out of nowhere," Ecker explains. "In one case, for example, a man who had been harassed by MIBs attempted to chase them, running after their car as it drove down the street. He reported that the car disappeared into thin air."

In every case, MIBs have a clear-cut agenda. They want eyewitnesses to turn over information and keep quiet. Although the MIBs threaten physical harm if an eyewitness is uncooperative, reports of death are infrequent and apocryphal. "Even though there has never been any direct link between MIBs and these particular deaths, the paranoia thread is intertwined throughout it all," Ecker says. "In one particular case, a New Jersey UFO investigator who had just had a rather dramatic UFO sighting was approached by a very saturnine man who sat down next to him in a diner and just starting talking about innocuous things. Suddenly, he looked at the witness and said, 'You know, people that look for UFOs sometimes find problems.' And the witness claimed the MIB then picked up a quarter, held it in his hand, and the quarter disintegrated. The man was terrified, and about six months later, according to [UFO researcher] John Keel, who investigated the case, the man had a heart attack and died. He was only thirty-five years old. Of course, after this incident, the paranoia factor immediately built up."

In 1967, the United States government officially acknowledged the possible existence of MIBs in a top-secret Air Force memorandum written by the assistant vice chief of staff, Lt. Gen. Hewitt T. Wheless:

> Information, not verifiable, has reached Hq USAF that persons claiming to represent the Air Force or other Defense Establishments have contacted citizens who have sighted unidentified flying objects. In one reported case an individual in civilian clothes, who represented himself as a member of NORAD, de-

manded and received photos belonging to a private citizen. In another, a person in Air Force uniform approached local police and other citizens who had sighted a UFO, assembled them in a schoolroom and told them that they did not see what they thought they saw and that they should not talk to anyone about the sighting. All military and civilian personnel . . . who hear of such reports should immediately notify their local OSI [Office of Special Investigations] offices.

According to Don Ecker, the FBI was also "very heavily involved in tracking down MIB cases and attempting to arrest individuals impersonating federal agents, but no one was ever caught." When *Sightings* first began to explore the MIB phenomenon in 1992, few people were willing to speak publicly about their encounters. Most of the stories of MIB contact dated back to the 1970s and came secondhand or from anonymous sources. Ufologist Larry Fenwick was one of only a handful of eyewitnesses who agreed to share his experiences on camera. "On November 16, 1977, I was walking on Bather Street in Toronto, Canada," Fenwick recounts. "And there it was: a long lit-up cigar-shaped object heading just over the rooftops on the west side of the street. It was silent, glowing from one end to the other, and moving steadily to the north at about three miles per hour. There was a police cruiser parked at the curb, and one of the police officers got out of his car and stood with his mouth hanging open. I was astounded by the beauty of the UFO. I was not frightened, because it was so beautiful. I was just overwhelmed with the aesthetics of the thing.

"But when I got home," Fenwick continues, "my wife said, 'You just got a phone call.' They told my wife that if I talked to the media about this sighting, 'Your daughter will die.' Well, about a month later my wife contracted cancer. Whether that's a coincidence or not I don't know. Maybe Men In Black were involved, because I can't imagine who could have made that phone call. I hadn't told anyone yet about my UFO sighting."

After his own encounter in 1977, Fenwick intensified his interest in the MIB phenomenon and interviewed a number of Canadians who had all had some kind of interaction with the Men In Black. Pat De La Franier, a UFO researcher from Stratford, Ontario, was persuaded to retell her MIB story for *Sightings:* "On April 25, 1978, I was a member of CUFORN, the Canadian UFO Research Network, preparing my research notes for a radio interview at a local station. I was in my office, going over some detailed UFO reports I wanted to present on the program, when there was a knock at my office door. Now, where my office is located, I can hear everyone coming in the main door, being admitted, and then walking down the hall. But this knock came from nowhere, and when I opened the door, there was a very odd-looking man standing there.

"He was dressed entirely in black. He was about five feet six, extremely thin, with a slightly enlarged head. His hair was just nubs, as if he had been completely shaved and the hair was just growing back. His skin was a strange olive hue. His lips were very thin, and his cheeks were so sunken in that they looked like they were pinned on the inside. His eyes were dark and extremely long; they literally wrapped around his temples. I've never seen eyes like that. They just bored into me. He just stood there staring at me. I didn't move. I was fixated on his eyes, and I felt intruded upon on a mental level. Finally, after a full minute, he spoke.

"He said, 'Would you like a photograph of your family?' It was a strange question, and his voice was very strange, too. It was low and hesitant, and this man had absolutely no conception of how to speak, how to put a sentence together. It was not that he had a foreign accent. His English was impeccable, but he was struggling to get through the sentence. I said, 'No, I have enough pictures.' And with that he stepped back, turned, and just disappeared. The man was completely gone. Later, I discovered that many [of my] files and papers were missing."

By the 1980s, MIB encounters were being reported with less and less frequency. There were still sightings of Men In Black driving black sedans with tinted windows and there were accounts of veiled threats from ominous strangers, but most researchers who had followed MIB reports from the beginning declared that the MIBs were a thing of the past and the phenomenon was over.

However, while the classic MIB profile may have faded from the UFO scene, new varieties of people and vehicles with the same methods of harassment and intimidation have since emerged to take the place of the MIB.

When *Sightings* interviewed Shirley and George Coyne in 1992, they were state directors for MUFON (Mutual UFO Network). The Coynes told a *Sightings* investigative team that they had been pursued not by black cars but by sinister black helicopters on a number of occasions going back as far as 1988. They also revealed that since then, important files and original audiotapes had been disappearing from their home. "I certainly believe that we are being pursued by aliens, and I think what has happened is that they've left their black Cadillacs behind and have taken to using black helicopters," Shirley Coyne said in 1992.

"The helicopters look like modified Hueys," she described, "with the nose more streamlined, so that it slopes down and comes almost to a point. The entire helicopter is black. Even the windows are black. There is some kind of a cable running from the tail assembly to the cabin, which we have been told is probably some kind of low-frequency antenna. The helicopters don't have any numbers on them; there are no markings of any kind, except for a strange emblem or insignia on the side, a small white circle with a smaller black circle inside. Sometimes a helicopter will circle the house maybe three or four times in a tight, tight circle just over the roof. Other times, when we're driving, they'll be hovering behind a bridge or an embankment, and just as soon as we go past, the helicopter will come up and go after us, pacing our car."

Shirley Coyne's first encounter with the black helicopters occurred on January 10, 1988, while she was participating in the hypnotic regression of a woman who believed she had been abducted by extraterrestrials. While a hypnotherapist regressed the woman, Shirley took notes and also recorded the session on audiotape. "The regression had just begun," Shirley recalled, "when all of a sudden I heard a helicopter coming. It was getting closer and noisier by the minute, so I got up and went outside to see what was going on. A black helicopter was hovering above the house, and it had its nose pulled down. It was really frightening. I felt that it was trying to intimidate me. It made me angry, too, because here I was trying to help someone who was going through a traumatic experience, and this was the payback I was getting, this black helicopter harassing us. I fully believe this had something to do with the Men In Black."

After the session, the helicopter left. A few weeks later, Shirley Coyne played her audiotape at a MUFON meeting, so the assembled researchers could hear the sound of the intimidating helicopter. "I started to play the tape of the regression, and just before the black helicopter appeared and should have been audible on the tape, there was no sound on the tape whatsoever," Shirley explained. "Someone had erased just the section of the tape from where the chopper arrived to just after it left. Now, we weren't stupid. George and I had made three other copies of that tape, so we still have the chopper sound, but the original was erased." It was the beginning of a pattern: see a black helicopter, then discover that tapes and important files had been disturbed or stolen. "We had a lot of very expensive antique pieces in our house," Shirley said. "I had a collection of antique dolls; George had all kinds of coin and stamp collections. Nothing ever came up missing except for UFO files."

The Coynes reported that they never came face-to-face with any Men In Black, but feared that the black helicopters were piloted by MIBs. "I remember one time, a black helicopter hovered so low above our back porch that I could have reached out and hit it with a long pole," Shirley remembered. "It was just sitting there with its nose down as if it were staring at us. It was completely matte black, including the windows. I didn't like the idea of somebody staring at me and not being able to stare back at him. It was frightening to have this big, black thing less than seventy feet away and you don't know what's inside. George ran off the porch and went to his car to get his camera, and just as soon as he got it out of the car, the helicopter turned and sped away going really fast."

George Coyne vowed to never miss a chance like that again. On May 1, 1992, he had a camera at the ready and was able to videotape one of the black helicopters. (See Photo 39.) "We were on our way to a MUFON planning meeting in Lansing, Michigan, and one of the black helicopters followed us all the way there," George recounted. "It was hovering low behind an embankment, and as we pulled onto the expressway it crossed in front of us and paced the car all the way to Lansing. When we got to the meeting, the helicopter started doing figure eights over the parking lot. I pulled out everyone who was already inside for the meeting and had fifty-three witnesses standing there watching this thing hover. We had a video camera there and started taping right away. Later, I showed that tape to four National Guard airmen, and they all said that it was not one of their helicopters or at all similar to any chopper they'd ever seen. They also told us it was against the law for any chopper to fly that low."

Why didn't the Coynes immediately report the incident to the FAA or other authorities? Shirley said it was because they had been burned before. "It doesn't do any good to call anybody," she said with resignation. "When we saw the first helicopter on the tenth, we contacted the airports, Metro police, and the FAA. The guy from the FAA told us it was the newscopter from NBC. Well, we had a friend who also worked at the FAA, and we asked him to check it out. He told us that he called and asked if it was a helicopter from NBC, and the guy we spoke with said, 'Of course not.' Our friend said, 'Why did you tell the Coynes that it was?' And he replied, 'Just to get them off my you-know-what.' That's why he told us that story."

Despite ridicule from many nonbelievers in their community and the constant intimidation from black helicopters, Shirley and George said they were not afraid of MIBs. Shirley said, "They haven't done anything to us yet. And I feel that the more vocal I am, the less I have to be afraid of. If I have to live with them, then I have to live with them. But I do plan on continuing to do the work we're doing. There are thousands of witnesses and abductees out there who need help, and by God, I'm going to help them. I just won't be intimidated." Despite this vehement pledge, soon after their *Sightings* interview, both George and Shirley Coyne resigned from MUFON and ended their involvement with any kind of UFO research. When George died, Shirley remarried and continues to distance herself from the UFO community.

More evidence of the changing face of MIBs can be found in the experiences of two women, one a newspaper reporter, the other a UFO researcher, who encountered mysterious strangers during their investigation of a series of UFO sightings north of Scranton, Pennsylvania. The sightings began in 1991, and for more than a year, dozens of people—including state and local police—witnessed a spectacular display of lights over Newton Township. Christy Steier was the first to observe the UFOs while she was driving home late at night. "At first I thought it was another car following, but when I looked back, there was no car, and as I adjusted my mirror, I saw that it was an object in the sky—bright, bright points of light. It kept following me as I drove down the road, and when I made a right-hand turn, this object made a right-hand turn and followed me right to my house. By this time I was really scared," Christy remembers. On that first occasion, Christy was the only one who claimed to have seen a UFO. Her family believed her story but thought she had probably misidentified an aircraft or a planet. Then, a few months later, the lights returned, and this time, Christy's father, Gary Steier, got the UFO on videotape. (See Photo 40.)

"It was a feeling of great excitement," Gary recalls of the night he saw his first UFOs. "This thing was happening right before my eyes. I didn't know what the lights were or what was happening, but it felt like a great adventure." Gary Steier called the Newton Township police, and Sgt. Anthony Cali, Jr., was dispatched to the site. "I didn't believe initially when I got the call that there would be anything of substance to see out there," Sergeant Cali says. "But immediately upon exiting my police vehicle at the scene, I looked up in the sky and saw four or five bright objects up in the air."

Sergeant Cali called in to his dispatcher and asked him to check with the local airport tower to see if they were picking up anything on radar. The tower reported that they had no unknowns on their radar screen, but air traffic controller William Wallick sighted the UFOs through his binoculars. "When the dispatcher called," Wallick explains, "I said, 'Lights? What lights?' I had nothing on radar. But I said, 'All right, let me look.' It was one of those real crystal-clear nights. There wasn't a cloud in the sky. I looked out the window over toward where he was talking about, and sure enough, there were lights out there. We had no reported aircraft in the area at that time and nothing on radar."

During 1991 and 1992, the lights appeared to hover most often over Bald Mountain, the area's highest point. Pam Zikoski was the local newspaper reporter who first broke the UFO story—and the first to attempt to climb to the top of Bald Mountain to search for clues to the mystery. She was accompanied by UFO investigator Irene McDonald. The two women were nearly at the summit when they had a terrifying encounter with two men. The men were not in black but appeared to be officials of some kind—perhaps, the women thought, forest service employees. "We were merely poking around, trying to see if we could find Gary Steier's house from the top of Bald Mountain. Two men in a pickup truck drove up the access road, pulled up to us, and got out. There was a younger man and an older man, no one I had ever seen in town," says Zikoski, a reporter who makes it her job to know the people in her town.

"They both had guns," ufologist Irene McDonald remembers. "They said, 'You're trespassing. You know you're trespassing. What are you doing here?' I said we were just taking a walk. I wasn't going to say we were up there looking for evidence of UFOs. When I saw their intense anger and their guns, I knew in thirty seconds I would either be alive or I wouldn't." Zikoski continues, "We agreed to leave, even though we had only been up there maybe five minutes at the most. What's really unusual about this encounter is that almost everybody around here at one time or another has climbed that mountain for exercise or recreation, and no one has ever been threatened by anyone, and certainly not with a gun." Zikoski and McDonald never saw the two men again. Pam Zikoski ran a search on the license plate number on the pickup truck, but that only deepened the mystery and again reminded the women of the encounter's MIB overtones. The plate number did not exist in any Pennsylvania motor vehicle record, past or present. The identity of the men has never been uncovered.

Were they MIBs? Journalist Mark Farmer, who has researched many secret military projects, has a cogent theory: "In the mental

landscape of the '50s and '60s, there was a stereotypical percep-
tion of MIBs based on the very real observation that government
officials wore dark suits and drove older-model sedans. Maybe
MIBs or government agents—or whatever you want to call
them—have simply changed the way they do business and have
thus become less visible. Just look at Secret Service guys today.
They wear brown shoes and loud ties. Times change."

Epilogue:
The Ultimate
Apocrypha—
A Ufologist Fights Back

In 1992, Don Ecker recounted for *Sightings* the details of a terrifying MIB encounter as told to him by a fellow investigator whom Ecker knew and trusted. It illustrates the fine line between knowledge and belief:

"One researcher got out of the Army about a year and a half ago and claimed to have received a lot of harassment during his military career because of his UFO interest. He returned home after twenty years of service and continued his research into UFOs. One day, he was out in his backyard doing chores, and a man—perhaps this was a MIB—jumped over his fence, walked up to him, and began talking about his UFO experience. The stranger said that he wanted to drive this investigator out to the desert to see a flying saucer. As they were leaving, the investigator slipped a revolver into his coat. They drove out to the site, and this man claimed that he saw a UFO land about fifty yards in front of them. An entity got off the UFO and began walking toward them. The investigator felt very threatened and pulled his revolver out. The entity kept walking at him. This investigator claimed that he fired six shots directly into the body of the entity, with no effect whatsoever. He claimed that his bullets didn't even touch the individual.

"This is the kind of story where it's very hard to fathom whether there is a basis in reality or whether it's someone's imagination. It sounds ludicrous, but that's what you're left to work with unless it happens to you."

1877–Present

Life on Mars

Signs of a Martian Civilization Revealed

> It's quite possible that NASA knows more about anomalous structures on Mars and the existence of extraterrestrials than they're telling us.
>
> —David Childress, archaeologist

It has long been thought that Earth is a singular outpost in our vast solar system, that this green planet is the only one of the nine planets capable of sustaining sentient life-forms. If extraterrestrials exist, mainstream scientists have long argued, they would have to come from somewhere else in the infinite metagalaxy. Mercury, Venus, Mars, Jupiter, Saturn, Uranus, Neptune, and Pluto are all just gigantic rocks with atmospheres incapable of sustaining anything more advanced than an amoeba, if that. That means that the closest possible home planet for an extraterrestrial visitor would be more than 800 million miles away, an impossible distance to cover in any lifetime.

Theories about intergalactic time travel and ultradimensional space warp aside, new scientific findings have everyone—ufologists and mainstream scientists alike—rethinking the prospect of alien life forms within our solar system. The focus right now is on

Mars, and the question being posed is no longer, Is there life on Mars, but, Just how much life is there?

It started in 1995, astronomers made a startling announcement. They had discovered one of the essential raw materials of life floating in space: an amino acid called glycine. Keay Davidson, science writer for the *San Francisco Examiner,* describes the importance of the discovery this way: "It was sort of like finding a brick floating around in space; from that brick, you could infer the existence of brick houses in outer space. Now we don't know for sure that the discovery of glycine means that larger amino acid structures are forming in space, but it's a clue that the formation of the building blocks of life is a routine thing in the universe."

Then, in 1996, NASA researchers announced that a chunk of Mars, which had fallen to Earth in the form of a meteorite, contained carbonate globules, carbon-containing compounds, and microscopic structures that looked like fossil bacteria. (See Photo 41.) Each of these compounds alone could have other explanations, but taken together, NASA said cautiously, the compounds strongly suggest that life was once present on Mars. Summing up the feelings of the worldwide scientific community, NASA chief Dan Goldin had a one-word answer at his August 7, 1996, press conference. He said, "Wow!"

Jeff Kargel, an astrogeologist with the U.S. Geological Survey, offers an intriguing scenario for the potential of life on Mars. "On Earth there has been a long period of evolution, which has allowed microorganisms to survive and adapt to the changing conditions on Earth. We've had 3.8 billion years of trial and error to adapt to these conditions. Whether or not the microorganisms on Mars have had a similar period of adapting isn't known, but at the optimistic end of things, it's possible. Life is very imaginative, and it finds ways of adapting to an extraordinary range of environments. We find living creatures in hot springs in Yellowstone. We find them living beneath the ice of Antarctica. I have no doubt that given enough time, life forms could exist on Mars just as they exist on Earth."

The opinions of Kargel, Davidson, Goldin, and others are acceptable to the general public now because of the discovery of just one rock; but they are not the first scientists to postulate the existence of life on Mars. Long before the discovery of possible organic fossils in a Martian meteorite made headlines worldwide, there were scientists who believed in life on Mars and throughout their entire careers fought against the ridicule their eccentric theories engendered. Is mainstream science just now beginning to catch up with these pioneers?

In 1877, Mars came the closest to Earth it had ever been since the invention of the telescope, enabling American astronomer Asaph Hall to discover that Mars had two moons; however, Hall's important discovery was almost entirely overshadowed by discoveries made at the same time by Italian astronomer Giovanni Schiaparelli, who claimed to have found artificial structures on the surface of Mars. Schiaparelli rocked Earth's entire cosmic view with the declaration that someone may have built an elaborate system of canals on Mars. "At the time Schiaparelli first was observing the planet, it was believed that the dark areas on Mars were bodies of water. They called them oceans and seas," explains Leonard Martin, planetary researcher for the Lowell Observatory in Flagstaff, Arizona. "What Schiaparelli thought he saw were lines connecting these bodies of water, and he interpreted them to be waterways connecting the different seas and oceans. Later on, when it was decided that the dark areas probably were not bodies of water, this changed the interpretation of the lines as waterways—but the word 'canals' sort of stuck."

Schiaparelli may have discovered the canals, but it was American astronomer Percival Lowell who popularized the notion that the Martian canals were created by dint of labor, not geology. Lowell made his first observations of the Martian canals from an observatory he built himself in Arizona in 1894. While cowboys roamed the great plains, prairies, and deserts of the Wild West, Lowell was sitting at a telescope dreaming about Martians.

"Lowell was the major proponent of the idea that the canals might be artificially made by intelligent beings. And he spent a great deal of his time trying to sell this idea to both the scientific community and the general public. He thought that there were Martians," says Leonard Martin.

Lowell Observatory archivist Martin Hecht is responsible for maintaining the vast number of documents, sketches, and globes created by Lowell during his lifetime. "Percival Lowell created Mars log books that he used at the telescope to record his findings," Hecht explains. "He also included sketches of his observations. The sketches were necessary, because in the late 1800s and the early 1900s, photography was not yet developed to take pictures through telescopes. If you look closely at Lowell's sketches, you can see what he considered canals. [See Photo 42.] These sketches were later transferred onto Mars globes, which are a real treasure of the Lowell observatory."

Several important discoveries, including the discovery of the planet Pluto, were made at the Lowell Observatory, now a museum open to the public, but Percival Lowell's greatest legacy may very well be that he got the world thinking about the possibility of life on other planets. "I think people believed in Martians before Lowell," Martin concedes, "but certainly Lowell brought the possibility that life could exist someplace else within our solar system to the attention of a lot of people. And Percival Lowell felt that the best prospect for life to happen was on Mars. I think that any search for extraterrestrial life has to include Lowell as a player, because he created a lot of excitement about extraterrestrial life, and certainly his influence is still felt today and always will be."

Lowell remained at the forefront of Martian life studies until an amazing discovery in 1924 eclipsed his theories about the Martian canals. On August 24, 1924, two American scientists, one an astronomer, the other a mechanical genius, ascended in a balloon high above Washington, D.C., and when they returned to Earth, they claimed that they had successfully made contact with Mars. "It is reasonably certain that Mars has been inhabited in the past and is inhabited now," wrote David Todd, the astronomer who ascended in that balloon to prove his outrageous theory to the world.

"David Todd was an astronomer at Amherst College one hundred years ago and, like many people of the time, was a believer in the existence of intelligent being[s] on Mars because of the apparent existence of features that seemed to be not natural but engineered," explains David A. Blerkon, Ph.D., an astronomer at the University of Massachusetts who has written a biography of Todd. "Todd felt that if there were intelligent beings on Mars, they would have been more advanced than we were at the time. We had just developed radio, and therefore, Todd reasoned, the Martians must have developed radio long before and were probably signaling to us and wondering why we were so stupid that we weren't sending any return answer. So his idea was in fact to listen to Mars and see if we could pick up radio signals directed toward us."

Today, high-powered radio telescopes and computerized receivers continue to scan the cosmos for signs of intelligent life in space, but in 1924, things were quite different. There were no radio telescopes, computers, or even tape recorders. To receive and preserve signals from space was a daunting task, and Dr. Todd knew there was only one man who could help him realize his dream of contact: C. Francis Jenkins. "If there was anyone in the world of invention at that time who had all the tools to do the kind of thing that Todd wanted to have done, I think Jenkins was the logical choice," says David Hollenbeck, Ph.D., assistant professor of communications at the University of New York, Cortland. "Jenkins had over 300 patents, in both radio and optics. In 1923, it was Jenkins who actually sent the very first definable television image that we know of."

Jenkins was fascinated by the challenge presented to him by Todd: build a machine that would record signals from space. "Jenkins created a strange device called a radio detective to listen for signals from Mars and record those signals optically," Dr. Hollenbeck explains, "because if you have radio signals coming in, you have to somehow be able to reproduce them. It's easy for us nowadays. We have tape recorders and even digital recorders. But in those days it was a lot more difficult. Jenkins had to come up with a device that converted the radio signals to light and then put it on film."

So up in the balloon they flew with their newly invented radio detective. They picked August 24, 1924, because Mars was then at its closest point to Earth. Dr. Todd asked for complete radio silence from the armed services of the United States and received it. No transmissions were made from Earth during his flight. "Effectively, from what I understand, Todd and Jenkins used the device by aiming it at Mars and trying to record signals of some kind coming from that direction. They were hoping to make contact."

Astonishingly, contact was made. For the first and only time in human history, a strange message coming from the direction of Mars was actually recorded on film. (See Photo 43.) "They brought the film back," Dr. Blerkon says, "and then began to analyze the markings on the film, which were very hard to decipher. There was apparently something that looked like a face that was constantly repeated along one edge of the film." It was this so-called face-on-Mars code that was the number one topic of conversation in scientific circles in 1924. Many people began calling it Martian code and demanded that it be deciphered. David Todd submitted the film to William Friedman, the country's leading cryptologist. Friedman would later become the United States government's master of decoded military secrets and the acknowledged godfather of the CIA.

"William Friedman is one of the most important figures in twentieth-century cryptology because of national security issues," says Thomas Camden, a director of research at the Virginia Military Institute. "He was working for the government in the security arena, decoding messages in World War I and World War II, including the famous deciphering of the Japanese Purple Code. He also worked on Egyptian hieroglyphics and Mayan code his entire life. Jenkins and Todd felt that they had an extraterrestrial message, and they felt that the only person who might be able to help decode that message was William Friedman."

What happened when two of America's best scientists met the master of cryptology? The answer remained shrouded in mystery until a *Sightings* investigative team finally tracked down Jenkins's long-lost Mars film. It was in William Friedman's personal archive at VMI in a dog-eared folder labeled "Can We Decode Mars Messages?" "William Friedman looked at the code and made an attempt to decipher it," Thomas Camden explains. "But there's no evidence in the file that indicates that he actually broke the code. There's nothing to indicate in our records that he confirmed the existence of extraterrestrials through this particular coded message, but he did not dispose of the information. He kept the information in his files—and why he did not return it to the gentlemen who brought the whole subject to his attention is not known." Although Friedman's archives have been purged of their most important correspondence by the National Security Agency, there was one letter in the Mars file. The letter, dated September 5, 1924, was written by a friend of Friedman's then serving as a captain in the U.S. Signal Corps. Camden explains, "A man named Captain John P. Ferriter writes to Friedman, 'During the time that Mars was closest to Earth, we had three radio stations here watching for possible signals. On the night of the twenty-fourth, we heard some peculiar signals and . . . as well as I can tell, they are the same signals that have been reported. They consisted in part of dashes of six seconds' duration separated by intervals of seven seconds. They were followed by a voice pronouncing words which were isolated words of one to four syllables.' He makes mention of the fact that he assumes they were some sort of radio test, but he says that they could not determine what language was being used."

Does the existence of Todd and Jenkins's face-on-Mars code—and the letter from Captain Ferriter—indicate that Friedman knew more about the code than he was willing to tell? Thomas Camden won't venture a guess, but he does say, "To decode a message from another planet that may indicate extraterrestrial life—I believe William Friedman would have seen that as the ultimate code." The details of any code work Friedman may have done on the 1924 signals are lost. The idea of Martians, the face-on-Mars code, and extraterrestrial radio waves has disappeared into obscurity, along with David Todd and C. Francis Jenkins.

The next clue to the life-on-Mars mystery didn't come until fifty-two years later, when the *Viking I* mission to Mars sent back the first high-resolution photographs of the Martian surface. There, for everyone to see, were the red rocks and dust, the hydrogen permafrost, and the boulder-strewn landscape the astronomers had predicted. There was also something there that the scientists hadn't predicted, which harked back to the code of Todd and Jenkins. *Viking I* sent back a picture of what looked like a face on the surface of Mars. (See Photo 44.)

Was it a case of cosmic simulacra, a rock that simply looked like a face? Or was it built by unknown hands as a totem or possibly a signal to the Martians' earthly neighbors? "The image of the face is very compelling," says Stanley McDaniel, professor emeritus at Sonoma State University, who has made a comprehensive study of the *Viking I* photographs. "It was the upfront likeness to a humanoid image that really drew my attention and made me quite interested in it. The face has been measured anthropometrically, which is measuring it according to standard human proportions, and the face on Mars falls within the tolerance ranges for humanoid proportions. That isn't likely to happen for something that is simply geological or a trick of lighting. There are two eye hollows and deep set in the clearest eye hollow is an eye pupil. This has been brought out by very careful image enhancement work. But I've had NASA horselaugh at the entire project and tell me, 'An eyeball, ha-ha-ha! There just couldn't be one, so I'm not going to look at the data.' It reminds me of the church fathers who wouldn't look through Galileo's telescope."

McDaniel and many others who have studied the area surrounding the mile-long face believe that there are many more potentially earthshaking structures within the region of Martian topography known as Cydonia. "Most people have heard only of the face, and NASA acts as though the face is the only object that is of any interest, but actually there's an entire group of objects close to one another." McDaniel continues. "There is sufficient evidence to indicate that some of these objects on Mars may be artificial. I've been operating under the ethical idea that if there's even the slightest possibility of life on Mars, a high priority should be given to investigating it, but there has not been a single formal NASA study of the objects on Mars.

"There's the face itself and then about eight miles to the west, there's a complex of structures that includes a very peculiar object called the fort," McDaniel continues. "Now, these names like 'the fort' are just intended to be suggestive. It doesn't mean that anyone knows whether it really was a fort. There is also what we call the main pyramid and smaller pyramidal shapes one hundred feet high arranged in an orderly manner that's been called the city square. [See Photo 45.] Also, on the other side of the face to the east is another unusual set of objects called the cliff, the crater pyramid, and a five-sided object called the D&M pyramid [for Vincent DiPietro and Gregory Molenaar, who originally discovered it]. The D&M pyramid is quite large, about 1.6 miles long, over a mile wide, and about 1,600 feet high. It's a very unusual geometric figure. The chances of finding a natural mountain at random that fits that unique geometry would be very, very slim."

NASA's official position is that nothing has ever been constructed on the surface of Mars and that the face, pyramids, and other seemingly artificial structures are only tricks of light and shadow. Mars researchers, however, point to computer-enhanced 3-D images of the face on Mars that show that the face is clearly visible, no matter where it is in relation to the sun. "I was quite interested with the first photos in release of the face on Mars," says archaeologist David Childress, author of *Extraterrestrial Archaeology*. "But I was particularly interested in the pyramidal structures, because some of these pyramids appear to have a central stairway running up and down them. The more we look at these structures, the more we can see that there's something amazing here."

It is the deliberate and mathematically exact placement of the pyramids in the complex that Stanley McDaniel finds the most compelling. "These objects, if you measure carefully from the tops of the five pyramids that surround the city square, form an almost perfectly symmetrical pentagon," McDaniel has found. "It's as if it had been done by an architectural designer. A professor of physics has since calculated that the chance of this happening in nature is 1 in 50,000."

David Percy is an author and paranormal researcher who has also studied the Mars complex extensively. Percy believes that the Mars complex was deliberately designed and built by extraterrestrials and has discovered a startling connection between the mysterious structures on Mars and equally mysterious monuments right here on Earth. In the countryside of south-central England, in a hamlet named Avebury, stand 5,000-year-old stone structures of unknown origin. There are also enormous circular mounds constructed for a purpose no one has yet deciphered. The Avebury area has been the site of hundreds of UFO sightings dating back to the sixteenth century and has the largest concentration of crop circles in the world. It is a paranormal researcher's paradise, and it was while researching crop circles in Avebury in 1991 that David Percy believes he discovered the area's link to Mars.

"The complex on Mars is exceedingly important in my view," says Percy. "And when I was studying the Avebury stone circle and the mound at Silbury Hill nearby, something about the relative position of these two structures reminded me of the structures on Mars. I took an ordinary survey map of the Avebury area and superimposed it over a NASA photograph of the complex in its entirety, and to my surprise, found that it matched. [See Photo 46.] Particularly compelling is the match between the Mars crater on the east side of the complex and the Avebury stone circle, and the match between the Mars spiral mound and Silbury Hill.

"The Avebury stone circle," Percy explains, "is about a quarter of a mile in diameter, nearly the same size as the Mars crater. Around 5,000 years ago, some group here shifted approximately four million cubic feet of material, and one has to ask, Why? My theory is that this is a copy of the crater on Mars. Now a short distance away, we have Silbury Hill. It's the same relative size as the spiral mound on Mars, and it's the same relative distance to the crater as it is to the Avebury circle. Further, if you draw a line from what they call the Mars cliff or the Mars wall down to the southern end of the spiral mound, and then up again to the five-sided pyramid, you get a measurement just under 19.5 degrees. If you do the same thing at Avebury, you get precisely the same measurement. [See Photo 47.] You cannot get such a correspondence just by wishful thinking."

Perhaps the most intriguing piece in his puzzle is one that Percy discovered after he had already made his calculation on the matches between Mars and Avebury. "In a document from the

1700s, I discovered that for a very long time Silbury Hill was called the Hill of Mars. It's an ancient name; nobody knows how old it is. Now you have an ancient connection to Mars and the modern overlay between the two maps that matches up remarkably well. I have to say this looks like an intentional relationship, and I believe that what we have here in Avebury is a model of Cydonia on Earth. The purpose may have been to verify the finding of Martian spacecraft, but when and if that ever happened, we cannot say."

Percy's thought-provoking theory notwithstanding, Stan McDaniel firmly believes that the jury is still out on the origin of the Martian complex. "I don't believe that the structures are necessarily man-made," he says, "But I believe that there is enough evidence that they might be man-made, and for that reason alone, we need to look at these objects more closely." When later space probes did go in for a closer look, something strange happened: something that has Mars complex researchers crying foul.

In 1990 a Russian Mars probe called *Phobos II* attempted to take additional pictures of Cydonia, but the probe disappeared before it even reached Mars's orbit. In 1993, a U.S. probe called the *Mars Observer* met a similar fate. Just when the *Mars Observer* seemed to be moving in for a closer look at Cydonia, NASA announced there had been a technical malfunction and there were no more pictures. "It's quite possible that NASA knows more about anomalous structures on Mars and the existence of extraterrestrials than they're telling us," David Childress suggests. Many researchers agree that NASA is withholding important photographs and data taken in the Cydonia region. It has been suggested that NASA created the *Mars Observer* malfunction story to hide the greatest archaeological discovery of all time.

"Some people want to go far beyond the edge of what's accepted in terms of Martian imagery," says James Oberg, an engineer, computer scientist, and space program subcontractor who doesn't believe that NASA is covering up anything. "If people want to see patterns on the rocks on Mars or on the moon or in the rings of Saturn, my view to that is, *mazel tov,* go ahead and make your proposals. I have a favorite quotation from British physicist J. B. S. Haldane, who said that 'the universe is not only queerer than we imagine. It's queerer than we can imagine.' There are bizarre things out there. I just don't think pyramids on Mars is one of them."

If NASA does have new information about these reportedly artificial structures, why would they be hiding their findings from the American public? An advisory report from the Brookings Institute, a Washington, D.C.–based think tank, may hold the answer. "There is a section on what might occur if evidence of extraterrestrial existence is found on other planets," Stanley McDaniel explains. "They said that NASA or the government might want to consider keeping the information from the public, the reason being that it could cause widespread social unrest and possible deterioration of government control."

According to NASA, the *Mars Observer* suffered a catastrophic electrical failure, rendering it inoperable. "I know a lot of people like to think there is a secret NASA program out there that is actually studying pictures from Cydonia and keeping the results secret, that all the scientists we see in public are either stooges or second-rate stand-ins for the secret establishment," says James Oberg. "Sometimes I wish there were. I wish we had the funds to do that, but I think that we as a society and the scientists as individuals don't have either the mental framework or the desire to sustain a cover-up like that. Life is more complex than even our imaginations. Stupid things are done; spacecraft do blow up, especially ones, as we can now tell in hindsight, [that] were as poorly designed as the *Mars Observer*."

Stan McDaniel adamantly disagrees. "The *Mars Observer* did not lose transmission. They turned it off. And they turned it off after the instructions for going into orbit had been uploaded to the spacecraft. It was possible that the spacecraft could go ahead, follow out its instructions, and go into orbit and no one would know about it because NASA had turned off the radio." James Oberg counters: "We have to keep realizing just how tough these projects are. We're doing things out there in space, every time we do it, that no one even thought was possible even a few years ago. These are really tough missions to accomplish." McDaniel re-

mains unconvinced. "All I know is that I've had secondhand reports that people within NASA who would not give their names
have said that the *Mars Observer* is still operative, and it is sending
back clandestine reports."

Soon, we will have another chance to learn more about the
tantalizing mysteries on Mars. As of this writing, NASA has
launched the *Mars Global Observer,* which will orbit Mars and take
new higher-resolution pictures. They are also planning the
launch of the *Mars Pathfinder,* which will send a land rover down
to explore the Martian surface. "We're living beings, conscious of
this magnificent universe around us," astrogeologist Jeff Kargel
sums up philosophically. "We use our intellect to try to understand our place in the universe. Why do we exist? *Mars Pathfinder*
isn't going to tell us the answer to that; nevertheless, all human
beings share this fascination with existence, and Mars is a world
that clearly has the key ingredients of life. Mars has [captured] in
the past and will continue to capture human imagination."

Less than one hundred years ago, a nanosecond in cosmic
time, we rode in horse-drawn buggies and depended on the pony
express. Today, we are sending a robot to mine the surface of
Mars. It may be sooner than we think before we have the ability to
make contact with alien life forms we can now only imagine.

The Roswell Autopsy Film

Cyberbunk

This is indeed a human corpse, undoubtedly somewhat doctored. And that makes it one of the most despicable hoaxes ever perpetrated.

—Kent Jeffrey, Roswell Declaration

I'm ultimately confident that the film is genuine. If it wasn't, I wouldn't be so foolish as to place myself in the limelight that I'm in right now, especially when we're not making a great deal of money out of it.

—Ray Santilli, promoter

In the summer of 1995, bizarre and graphic images of a humanoid creature exploded across the World Wide Web. Within hours, thousands of Internet users were transmitting and downloading pictures of what was being touted as the first hard evidence that alien bodies had been recovered, examined, and hidden from the public by the U.S. military. For nearly fifty years, UFO researchers had been looking for the smoking gun that would prove once and for all that the government was lying about what crashed seventy-five miles northwest of Roswell, New Mexico, in July 1947. The first pictures that appeared on the Internet looked like the missing link in the Roswell story, but since then the origin of the stills and the controversy over their authenticity has eclipsed the original Roswell incident as the most compelling and Byzantine UFO story of the century.

Sometime between July 3 and July 7, 1947, something crashed into the desert near Roswell, New Mexico. The first information released by the 509th Bombardment group intelligence office at Roswell Army Air Force Base stated that the object was a "crashed disc." The *Roswell Daily Record* embellished that report just enough to trigger the most famous UFO incident in history when they went to press on July 8, 1947, with the headline: RAAF CAPTURES FLYING SAUCER ON RANCH IN ROSWELL REGION. Despite vehement denials from first Air Force General Roger Ramey and then every subsequent Air Force spokesperson to date, nearly every researcher in the international UFO community believes the government is still hiding what they know: An alien spacecraft crashed in 1947, and the Air Force is holding on to the wreckage. When the Air Force released its 1,000-plus-page "Report on Roswell" in 1994 and admitted that the Roswell craft was not a weather balloon—as they originally stated—but a top-secret Project Mogul balloon, ufologists cried foul, and their commitment to a global cover-up only deepened.

From the beginning, witnesses have come forward with intriguing stories about the location and disposition of flying saucer crash debris. However, none of the witnesses from the original crash site ever reported seeing bodies, including Major Jesse Marcel, the staff intelligence officer who accompanied the wreckage as far as Carswell Army Air Force Base in Fort Worth, Texas, and who would later reveal that he believed the craft was extraterrestrial in origin. The first hint that bodies from another world had been recovered at the crash site didn't occur until 1984, when an unauthenticated government document was discovered and released to the public. Called the Majestic-12 or MJ-12 document, it is purported to be a leaked top-secret memo from November 18, 1952, briefing President Truman on the status of UFO affairs in the United States.

The MJ-12 document (which the Air Force maintains is a hoax) begins with a brief description of Kenneth Arnold's saucer sighting of 1947 (see the chapter "Flying Saucers Are Real"), then moves on to a detailed report on the Roswell incident, including the following stunning statements:

> During the course of this operation aerial reconnaissance discovered that four small human-like beings had apparently ejected from the craft at some point before it exploded. These had fallen to earth about two miles east of the wreckage site. All four were dead and badly decomposed due to action by predators and exposure to the elements during the approximately one week time period which had elapsed before their discovery. A special scientific team took charge of removing these bodies for study. The wreckage of the craft was also removed to several different locations. Civilian and military witnesses in the area were debriefed and news reporters were given the effective cover story that the object had been a misguided weather research balloon.
>
> It was the tentative conclusion [of the special scientific team headed by Dr. Detlev Bronk, chairman of the National Research Council] that although these creatures are human-like in appearance, the biological and evolutionary processes responsible for their development has apparently been quite different from those observed or postulated in homo sapiens. Dr. Bronk's team has suggested the term "Extra-terrestrial Biological Entities," or "ERBs," be adopted as the standard term of reference for these creatures until such time as a more definitive designation can be agreed upon.

In 1989, during a *Sightings* interview with alleged Area 51 physicist Bob Lazar, the possibility that photos existed from an "alien autopsy" was discussed. Lazar said that when he first arrived at the Air Force's supersecret aircraft design and testing facility at Area 51, he was given a series of briefing documents to study. According to Lazar, the briefings were arranged as short pamphlets, each on a different extraterrestrial subject. Lazar admitted that he did not know if these pamphlets were real or if they were designed to test his ability to keep secrets, but he recalled for *Sightings* the contents of one of those briefings.

"The photographs that I saw were from an autopsy report, presumably of a dead alien," Lazar said. "The alien appeared to be lying on some sort of table. There was a T-cut in the chest section with the skin peeled back. There were also photographs of one large central organ that was removed, which I would describe as a liver you would see in a grocery store. It was a wet-looking mass; a liver is the only way I can describe it. The face was mildly triangular, with very large dark eyes, a slit for a mouth, no nose, and essentially no ears. Also, it was hairless."

Then, in 1995, *Sightings* interviewed a man who claimed that his uncle had actually seen alien bodies being examined at Wright-Patterson Air Force Base in Dayton, Ohio. Now that his uncle had passed away, Ohio horticulturist James Donohoe told *Sightings*, he was ready to reveal the family secret. "My uncle Jack had a top-secret security clearance when he worked at Wright-Patterson," Donohoe begins. "The strangest story that he ever recounted to me was the day that he asked me if I had heard of a UFO crash out in Arizona. He said, 'We have the bodies from the crash.'" Donohoe claims that his uncle Jack Donohoe told him that in 1953 he was led down a series of twisting hallways to a secret room.

"There was a stainless-steel table in this room that was arranged a little bit like a laboratory. A man said, 'Look at this.' And Uncle Jack told me that he looked at the body, and they were doing full autopsies on the bodies. The head was shaped basically like a human head, only it was small. He said, 'We better not spend very much time here.' And they left the room. I tried to bring the story up with my uncle many times after he told it to me originally, but he always said, 'Forget about it, forget about the whole incident.' And I said, 'What do you mean, forget it?' And he said, 'Just forget it. It never happened.'"

Rumors about alien bodies at Wright-Patterson have been circulating for a number of years. As legendary UFO researcher Leonard Stringfield told *Sightings* shortly before his death, "I was told by one intelligence source here some years ago that they had thirty alien bodies underground at Wright-Patterson alone." Dayton news anchor and investigative reporter Carl Day's own research into the alien body stories yielded this information: "One of the most interesting discoveries has to be the alleged alien jawbone that we uncovered. Officials within the Air Force intelligence community have told me that they determined back in the 1970s, possibly before, that they had an alien jawbone. I can't have anybody go on record now, however, as saying that. I think the Air Force is hiding a lot of things."

The official U.S. government position is unequivocal. According to the United States Air Force's 1995 Roswell Report, no bodies, alien or otherwise, were recovered at Roswell—nor, for that matter, at any other alleged UFO crash site. Summarizing the Air Force findings, Col. Richard L. Weaver, director of security and special program oversight, writes:

> The Air Force research did not locate or develop any information that the "Roswell Incident" was a UFO event. Likewise, there was no indication in official records from the period that there was heightened military operational or security activity which should have been generated if this was, in fact, the first recovery of materials and/or persons from another world. The post-War U.S. Military (or today's for that matter) did not have the capability to rapidly identify, recover, coordinate, cover up, and quickly minimize public scrutiny of such an event. The claim that they did so without leaving even a little bit of a suspicious paper trail for 47 years is incredible.
>
> The pro-UFO groups who espouse the alien bodies theories cannot even agree among themselves as to what kind or how many, and where such bodies were supposedly recovered. Additionally, some of these claims have been shown to be hoaxes, even by other UFO researchers. Many of the persons making the biggest claims of "alien bodies" make their living from the "Roswell Incident." While having a commercial interest in something does not automatically make it suspect, it does raise interesting questions related to authenticity. Such persons should be

encouraged to present their evidence directly to the government . . . if honest fact-finding is what is wanted.

Although the U.S. Air Force summary was written before the release of the alleged "alien autopsy" film and no official comment has been made specifically about it, it is safe to assume that the official response would be identical to that stated above. But for tens of thousands of UFO enthusiasts and a few serious researchers, the "alien autopsy" film released by London music promoter and documentary producer Ray Santilli is hard evidence that there have been extraterrestrials among us. Nuclear physicist and renowned UFO researcher Stanton Friedman asserts, "If the autopsy film is truly genuine, then it becomes the focus of worldwide recognition that indeed our planet has been visited, that indeed governments have known for near half a century and haven't told us. The world will never be the same again."

Rumors of a Roswell autopsy film go back to 1993, when Ray Santilli told BUFORA, the British UFO Research Association, that he had unearthed twenty-two canisters of 16-millimeter film in the private vault of a former military cameraman. "Ray Santilli said, 'I have put my hands on some material,'" remembers BUFORA member Colin Andrews. "He told me, 'I know nothing about Roswell, but I'm being told by the man who sold this to me that he was a military cameraman with the United States in 1947, and he said that this was the official record of an event which occurred there,' i.e., a crashed UFO and the recovery of aliens and debris."

In a 1995 interview with *Sightings,* Ray Santilli described how he had come into possession of the amazing film footage. He was working on a film documentary about Elvis Presley when he heard that there was a former military cameraman who had never-before-seen footage of Elvis in the U.S. Army. During his visit with the cameraman, Santilli claimed he was shown twenty-two canisters of black-and-white film that the cameraman had taken after the Roswell crash. It is rumored that Santilli paid $150,000 for the footage. According to Santilli, the man decided to sell the footage because he was getting old and wanted to buy his granddaughter a home before he passed away. Why didn't he release the footage himself and reap even greater rewards? San-tilli says it is because the cameraman may have broken the law by holding on to government property. "This guy's in his mid-eighties," Santilli told *Sightings*. "He's not interested in the subject of UFOs. He's got his family to consider, and his family is his only consideration. He's also a veteran and doesn't want to lose his pension. You know, technically, he sold something which be-longed to the U.S. government, and he could be regarded as a traitor." For the man's own protection, Santilli insists he will not be the one to publicly reveal the identity of the cameraman.

As soon as word of the alleged autopsy film reached the UFO community, excitement was tempered by skepticism. How could this cameraman have kept more than an hour of highly classi-fied film about the world's most stunning extraterrestrial event? It seemed unfathomable to researchers who had spent decades trying to squeeze a few classified Roswell documents out of the military.

"He shot hundreds of canisters of film during the event itself," Santilli explained. "Each of the canisters contained a reel of film three minutes in duration. During the filming, he separated reels that he felt were problem reels, reels where the film had jammed, where there were focus problems or exposure problems. He sepa-rated out film he would need more time in processing. He sent the remainder—the bulk of the film—on to Washington. He spent more time on the twenty-two reels of film, which he processed or whatever. And once he'd got to the stage where he felt he could send them on, he called Washington and asked them to pick up the film, and they just failed to do so."

Among the first to see the "alien autopsy" film was Colin An-drews. "I traveled to London with [ufologist and former lead singer with The Troggs] Reg Presley and was introduced to Ray Santilli. We watched a film in which there was an unusual hu-manoid creature and a procedure was underway. We watched this very, very bizarre object, including the full autopsy itself. Key line researchers like myself had always speculated that in 1947 of course camera and film technology existed, so an official film record had to exist. It wasn't just notepads and pens. And after watching the film, one would have to say that quite conceivably this is the record."

Andrews provided a vivid description of the footage he saw in early January 1995: "The being was approximately four feet, six inches, perhaps five feet long, lying on a flat surface in a room perhaps eighteen to twenty feet square. There were two personnel there attending to this body. They were fully clad in white one-piece suits with visors. One end wall had a very large glass panel, and one could see one more individual observing everything that was going on. The personnel had a very close look at the right leg, which was seriously wounded. It was a very deep wound; one could see that the leg had been split open all the way down to the bone structure. The female genitalia was visible, but secondary sexual organs were not. It was humanoid, with a large head, large black eyes, a small nose, small mouth. The ears were set much lower down than on a normal human being. The legs were muscular. The stomach was expanded, perhaps gas-filled, I don't know, but it was distended. There were six fingers on each hand, six toes on each foot. When the autopsy commenced, the heart was removed. There was an unidentifiable organ removed from the solar plexus area. The head was incised around the skull, and a brain was removed."

After still frames from the film were leaked onto the Internet, *Sightings* televised several startling frames from Santilli's film. (See Photos 48–50.) At the same time, portions of the film were being screened for researchers, medical and film technicians, press, and potential buyers. As the film reached more and more people, the buzz turned from exhilaration to condemnation. Kent Jeffrey is an international airline pilot, UFO enthusiast, and the author of the Roswell Declaration, a petition calling for the declassification of all government documents on Roswell. He had eagerly anticipated the release of Santilli's film. "We were told that the film was in fifteen ten-minute reels in its original canisters. To me, this sounded very encouraging, because my thought was that if somebody was going to hoax a film they wouldn't do 150 minutes' worth. I was very hopeful. I thought that if this film were genuine, it would be the holy grail of evidence that would break the

Roswell case wide open. But after just a few seconds of watching the film, I knew that this was a hoax. That was a human body on that autopsy table. There was no doubt in my mind. Now I do believe that there is a very high degree of probability that the crash of a flying saucer did occur at Roswell as originally reported. I also believe there is no probability that this film is a documentation of any part of that event."

Jesse Marcel, Jr., the son of Major Marcel, an original Roswell eyewitness, echoes Jeffrey's sentiments. "I believe in July 1947 that a craft not of this world crashed outside of Roswell, New Mexico. I believe the United States government orchestrated a major military operation, and I believe they recovered bodies. I would like to believe that the autopsy film is true, but my gut feeling is that the film is probably a hoax." And Walter Haut, the public information officer at Roswell Army Air Base in July 1947 agrees. "I think we had a crash of a UFO on the night of the fourth. Debris was picked up on the fifth and the sixth, and we played games with the press until the eighth. Okay, but now this film shows up, and frankly, I'm not impressed. I don't feel it was an actual autopsy. I think it was a hoax, and someone is probably making a little bit of money on it."

According to Kent Jeffrey, "Ray Santilli has said from the start that he's in it only for the money, and that's one of the few statements that Santilli has made which I believe." For his part, Santilli has never denied that his goal has been to make money, from the sale of videocassettes and broadcast rights to the "alien autopsy" film, but in his 1995 *Sightings* interview, he declared that he had yet to see a significant profit. "In terms of profit," Santilli said, "we haven't made our money back by any stretch of the imagination. The ultimate aim is commerciality, but we still have to get past the first hurdle—and that is to satisfy broadcasters, the world of ufology, and the general public that the film is genuine."

But, critics charge, Santilli has done little to authenticate the footage. "I have zero doubt that this film is a hoax, and I have little doubt that those presently in possession of it are well aware of that fact," says Jeffrey. "They're certainly not acting like people who are in possession of the genuine article. If you had something you considered to be the genuine article, wouldn't you do everything you could to have it authenticated? But Santilli has yet to release one scrap of original film to anyone. I haven't talked to anyone who has seen anything other than leader."

Santilli has heard criticism from Jeffrey and many others and counters that it is not his role as promoter to authenticate the film. "Let me just make one point very clear," Santilli insisted. "I have no interest in the subject of UFOs or the paranormal. Okay? I do not have the ability to research or investigate the footage. Therefore, we appointed broadcasters in various territories, and the responsibility is with them." The broadcasters that Santilli referred to include television networks and private production companies around the world who may have been "appointed" to investigate the film but who reportedly paid large sums of money for the privilege of being appointed. How can you expect a fair analysis, ufologists ask, when the vested interest of the distributor is in promoting the footage as an actual alien autopsy?

Although *Sightings* was not one of Santilli's appointees, we did attempt to investigate the authenticity of the autopsy film. Santilli claimed that original footage had been authenticated by Kodak, but in an open letter from Kodak to the Internet community, Kodak spokesperson P. G. Milson writes:

> We have seen sections of either the film or its projection leader in three Kodak locations. . . . The symbols we have seen on the Roswell film samples suggest that the film was manufactured in either 1927, 1947 or 1967. We are, therefore, unable to categorically confirm when the film was manufactured. It should also be remembered that even if the age of the film manufacture is confirmed, this does not necessarily indicate that the film was shot and processed in the same year. So, the bottom line is that although we would like to know if aliens actually exist, Kodak cannot categorically confirm either the age of the film or when it was shot and processed.

As for the body itself, *Sightings* found three deeply divided schools of thought. A few ufologists believe the body is truly extraterrestrial, but the majority believe that the creature on film is either a deformed human or a latex creation. "The opinion of the medical people I have spoken to or read about is that the being in the film is not a latex dummy," Kent Jeffrey says. "It was probably a woman who had some genetic deficiencies and possibly was altered using rubber or something like that to make it appear more freakish. The musculature of the arms and legs is obviously human. Even though the body had six fingers and six toes, the feet and hands were human. You could even see toenails on the feet. The eyes appeared larger than normal, but the eye sockets did not. The eyes had a dark membrane covering them. This membrane was removed by the surgeons very easily as if they knew what they were doing. They just lifted it right off like soft contact lenses. Medical experts have pointed out that if the membrane were part of the being, if it were an organic feature, it would not lift right off. It would be attached and quite difficult to remove.

"The human organism, like all forms of life on earth," Jeffrey adds, "is the result of billions of years of evolution. That means untold numbers of mutations and just trillions upon trillions of chance combinations of genes. The chances of another life form developing on another planet, even if its environment were identical to that of Earth, the chances of a life form developing so close to that of a human being would be nil to zero. It would just never happen. This is indeed a human corpse, undoubtedly somewhat doctored. And that makes it one of the most despicable hoaxes ever perpetrated."

Sightings asked special makeup effects artist Steve Johnson for his opinion on the origin of the "alien body" in the Santilli film. Johnson owns XFX, the company that designed the creatures for *A Nightmare on Elm Street IV, Poltergeist II,* and *Ghostbusters,* among other films. He is of the opinion that the creature in the autopsy film is entirely fabricated. "I expected from everything I had heard to walk away from this thing thinking that it might possibly have been a deformed child that had been altered with silicon injections. But I think this thing was never alive. To me and to most special makeup effects artists, it's pretty clearly a hoax that's really,

really well done. I'm considering now doing a full-scale Loch Ness monster," Johnson says facetiously. "At the risk of sounding pompous, I could have done it a lot better. The main thing is, it never proves it's a dead body. For instance, when they make an incision, they will cut away or cut in tighter so you never see the whole thing. From a special effects technician's point of view, they used every trick that I would've asked a director to use to do a great autopsy scene.

"There were a couple of weird things about it. The eyes: They go directly to it with a tweezerslike instrument, pull something off and then move on as though 'So what?' Well, maybe they had already dissected another alien and they knew what was coming up, but the physical point that's wrong with that is that I use lenses like that to change the entire look of the eye and they're big and have a pretty round shape, because it has to be tucked in under the eyelids. When these people remove these lenses, it's perfectly almond-shaped, saying to me it was just sitting on top of the eyeball. It would have been a lot more trouble to actually make it slide out from under the eyelids. That's a clear indication that something's fishy.

"Also, they don't move the body. And if they were indeed documenting this on film, why didn't they move the body? My guess is because it's hard to do. It would bend like rubber, or it wouldn't bend at all. They do move the head slightly, but no more than the rubber could take. And maybe the most interesting thing is that the Roswell alien was pretty clearly reported to have had four fingers on both hands. This one had six. Now, was that a mistake or was there a reason for that? I think the reason may be there are two close-ups that are pretty convincing. Did they just add a finger to a real person's hand? Possible. And they couldn't have taken one away. Making four fingers look realistic would have been kind of difficult."

Steve Johnson and many of his colleagues in the special makeup effects business have puzzled over who could have created the creature in the autopsy film. The special effects community is small, and most creators have signature effects that are easily identifiable. "It feels to me," Johnson surmises, "that this thing was built in the last five years, probably in England. The reason I say that is because this business is like high school, and secrecy is virtually impossible. Another possibility is that it is a well-known fact that there is a Hollywood effects guy who has done a lot of work with the CIA in direct relation to disguises, getting people in and out of countries, and this guy's come forward and admitted it. So we know it happened. Now, I'm not paranoid, but who knows? I prefer to think it's somebody in the business who just wanted to make a lot of money, because I know there's a lot of money being exchanged over this thing. And it would be exciting in a perverse way to be able to fool a lot of people like this."

In response to the comments of special-effects technicians like Johnson, Ray Santilli said, "It may be the opinion of some special effects companies that this is a hoax. However, a special-effects company can have you and me sitting in the car with John F. Kennedy driving down Dealey Plaza. That's the job they're in. They can recreate anything. But recreating something and the event itself are two separate issues."

After *Sightings* aired the findings of Kodak, Jeffrey, Johnson, and others, we received a firestorm of immediate and acerbic criticism. One caller to the *Sightings* hotline said, "The feeling of respect and integrity toward *Sightings* that my friends and I have held has been destroyed by your obvious cover-up and disinformation campaign concerning the alien autopsy." On the *Sightings* Internet site one viewer wrote: "You were totally slanted to it being a fake and made it sound like no expert believes it is real. That just isn't true."

Sightings is not part of a cover-up. *Sightings* has no vested interest in the ultimate judgment on the authenticity of the film. We believe that the Roswell autopsy film will eventually be revealed as a hoax and may damage serious research that continues to be done on the Roswell incident. "This is my biggest concern about the whole affair," Kent Jeffrey sums up. "What's going to happen as this film gets more and more publicity, more and more hype, is that people are going to start to relate the reality of the Roswell event with the authenticity of the film. People are going to assume that the entire Roswell event was a hoax. I think that would be a terrible injustice."

Sightings has always tried to bring forward the considered opinions of experts on all sides of the issues. The best way to get at the truth of any controversy is to explore the evidence in an open, educated forum. We ask the questions, you provide the answers. Is the film a hoax? Did a saucer crash at Roswell? Do UFOs exist?